Computing
for historians

Computing for historians

An introductory guide

Evan Mawdsley and **Thomas Munck**

Manchester University Press

Manchester and New York

Distributed exclusively in the USA and Canada by St. Martin's Press

Published by Manchester University Press
Oxford Road, Manchester M13 9PL, UK
and Room 400, 175 Fifth Avenue, New York, NY 10010, USA

Distributed exclusively in the USA and Canada
by St. Martin's Press, Inc., 175 Fifth Avenue, New York,
NY 10010, USA

British Library Cataloguing-in-Publication Data
A catalogue record for this book is available from the British Library

Library of Congress Cataloging-in-Publication Data
Mawdsley, Evan, 1945–
      Computing for historians: an introductory guide / Evan Mawdsley
and Thomas Munck.
          p.   cm.
      Includes bibliographical references and index.
      ISBN 0-7190-3547-3.—ISBN 0-7190-3548-1 (pbk.
      1. History—Data processing.   2. Data base management.   I. Munck,
Thomas.   II. Title.
D16.12.M385   1993
902.85—dc20   92-38789

ISBN 0 7190 3547 3 *hardback*
ISBN 0 7190 3548 1 *paperback*

Typeset in Hong Kong
by Best-set Typesetter Ltd
Printed in Great Britain
by Bell & Bain Ltd, Glasgow

Contents

Figures

Tables

Preface

The revolution in Information Technology (IT) applies as much to historical information as to any other type. This book is intended to introduce historians to some of the ways the computer revolution can be of benefit in dealing with their sources and presenting their findings. It is aimed especially at university students, and is based on wide experience in teaching them; it should also be useful in secondary schools at an advanced level. We hope, however, that it will serve as an introduction to anyone – inside or outside universities, colleges, and schools – who is contemplating the use of computers in historical work.

A preliminary definition of terms is important. We will use the word 'computer' to refer to the desktop computer that has revolutionised mass information technology in the decade and half since the appearance of the Apple II in 1977. The term 'microcomputer' or 'micro' is really no longer appropriate: laptop, notebook and palmtop computers are physically smaller and the great power of today's desktops could not be described as 'micro'. The term 'PC' (Personal Computer) is also not ideal, as it is often used to refer specifically to the IBM PC and its clones. Having said that, however, this book is very much a product of the microcomputer era, of the machines and software of the 1980s and 1990s. Neither of the authors was involved in the 'heroic age' of historical computing in the 1960s, the era of the mainframe and the punched card; neither of us have ever punched a punched card; we are ourselves children of the micro revolution.

Revolutionary changes in the nature and availability of computers and software over the last decade have unquestionably made them much more generally useful to everyone involved in historical work than they ever were in the 1960s and 1970s; that is the essence of the microcomputer revolution. Professional and amateur historians who are not using computers, at least for word processing, are forgoing a tool of great value. Students of history who are not exposed to some form of computer work are being deprived of an important part of their historical education; they are also not benefiting from one of the ways history can prepare students for a range of professions in the modern world.

The book is designed above all to be understandable to those who have never used a computer before; it is about 'entry-level' historical computing. We believe that there are many historians who sense that computing is somehow 'for them' but are unable to get background material to hasten their progress. We aim to provide that background. Where technical terms are used their meanings will be made clear to the reader; an extensive Glossary is also provided. We have had seven years of experience teaching 'historical computing' to students, most of whom had never touched a keyboard before; if we seem to labour some points, it is because we have in practice found it essential to do so.

The most important single theme of the present book will be the use of databases for the storage and analysis of historical sources. A database is a collection of conventional historical information of a more or less structured type which is stored in a computer and studied with the aid of computer programs. We also discuss at some length another fundamental aspect of computing that anyone studying history can exploit, the presentation of historical findings using a word processor.

What is the book *not* about? It is not narrowly about computing, nor does it say much about the history of computing technology. Computer programming is not one of our concerns; one of the advances of the microcomputer revolution has been the production and wide availability of ready-made programs (software) which are well suited to historians. We will not consider in any depth Computer-Assisted Learning (CAL) for historians or historical simulations. However valuable such programs are for the classroom, especially at secondary school level, they can speak for themselves.

While we both have an interest in economic history, the stress in this book is not in that direction, and certainly not on its quantitative or 'econometric' side. There is also no in-depth treatment of 'quantitative methods' and the use of statistical software and techniques. We are not champions of 'cliometrics', 'quantification', the 'new' history, 'scientific history', or even what is called 'social science history'. Some historians still think that computers and quantification should set the agenda for historical research. In our view this is the tail wagging the dog. This is certainly not a treatise on the computerisation or quantification of history. We are ourselves fairly traditional historians, but have come through personal experience to see the computer as an extremely useful *tool* – if one of many – for historians.

The book is also not about the most advanced (and expensive) techniques. It is based on that level of computer technology which is actually available in universities, schools, and even homes in the early 1990s. There is no point in an introductory text in emphasising the 'leading edge' of the field. We anticipate rapid developments over the next five years, but hope the present book will keep some of its value in terms of the general principles discussed.

This book is not a manual for users of particular products, but it is also not an abstract guide. We have tried to illustrate practical usage in a way which is independent of specific pieces of hardware and software. Readers should be thinking about the practical use of a computer now or in the near future. Ideally the book should be used with access to a computer either at home or in the classroom. As an aid to some of the techniques we have included as a source (in Appendix 1) a small amount of information from the 1851 British census. This can be entered into a computer by the reader, using whatever database management system is available; the process of data entry should not take more than a couple of hours. The new historical database can then be studied using the computer. There is no reason, however, why the book's main points about how sources are structured should not be understood *without* a computer.

The books falls into three parts. Part I is general background. Chapter 1 gives an introduction to how historians can use the computer; the starting point is the historian, not the computer. Chapter 2 is the nearest we get to a 'how to' guide and the farthest we get from history itself. It sets out the basic elements of a computer system. Chapter 3 is concerned mainly with word

processing and shows how historians can best use the word processor for what has always been a central part of the their craft –
presentation of results. We also use word processing as an example
to help the reader gain an understanding of computer systems
more generally (file structures, operating systems, etc.).

Chapters 4–7 make up Part II, and they are concerned with
the 'model' dataset created from the 1851 census. The idea is to
move through the essential stages from a 'raw' manuscript historical source to a study of that source in a computer. We look
at the way the source can be enriched by the computer, and
introduce some simple statistical techniques that exploit its
calculating power.

Computing should not, however, be confined to *social* history.
Part III extends our survey by bringing in examples from other
areas of the discipline. Although the examples come from what is
customarily called 'modern history', they cover a wide range of
periods and geographical areas. Chapter 8 is about how groups of
politicians and other professionals can be studied; the main
example involves the members of the French revolutionary Convention of 1792–95. Chapter 9 looks at sources on elections,
focusing on the 1917 election to the Russian Constituent Assembly;
it also introduces spreadsheet software. Chapter 10 introduces
the study of economic sources, taking as a starting point the
unique Danish records of shipping in and out of the Baltic Sea – a
main artery of European trade – in the late 1700s. Chapters 11
and 12 are an introduction to more advanced topics. They stress
the complex structures of the 'relational' historical database and
the potentials for studying historical texts, but also touch on the
array of other computer tools that can aid the historian now and
in the future.

We referred above to a model database from the 1851 census
which has been used as an example in this book, especially in
Part II. For this we are indebted to Alison Gray. The excellent teaching datasets she prepared under the auspices of the
Strathclyde Regional Archives and Scottish Office Education
Department showed us the value of census datasets as an introduction to historical computing; our data is essentially a subset of
a database she developed. We also wish to acknowledge the
General Register Office for Scotland for making available the

census material and note that it is reproduced in this book with the permission of the Controller of HMSO.

The support of the Economic and Social Research Council for a number of computer-based research products is also gratefully acknowledged; this support has indirectly played a valuable role in developing the use of computer techniques in history at Glasgow.

Both authors are part of a cheery, argumentative and at times embattled group of historians at Glasgow University who since 1985 have worked to make computers an integral part of the undergraduate curriculum there. The DISH Project (Development and Implementation of Software in History), as this consortium is known, was originally funded by the British universities' Computer Board; thanks to the continuing support of the university our 'dedicated' historical computing facilities and cumulative expertise are probably second to none in Britain.

While we cannot name everyone who was of direct or indirect help in the production of this book, some stand out. Don Spaeth, manager of the Glasgow-based Computers in Teaching Initiative Centre for History (CTICH), brought his wealth of experience of different approaches in historical computing to bear, not least by questioning some of our assumptions and forcing us to face up to issues that we had skated round. Michael Moss, one of the driving forces behind the DISH project, never failed to provide new impetus and helpful advice; his comments on the final draft were also much appreciated. We also benefited from the comments on all or part of the text by James Currall, Jacqueline Jenkinson, and David Liston. Whilst we cannot blame anyone but ourselves for shortcomings in the volume, these colleagues and friends can take much of the credit for its strengths.

We also owe special debt of thanks to Dan Greenstein, our colleague in the Modern History Department. Although working on his own more specialised book on historical computing, he has been very generous with his expertise and insights – even when this involved sending Ingres databases across JANET lines or discussing SGML in a sunny courtyard in Salzburg.

We learned much from two of the original DISH team, Rick Trainor (currently director of CTICH) and Nicholas Morgan; jointly they put a vast amount of time and effort into the early success of the project, and helped 'convert' a number of their traditionalist colleagues. Several programmers and lab managers have worked for DISH over the years. Mike Black, Francis Candlin, Brendan Hughes, Gavin Sinclair, and John Wood responded with unfailing enthusiasm to the sometimes misguided, sometimes Herculean tasks set on them – in the form of strange datasets in impossible formats and unintelligible languages, of lost files, or of freshly-baked exercises for students; they have been of immense help in coping with the peculiar hardware and software needs which historians have.

Glasgow University Computing Service has always been generous in its technical support and training provided to naive users in the histories; in addition to James Currall, already mentioned, we would wish to thank Peter Kemp, the Director, Paul Salotti, David Fildes, and Stephen Whitelaw. Inez McIntyre of Glasgow University Library provided much valuable advice in connection with CD-ROM and on-line bibliographies.

We have now, as part of the DISH team, spent seven years teaching skills like those outlined in this book to staff and students in our departments. We cannot emphasise enough the value of this. A healthy scepticism on the part of our fellow-historians, and a response ranging from patient forbearance to whole-hearted enthusiasm amongst several generations of students, have helped us realise what is feasible and what is not.

And on the subject of patience, we both owe a great deal to our respective spouses, who have suffered major intrusions on domestic peace. Whilst one computer might be a useful means of entertaining a child or two on a rainy day, there seemed at first glance no such obvious excuse for *two* computers running simultaneously, sometimes at half-past midnight, nor for husbands who invariably reverted to database-conversations in their spare moments. No doubt the computers are there to stay, but the book is dedicated to our children, Neil, Rhona, and Michael, who will soon take all of its contents for granted.

E. M.
T. M.

Part I

Background

Chapter 1

History and computing: the second revolution

see p. 6

This is the second age of 'historical computing'. The first computer revolution for historians took place in the 1960s. In 1968 Emmanuel Le Roy Ladurie wrote about the future of his profession; the French historical school was dominant in the field of economic, social and quantitative history, but American technology posed a great challenge. By the 1980s, if French historians did not keep pace with technical change, things might be different; in this area 'the historian of tomorrow will be a programmer or he will be nothing'.[1]

In the 1960s a vocal minority of historians in several countries argued that the big computers that were becoming available in universities and research institutes would provide a wonderful new route to the past. The creation of vast databases by teams of researchers, the use of modern statistical techniques, and a focus on the social foundations were central planks of a 'new' – scientific – history, sometimes called Cliometrics.

The counter-attack was not long in coming. Quantitative computer-based research, replied the traditionalists, touched only a narrow range of questions. 'Almost all important questions are important,' wrote Arthur Schlesinger, 'precisely because they are *not* susceptible to quantitative answers.' The style of the 'new history' was mocked; the Oxford historian Richard Cobb wrote about 'the armies of white-coated assistants employed in the clinical Historical Laboratories' and the research groups, 'more extensive and much more deferential than the teeming below-stairs population of an affluent mid-Victorian home'. Computer projects were criticised for not producing results. In 1979, a decade after Le Roy Ladurie, a prominent British social historian could dismiss the computer revolution:

It is just those projects that have been the most lavishly funded, the most ambitious in the assembly of vast quantities of data by armies of paid researchers, the most scientifically processed by the very latest in computer technology, the most mathematically sophisticated in presentation, which have so far turned out to be the most disappointing.[2]

The traditionalists were never tempted by the new methods; as for high-profile innovators, they turned in the 1970s and 1980s to *mentalités*, the family, the working of the political mind, or the history of everyday life.[3]

Computers and the quantitative methods did not, then, come to dominate historical studies. A second point about Le Roy Ladurie's prediction is less obvious but no less important. If the historian *does* now use a computer the wide availability of ready-made programs (software) means he or she need never be a *programmer*. This development is one of the main themes in the present book. There is a great irony in the whole tempest about history, quantification, and computing. Five or ten years after the 'quantification' debate had burned itself out, along came the *micro*computer and its software. Suddenly really powerful tools began to be placed – literally – at the historian's fingertips.

Before this, in 1971, Edward Shorter wrote an introductory book on historical computing which took would-be users through the stages of data preparation.

[N]ow we step from the book-lined study and head for the world of flashing lights in the computer center. The great grey machines lined up behind the glass, with their spinning tape drives and chattering high-speed printers, seem to symbolize renunciation of all values and modes of investigation for which the historical profession has stood.[4]

Shorter's book is still useful, but the picture drawn here seems almost comic today. The historian no longer has to leave 'the book-lined study'. Nearly all the specific technical equipment mentioned by Shorter has disappeared – the same things are done, but in different ways.

The 1960s was the decade of the 'great grey machines', big mainframe computers like the IBM 360. At the time these machines represented a great leap forward in the availability of computing facilities, but they were expensive to use and operated in an impersonal way. Effective use required a reasonable knowledge of programming (as Le Roy Ladurie rightly said) or access to a specialist.

This is not the place to summarise the microcomputer revolution, but the critical point to note is that it was about both hardware and software. The real starting point was the development of the hardware: small, relatively-affordable desktop computers based on the microprocessor – the silicon chip. The most important early microcomputers were the Apple II, introduced in 1977, and the IBM PC, which followed in 1981. The descendants of these machines and their clones have become progressively more powerful and less expensive, thanks to the further miniaturisation of components and mass production on the western side of the Pacific rim. Important add-ons like printers and disk drives have evolved in the same way, with greater capacity and lower price. The use of the keyboard, the video screen, and simple storage devices like the floppy disk have made computing interactive and personal.

The other side of the microcomputer revolution, equally important, was the extraordinary development of software for the new machines. The most striking single feature of the microcomputer revolution was that the user acquired a range of ready-made programs which simply had to be loaded into the machine and run; he or she did not have to know anything about programming. The first commercial word-processor software became available at the end of the 1970s, along with database managers and spreadsheets. Powerful mainframe database and statistics programs were adapted for use on the new micros. All these programs evolved rapidly through the 1980s, matching the greater power provided by newer generations of microcomputers, and driven by the demands of the commercial world. Built-in help systems were developed. Ease of use and standardisation, at least for IBM-type machines, was made possible by the dominance of the DOS operating system.

At the same time the greater power of the microcomputer and ingenuity of software designers led from the mid-1980s to a stress on software that was even easier to master. The Apple Macintosh, unveiled in 1984, had a revolutionary new operating system based on visual images; the first version of the similar IBM-based

Microsoft Windows environment was introduced in 1985, and the array of commercial programs written for this format was multi-plying in the 1990s.

The 1960s, then, were a false start. Whatever the pros and cons of the quantification debate, the technology was not easily available to large numbers of professional historians, let alone to students and local historians. In the 1990s, after the microcomputer revolution, powerful and easy-to-use tools are on hand. Most professional historians now use computers at some stage in their work – but not in the way the pioneers of the 1960s imagined. The computer can be the centre of an historical project, or it can be used as an auxiliary. There are topics – and approaches – that could not be considered without the computer, for example a large database or complex statistical analysis. There are many *more* projects where the computer is very useful, but 'only' as an important auxiliary like a foreign language or palaeography. In short, the computer does not need to create a new type of historian or a new methodology; it is a tool suitable for all historians.

Data for what?

One major use of the new technology is helping to get to grips with historical sources, and that is what the present book is mostly about. Before considering how a modern computer can deal with a source, there is an essential first question: what is the data needed for? Professional historians are often critical of those who gather information for its own sake. Computer technology, which makes it easy to amass large amounts of data, actually increases the temptation of what is sometimes called antiquarianism. Researchers can spend their time transcribing information without thinking about it until too late, or at least until a large amount of useless information has been gathered. The concept of a 'data cemetery' – a mass grave of information built up but never shared or even effectively used – is not a fantastic one.

Even for a relatively small project specific questions must be the starting point. There will not be one simple question; usually historians are exploring some general historical theme and will want to ask a number of related questions; other questions will naturally arise as the research progresses. The definition of the questions has to be made at the very beginning of a computer-based project, as decisions have to be made about what to leave out, how many records to use, how to sample, what to code, and so on.

The importance of the answer also needs to be considered. Le Roy Ladurie, in the same article where he spoke of the historian–programmer of the 1980s, made fun of one historian's computer-aided study of Wilhelm II's entourage; this simply showed that they were 'aristocrats born east of the Elbe. The computer told him the obvious.' The conclusion was that 'a computer is only interesting insofar as it allows one to tackle problems that are new and original in the subject matter, method and above all in their scope'.[5] That it true, but on the other hand the level of work must be kept in mind. Working historians and postgraduate students are supposed to be highly original, but the same kind of creativity need not necessarily be expected of local historians or history undergraduates. Students regularly write essays about questions that others have written about before. There is no reason why, using a database, they cannot usefully turn up results which are 'new and original' *to them*, and that is surely part of the learning process. Likewise local historians can come to terms with specific historical instances which are illustrative of more general developments.

In any event, assuming that some questions – important to the user – have been raised, the computer can be used to do three things with an historical source: store it, analyse it and present the findings of that analysis.

Storing data

Computers are superb at storing data and keeping track of it. If a project involves a lot of generally similar material on individuals, institutions or even sources, the computer is now almost certainly the best way of storing it. Essentially, this side of the computer's activities could be described as cataloguing, and the computer is now an excellent index-card catalogue. A very large amount of information can be stored in a physically small space, and back-up copies of the information can easily be created. The data can be in plain English (rather than in number codes as it was in the past), and constantly updated.

The data may well have to be *transcribed* by the researcher. Some critics see transcription or data entry as pure drudgery – hence 'the armies of white-coated assistants' to actually do the donkey work. It could be argued, however, that this only becomes a problem with very large projects. Data entry is much easier than it used to be. The equipment is compact and can be used in the library, archive, departmental cluster or 'book-lined study', using a desktop computer or even a portable. The information can be entered in any form, without the paraphernalia of codes and codebooks which was required in the punched card era. In any event the historian has to be the master of his or her sources, and this can only come with extensive contact with those sources.

Should the process of data entry be reduced by using other people's data? Should the benefits of data entry be multiplied by letting others use the data? *Potentially* it is very valuable to be able to access information that other historians have put into computers. The user can begin with analysis rather than with the tedium of keying in *all* the data. However, if someone else has done the transcription there are the problems of knowing how far it can be trusted, what decisions have been made by the original researchers about abbreviations, coding, sampling, etc. On the other hand, most first-time computer-based projects probably begin with the optimistic assumption that the information will be of general use; this is not always the case. Careful documentation is required before the data can be shared. The explanation of the different fields (and tables), the explanation of coding decisions, etc., all require painstaking work; it is also important, as with any kind of historical project, to document the source of individual items of information. All this requires time; in trying to create a general-purpose database the specific historical project may well suffer.

A collaborative computer project is also a tempting proposition, particularly for local history groups. Again, such joint work, while sharing out the problem of entering the information, requires rigorous agreed standards; it may even be helpful if the data can be tagged with the name of the person responsible for its entry. Documentation 'costs' for collaborative projects will be no less than for single-author ones.

Information retrieval and analysis

'Information retrieval' can simply mean recovering the one piece of information that is required. An historian might want to find the date of birth of an individual, the population of a particular town in a particular year, or the full text of a particular document. Any such piece of information can be stored in a database, and the ability to retrieve it quickly is obviously valuable; it is a sufficient reason for storing data on a computer.

Historical analysis, in contrast to simple information retrieval, normally means drawing some conclusions from the information *as a whole*, or at least from a part of the information larger than just one record. To continue the index-card analogy, it is not a question of looking at just one index card, but trying to make generalisations about many (or all) the cards. This may involve simple 'sorts', e.g. listing all the people of a certain age. Listing (or even counting) the contents of a database is one of the most tangible advantages of computing, even for the most traditional of historians.

Statistics takes this analysis one step further. This need not be complex; anyone studying members of a parliament might be interested in such a simple 'statistic' as their average age. Once information is in machine-readable form it is much easier to ask a wide range of different questions about the relations between aspects of the information. Here we are getting closer to the 'scientific' history of the 1960s, but the availability of statistical software on microcomputers makes the analysis much easier than it was then.

Graphics and tables are in a sense another tool of analysis which computers can provide. Although they might naturally be thought of as part of the presentation side (see below), they also provide an excellent means of seeing the overall 'shape' of the data. They can provide a basis for the hypothesis-building which is an essential part of further analysis. Related to this is geographical analysis, which looks at the way different characteristics are distributed spatially. At the moment mapping software is relatively demanding in a technical sense, but its potential future value for historians is great.

Presentation

The last functional area of historical computing is the presentation of findings. The most common example of this by far is word processing, which needs little more explanation. Desktop publishing is a further stage which allows a professional layout. And the graphical presentation of findings is one of the most exciting uses of computers. Pie charts, bar charts, line graphs, and tables are quickly generated and incorporated into a text with modern software.

Computers, learning, and training

How do computers fit into the educational process in the 1990s? As we have seen, one definition of the task of historians – whether university professors, local historians, or history students – involves the asking of intelligent questions about the past and the attempt to provide answers to those questions.

The early stages of historical training traditionally assume that the question-asking has been done by someone other than the student; the intelligent *answer* is the measure of success. This answer is supposed to show how much historical information the student has absorbed, usually from books by historians. The presentation of a well-formulated and supported 'answer' can be greatly aided by word processing and graphics. In addition the factual side of historical learning can be aided by computerised tutorial (CAL) programs.

The source-oriented, database side of computing really comes into its own at a later stage. In project work and dissertations, there is more freedom to pick topics and questions, and computers are valuable for marshalling evidence. At this point, indeed, an ability to ask the right questions is often a major part of what assessors are looking at. Topics tend to be narrower, a greater premium is put on the use of primary sources, and those sources may well be in a database or textbase.

Finally, training in the use of computers provides 'transferable skills'. Historical problems are complex, and reflect many of those in the real world; the use of computers to solve those problems provides valuable lessons. It is also clearly valuable to understand the basic processes involved in information technology; once the principles behind *any* database manager are understood, any other database manager can be mastered much more quickly. The same is true for word processors, spreadsheets, statistics software, and – in general – the way that computer systems operate. What can be learned is an approach and what can be overcome are the inhibitions of 'technophobia'.

The criticisms of computing and the 'new history' in the 1960s and 1970s had much to do with the scale and organisation of the work, the time required to master the technology, the exaggerated extent of the claims, the redundancy of the results, and the obscurity of the presentation. Our argument is that some of the criticisms may have been justified, but are now irrelevant to the 1990s, after the microcomputer revolution.

The storage and analysis of historical sources is a basic part of the discipline, and the modern desktop computer makes those tasks easier; small computers are easy to master and data entry is simple. Many projects will make their points by combining conventional analysis with a computer analysis, and perhaps qualitative and quantitative sources. The exhalted 'scale' so criticised in the first generation of projects is not a necessary part of modern computer-based work. Less of an argument surely has to be made about the value of modern systems for presentation; the advantages of word processing are already obvious to most historians.

There is no reason to argue that in the 1990s 'the historian will be a programmer or he will be nothing'. Historians and history students will do what they have always done, but modern desktop computers can help them do it better or faster (or both). The object of the chapters that follow is to suggest ways that the computer can help.

Notes

1 E. Le Roy Ladurie, *Le territoire de l'historien*, Paris, 1973, 1, p. 14. This comment has sometimes been taken out of context to suggest that Le Roy Ladurie was referring to *all* historians – rather than just

quantitative historians. Lawrence Stone is an example of someone who perhaps interprets Le Roy Ladurie too broadly; see his 'The revival of narrative' (*Past and Present*, LXXXV, 1979, p. 13).

2 A. Schlesinger, 'The humanist looks at empirical social research', in *Quantification in American History*, ed. Robert P. Swierenga, New York, 1970, p. 33; R. Cobb, 'Historians in white coats', *Times Literary Supplement*, 3 December 1971, p. 1527f; Stone, p. 12f.

3 Le Roy Ladurie himself became a student of *mentalités*, with works like *Montaillou* and *Le carnaval de Romans*.

4 Edward Shorter, *The Historian and the Computer*, Englewood Cliffs, 1971, p. 49.

5 Le Roy Ladurie, p. 11.

Chapter 2

Computer systems: an introduction

This chapter gives a basic description of what a computer does; it is the least 'historical' chapter in this book. Nevertheless it is written with historians in mind, and based on the uses to which computers are likely to be put in the study of history.

Hardware and software are the two main elements of computing.

Hardware is the physical machinery of the computer.

Software is the electronic instructions given to the computer, and it usually takes the form of programs. There are various kinds of software, for example word-processing software and database management software; these are also called *applications*.

Hardware

Five major elements of a basic desktop computer system need to be considered.

- The *computer* itself is the base unit. It contains the main working parts such as the processor and the memory.
- The *keyboard* is the main means by which the user communicates with the computer.
- The *monitor* or television screen is the most important form of immediate output – the way the computer communicates with the user.
- The *printer*, a second destination to which output can be sent, is basically an electric typewriter. The system will work without the printer – the results can be seen on the monitor – but in reality a printer is nearly an essential part.
- Some kind of electronic storage device for holding data and programs is the final element. Currently the main devices are

the floppy disk, which fits into a slot called a disk drive, and
the hard disk, which is usually inside the computer. Some
kind of storage device is required for nearly all serious use of
computers.

The computer/processor

The *processor* is the core element of a computer, like the motor
of a car. Other names are *CPU* (central processing unit) or
microprocessor; in any event it is a tiny layer cake of silicon
crystal (a silicon chip) containing thousands of electronic circuits.
It is not important to know exactly how it works, but it is useful
to have a sense of its relative power.

Computer processing power is important. The more powerful
the computer the more complex programs it can run; paradoxically
the more powerful the computer the easier it may be to operate.
A standard concept that relates to the power of a microprocessor
is how many *bits* of information it can handle. A bit is a *bi*nary
digi*t*, 1 or 0. A '16-bit' CPU can transfer 16 bits of information to or
from memory at one time. The first generation of microcomputers
had 8-bit chips; powerful modern computers have 32-bit chips.
Also important is the speed (*clock speed*) at which the computer's
CPU operates. A *hertz* is a measure of frequency, i.e. one cycle
per second; a *megahertz* (*MHz*) is a million hertz. A powerful
modern microcomputer would operate at 25 MHz or more.

Memory is where programs and data are held when they are
being executed or processed. *Random Access Memory* (*RAM*),
measured in *bytes*, is a basic measure of a computer's potential.
There are roughly a thousand bytes in a *kilobyte* (*KB*), and
roughly a million bytes in a *megabyte (MB)*. The most common
type of desktop computer, the IBM PC or one of its clones, is
now relatively small in terms of RAM: it has between 640 kilobytes
(.64 megabytes) and 2 megabytes. RAM should not be confused
with the capacity of a computer system to store electronic *files*
(whether program files or files of historical data). RAM and file
store are both measured in bytes: a computer might have 30
megabytes of file storage capacity on its hard disk, but only .64
megabytes of RAM.

One basic division between micros is between those that are
compatible with the IBM 'Personal Computer' (PC) and those

that are not. Since its introduction in 1981 the PC has been the 'industry standard' and a great deal of software – much of it useful for historians – is available for *IBM PC compatibles*. Different kinds of generally affordable PC exist, divided into generations by their processor chip, produced by Intel: the 8808 or 8086 (PC/XT), the 80286 ('286 machines' or PC/AT), the 80386 ('386 machines'), and currently the i486 ('486 machines').

Space does not permit much discussion of larger computers, which are in any event too expensive and complex for the beginner. But with rapidly increasing processor power today's small computer may be as powerful as yesterday's big one. *Workstations* are the next step up from the basic micro, but generally are outside the financial resources of an individual; the distinction between the most powerful microcomputers and workstations is increasingly blurred, but the latter are especially useful for graphics programs, including *desktop publishing* (*DTP*) and *computer-aided design* (*CAD*). Beyond workstations are larger computers, with a number of users, each on a *terminal*. *Mainframes* (so-called after the structure of their CPUs) are big, powerful but very expensive machines with only one or two available to a major educational institution. *Minicomputers* ('minis') were developed in the 1960s, long before the micro, as a relatively inexpensive integrated circuit-based alternative to mainframes; they were still centralised machines accessed by terminals. In many settings the processing power of minis and even mainframes is now being provided by 'distributed' facilities in the form of networked workstations or powerful micros.

Input devices

The keyboard is the standard device for communicating with the computer. The keyboard has a number of elements. It includes something very like a typewriter keyboard, often called a *QWERTY* keyboard after the letter-keys on the top left. If a lot of typing is planned there is a strong case for doing a self-taught touch-typing program first; institutions should have computer-based typing tutorials with names like 'Touch 'n' Go'.

Various other keys are not found on a typewriter, and their layout will vary from computer to computer. There may often be a square *numeric pad* with keys for numbers and mathematical functions; these keys are actuated by pressing the *Num Lock* key and they are extremely useful for rapid entry of numbers. Most keyboards will have *function keys*, labelled 'F1', 'F2', and so on. These can be assigned to perform particular tasks; their function will vary from program to program.

Because there are only a limited number of keys available, each must have several uses. As in a conventional keyboard the user can change the meaning of a key by pressing it together with the *Shift* key (shift + 'a' = 'A' or shift + ';' = ':'). On a computer keyboard the *Alt* and *Control* (Ctrl) key work the same way to provide more possibilities. For the sake of convenience there may be several Shift, Alt, and Ctrl keys on the keyboard.

Arrow/direction keys allow the user to choose the active part of the screen by moving the visual indicator called the *cursor*. Another key familiar from the typewriter is the *tabulator* (tab) key, which allows movement a set distance (say five character spaces) along a line – or to indent paragraphs. The *Escape* (Esc) gives an escape from a particular situation. The *backspace* key is used for moving backwards. There will be some means of either overtyping text on the screen or inserting at any point on the screen. The *Insert* and *Delete* keys allow the insertion and removal of text.

Finally, there will be a key called variously: *Enter*, Carriage Return, or *Return*. This is an extremely important key, and is used in most programs to tell the computer to execute a command.

The keyboard is still the primary means to enter instructions (text, data) into the computer. One objection to it is that the user has to know where the various keys are; to take advantage of the keyboard the user needs a second skill, the ability to type. Also, to move the cursor around the screen, using the keyboard, the user has to use the awkward direction/arrow keys.

The most common alternative to the keyboard is the *mouse*. The idea behind the mouse is to allow the user very quickly to select any point (or area) on the screen. The mouse is a little box on a roller, and as it is rolled over the desk surface it moves an electronic pointer on the screen; pressing one of the buttons of the mouse then performs certain actions (also called 'point and shoot'). In graphics-based systems the pointer can be moved to an *icon* to select a particular computer operation. In word-processor programs the mouse can be used to select and then move or alter chunks of text. Typically the mouse is used together with the keyboard.

Since input is being discussed here it should be mentioned that it is also possible to input data into a computer by transferring it in bulk from files, or by *scanning* it in using an electro-optical *scanner*. These methods will be discussed more fully later.

Output devices

The most important output device is the *monitor* or television screen. The monitor is sometimes referred to as a *VDU* (Visual Display Unit). It is normally based on the same technology as a television screen or *CRT* (Cathode Ray Tube), but a 'dedicated' monitor gives better definition than a domestic television. The standard monitor screen is about 80 characters (or 'columns') wide and 24 rows down. The small flat fold-down screen on most portable computers uses a different technology known as *LCD* (Liquid Crystal Display), but the principles of displaying output are the same. Monitors come in monochrome (black and white, black and green, etc.) or colour; colour monitors are better for most modern software. There are a number of graphics standards, based on the *video adaptor* fitted to the computer; *CGA*, *EGA*, *VGA*, and *SVGA* are common, with CGA being the oldest and producing the lowest definition.

What appears on the monitor screen can also appear as a different kind of output: on paper using a printer. There are several types of printers, varying in speed of printing, noise, expense, and quality of type. Speed is normally reckoned in *CPS* (characters per second). Printers are most commonly thought of as part of a word-processing system, but they can also be used for printing the results of the manipulation of historical data or for printing images (graphics).

Daisy-wheel printers have largely been superseded, and *dot matrix* printers are now the most common inexpensive type. The printheads of dot matrix printers consist of a number (9 or 24) of pins which strike the paper through a ribbon. They build up letters from points made by the pins; the more pins the better the resolution (clarity) of the print. Printers have both draft mode and NLQ mode. *Draft mode* is fast, but the letters are coarse.

B

NLQ (Near Letter Quality) mode is slower, to allow overlapping pin strikes; the resulting higher quality print is adequate for most purposes. Dot matrix printers can also be used to print graphics built up from dots, like the photographs in a newspaper. *Laser printers* are much quieter and faster, and have excellent quality print for text and graphics; they are, however, substantially more expensive. *Ink jet* printers are a relatively new development, quieter and of better quality than dot matrix printers, and costing less than laser printers.

Various kinds of paper can be used in printers. Standard British single sheet A4 (11.7 in × 8.26 in) paper can be used in most types of printer. *Fanfold* paper is paper connected with perforations to allow easy feed of sheets. Fanfold paper usually has a perforated margin on either side, like camera film; the perforation fits on the sprockets of the printer's paper feeder, or *tractor feed*.

More sophisticated output devices exist, such as the *plotter*, which can be used for drawing graphics.

Storage devices

Data is manipulated in the *memory* (RAM) of the computer; the problem is that as soon as the computer is switched off all the data in memory is lost. As a result some kind of storage device for programs and data is essential.

Floppy disks can be used to store programs and data (text, etc.). The disk itself is protected by a hard square plastic casing; 'floppies' come in two main sizes, the larger and thinner 5.25 in. diameter and the smaller and thicker 3.5 in. diameter; the smaller disks actually have more capacity. There are also some non-standard disks, like the 3 in. disk for the original Amstrad PCW. Floppy disks of all types can hold large amounts of information. A 3.5 in. *double density* disk can hold 720 kilobytes of data, over 720,000 bytes (actually 720 × 1,024 bytes = 737,280 bytes). A byte can store one letter or number, so given a text with an average of seven letters per word, one floppy disk could hold over 100,000 words of text, which would be the size of a medium-sized printed book. A *high-density* 3.5 in. floppy can hold twice as much, 1.4 megabytes (1,400 kilobytes).

Disks fit into the *disk drive* of the computer. Usually these disk drives have electronic designations like 'A' or 'B'. Disks will only fit into the correct size disk-drive slot. Some machines have slots for both 3.5 in. and 5.25 in. disks. Regardless of their size, disks will only work on the type of computer for which they have been *formatted*. Floppy disks straight out of the box are unformatted. It is necessary to arrange (format) the tracks and sectors of a floppy disk so that it can be used with a particular kind of computer. This is done by placing them in a disk drive and typing in the required command.

One of the first rules of computing is to 'back up' – make a copy of – everything important. This is especially true of floppy disks, which not only can be mislaid but also can become electronically corrupted. Utility programs exist to help 'un-corrupt' floppies but they can still be lost or physically damaged, so the best rule is always to copy the contents of the floppy to a back-up floppy which is stored in a different place.

Floppy disks are only one kind of storage device. They are very convenient, but their capacity is limited, and they are relatively slow; physical movement is required to *read* data from a floppy or to *write* to it. At the beginning of the 1990s the *hard disk* (also called a *Winchester*) became a standard part of the microcomputer systems. Hard disks are faster than floppy disks, and they have very large capacity – 20 to 300 megabytes (even the smallest is 25 times the size of a floppy disk). The hard disk is a permanent storage device; the data is not lost if the machine is turned off. Hard disks are so large that they create a problem of back-up. Like floppies, hard disks can fail, and the potential loss is much greater. Backing up individual files to floppies is time-consuming. One useful – but expensive – tool is a *tape streamer*, which copies the contents of the hard disk on to magnetic tape. Hard disks are delicate pieces of machinery and it is important to 'park' the hard disk before moving the computer; instructions will be given with individual machines.

Other storage devices exist. The first generation of computer-minded historians relied on *punched cards*. Awkward and now obsolete, these were perforated 7.375 in. by 3.25 in. cards which were used to feed programs and data into a mainframe computer (rather like the paper music rolls fed into a player piano). At the beginning of the microcomputer era audio cassettes were used for data storage. Much more powerful storage devices than the floppy and hard disk are now becoming available. *Optical disks* can hold very large amounts of information; the most common form available now is the *CD-ROM* (Compact Disc, Read-only Memory), similar to the common audio compact disk. Currently such devices are used for reading data into the computer, i.e. they are *read-only*, but in the near future the general user will be able to write data to storage devices holding *gigabytes* of data – one gigabyte equalling roughly a thousand megabytes, or twenty times the size of a conventional hard disk. This greater capacity will become increasingly important when images – which require a great deal of space – are being stored or manipulated.

Networks

So far the discussion has been about a computer on its own (in *standalone* mode). A computer in a university or school will probably be part of a *network* or *Local Area Network* (*LAN*). A network means that expensive equipment (*peripherals*) like printers can be shared between several users. A computer which controls an entire network, and which may be the source of programs and data, is called a file *server*.

Another advantage of being part of a larger network is that users have access to even more powerful computers (or *remote hosts*). A networked microcomputer can be used as a *terminal* to a more powerful mini- or mainframe computer elsewhere in the institution or even at another institution (a *remote host* in a 'remote site'); this can allow access to very large databases and to greater processing power. Increasingly it will be possible to have access to other computers without users going through complex connection procedures or even realising that they are on another computer; the link will be 'transparent'. A final advantage of networking, especially through a larger computer, is access to 'electronic mail' or *E-MAIL*. There may be E-MAIL on a local network or even a national system. The main system in Britain is called JANET (Joint Academic Network), while in the USA INTERNET is a commonly used network.

Networks raise the complex issue of security. The network has to know which of many possible network users it is dealing with, and users need guarantees that other people cannot get access to their data and programs. Network users are often assigned a user identity (rather like a telephone number) and also a secret password known only to the user (and the network manager). An analogy is with a hotel, where guests' room numbers (user identities) may be generally known, but only they (and the hotel manager – network manager) have the key (password) to open the door.

Once users have identities and passwords they can *log on* to the network for a session, and *log off* afterwards. When they log on they are telling the system who it is talking to, and whether that person has the right to use the network and the particular data and programs.

Software

Software is the programs that *run* on the hardware. Basically, programs are *loaded* in the computer's memory and then run. Material loaded into the computer consists of *files*. A complex program – for say a word processor or a database manager – will be stored in a considerable number of files (comparable to several floppy disks). Computerised data, historical or otherwise, also exists as files.

Computers have *operating systems* which, among other things, look after the storage, loading, and transfer of files. The operating system will usually tell the user the name and type of each file (e.g. whether it is text or a program), how big it is, and when it was created. Currently the most common operating system for desktop computers is called *DOS* (pronounced 'doss'), for Disk Operating System, which involves a range of standard and abbreviated commands for most kinds of computer 'housekeeping' operations. *MS-DOS* (Microsoft DOS) is the most common variant on PC compatible computers. There are other operating systems – like IBM's *OS/2* (originally announced in 1987) – but these are not so common for the smaller microcomputers.

Increasingly, operating-system functions are handled by the user through a *graphical user interface (GUI)* which, for example, allows the user to select files and programs by clicking on icons (graphical symbols) with a mouse. The 'buzz word' for these systems is *WIMPS*, which means Windows, Icons, Mouse, and Pull-down menu (or Windows, Icons, Menus, and Pointer). The general idea was pioneered by the Apple Macintosh in 1984. Everything is there on the screen, ready to be clicked on or, in the case of some menus, pulled down (made visible). Various versions of the similar Microsoft Windows environment are widely used with IBM PCs and compatibles (Windows actually sits on top of DOS). The new version of OS/2 is also a GUI.

Part of the appeal of GUIs is that they are intuitive, easy to use. File handling is simple and, within a particular GUI, different programs will work in the same way. The drawback is that such ease of use requires a relatively powerful computer; on machines with slow clock speed or limited RAM GUIs may be very slow or not run at all.

Most systems, graphical or not, will store files in different *directories*. The computer can be imagined as a filing cabinet; each drawer is a disk drive, and within each drawer there are labelled sections (directories) which contain files of a particular type, or relating to a particular topic – depending on how the user wants to store the files.

Programs

There are two different kinds of file to consider. Some contain programs, and others contain the information that will be (or has been) processed by the programs.

Complex manipulations of historical material used to require programming; this is no longer the case. Many different kinds of program are commercially available, including many that are relevant to historical work. One example would be a word-processing program or *word processor*, which allows the production of text; *desktop publishing* (DTP) programs are similar but concerned especially with page layout (see Chapter 3). Another type – the main focus of this book – is a *database management system* or *DBMS* (see Chapter 5 onwards). There is also *spreadsheet* software and *statistical* software which is used with numerical data; *textbase* software is used for the content-analysis of textual material. Usually a program can be brought into operation simply by typing its name at the operating system prompt, or in a graphical user interface like Microsoft Windows, by clicking on the icon that corresponds to the program.

Files are created by the user using the software. For example, a chapter of a dissertation or book would be created by the writer in a word-processing program and *saved* into a file. The next time the writer wanted to *edit* the chapter this file would be loaded back into the word processor, added to or modified (*edited*), and then saved again. Exactly the same procedure occurs with data entered into database software or numbers entered in a spreadsheet.

Files generally have a particular software format and their names have suffixes which indicates their type, e.g. FILENAME. DOC for a Microsoft Word word-processing file or FILENAME. DB for a Borland Paradox database file. It is the case, however, that in limited and well-defined circumstances files can be transferred from one program to another. A document could be created in Microsoft Word and later edited in another word-processing program, such as WordPerfect. Data in one type of software can be transferred to another type of software: the output of a database program could be exported to a word-processing program and edited there. However, even without fancy equipment or software it is often possible – although laborious – to *export* data or text in a raw form called ASCII, and then to *import* it in the same form into another application.

What kind of hardware and software?

In one sense a computer system is not an investment like a house – or a library book; prices fall, computer technology advances very rapidly, and chances of re-sale are limited. On the other hand a computer is an investment in the sense of being a tool, a 'means of production'. If a computer saves very substantial time in drafting and redrafting typescripts, if it provides a cheaper and more flexible alternative to professional typists, then it has an appreciable and permanent value. The same is true if it allows the user to store, manipulate and present historical information that would be handled only with great difficulty (if at all) by any other means – e.g. with index cards. The 'icing on the cake' is the non-historical uses to which a personal computer can be put and the value of everyday involvement in the information revolution.

This book is not the place to offer detailed advice on what kind of hardware and software the self-respecting computerised historian should purchase. Needs and budgets differ, and technical advice given here will in any event quickly be dated. Individuals have varied (although usually limited) resources, and institutions have institutional procurement and support policies. The shelves of newsagents are heavy with computer magazines offering general advice – although these can be aimed at the more knowledgeable enthusiast.[1] Within educational institutions technical specialists (and computer-minded colleagues) are on hand for consultation – but they, too, can talk over the questioner's head.

Looking first at hardware, however, the general advice for individuals would be to buy something better than the bare minimum. A long working life can be ensured if the machine is as near as possible to the 'state of the art'.

The computer should match required tasks. It can be assumed that a 'history' user will intend to write a good deal and to use some of the tools and methods described later in this book – databases, spreadsheets, perhaps even statistics and text analysis; this suggests a relatively powerful machine. Some of the most expensive add-ons – like laser printers or the more elaborate bits of software – may not need to be purchased at all, as they may be available from institutions. But this means that it is important that the equipment and software purchased for home use be generally compatible with that in the institution, and that data can be transferred back and forth with ease.

Given all this, a standard size (i.e. non-laptop) microcomputer with at least 2 megabytes of RAM and a 20 megabyte or larger hard disk would be the core; the hard disk is becoming an increasingly necessary addition to floppy disks for holding and quickly accessing modern software. The mouse is a strongly recommended addition, especially for word processing or for graphics-based systems. IBM compatible machines are attractive because they make up a large share of the machines in existence and much software is available for them. A name-brand IBM *clone* with a 80386sx processor and a VGA adaptor would – at the time or writing – be a cost-effective option, and one that would not date too quickly. Apple Macintosh-type systems have their own ardent followers; Macs are extremely easy to use, have many elegant technical strengths, and are now competitively priced. The range of software and peripherals available is substantially more limited than for the IBM types, but if institutional support exists for Macs then they are a very tempting option.[2]

Portable computers are an attractive option if extensive research work inside archives or libraries is planned, or if there is not sufficient space in a home or hall of residence to have a full-size machine permanently set up. *Laptops* and *notebooks* now may have the same features as full-size systems: the same processor, big hard disks, suitability for peripherals, QWERTY keyboard, etc. On the other hand they are more expensive than comparable non-portables, the keyboard may be cramped and – if not running off the mains – batteries need to be recharged every few hours. Another option, if library and archive use is a critical factor, is an inexpensive *pocket computer*, like the Sinclair Z88. This would not be at all comparable to standard IBM or Mac, but it would be a quarter the price of a laptop or notebook and suitable for note-taking and entry of raw data; the data can be *downloaded* (i.e. copied) to a conventional microcomputer for the more complex editing, manipulation, and presentation.

Turning to output, modern graphics-oriented software requires a colour monitor rather than a monochrome one to be used most effectively. An inexpensive dot matrix printer is also probably a requirement. As mentioned above, really fancy printing can hopefully be done on an institutional laser printer.

It is important to be careful about where the equipment is bought. For new users in particular after-sales 'support', including 'on-site' service, can be more valuable than high discounting of the retail price, e.g. from a mail-order company.

Advice for institutions is even more difficult to give than for individuals. The goal would probably be the same kinds of machines mentioned above, but networked together with a file-server (in effect, a master computer) so that they can share software and peripherals like printers. An additional shared por-table might be considered. For all this it is important to ensure that the key equipment is covered by warranty and/or service contracts.

The choice of software is even more dependent on an individual's or an institution's requirements and budget. Possible uses will be discussed later in this book. Software is not cheap – a basic suite (like a lounge suite) of software – word processor, database, spreadsheet, and statistics package would – at industry-standard quality and commercial prices – cost as much or more than a hard-disk standard micro with a printer and mouse. Even if it is anticipated that the major use of the computer will be word processing, a single-purpose system – a dedicated word processor – is not using the machine's potential fully; at the very least a database manager (DBMS) should be available. One answer may be an *integrated package* like Microsoft Works, which typically contains all the basic suite – except statistics software – in one package. Integrated packages often come 'bundled', i.e. 'free' with computer systems. (On the other hand, you get what you pay for.)

For UK higher education *CHEST* (Combined Higher Education Software Team) offer significant discounts on hardware and software; in general it is always important to look out for 'educational discounts'.

The aim of this chapter has been to introduce the elements of a standard microcomputer system – the hardware and the software. You should now have some understanding of the elementary aspects of running computer programs, and can begin to look at how they can be useful to historians.

Notes

1 The widely-available Consumers' Association magazine *Which?* regularly publishes simple and easy to understand articles for beginners on a few of the most commonly available products; these articles avoid the worst excesses of the trade/technical press. See, for example, 'Computing options', *Which?*, December 1991, pp. 709–13.

2 A clear comparison of the relative attractions of the PC and the Mac, written for historians and still not outdated, is Donald Spaeth, 'Which micro?', in *History and Computing*, I, 1989, pp. 145–8.

Chapter 3
Word processing for historians

Historians often come to the computer through word processing. Most historians write enough to feel the need sooner or later for direct access to some means of producing a typescript. Since even quite simple word-processing packages will allow infinite editing and re-drafting, easily controlled footnoting and searching, and some degree of control over the appearance of the final text, word processing has obvious value to all but those rare writers who can produce a perfect and definitive text on a typewriter without any preliminary drafts or intermediary editing. With at least a mid-range system there will be scope for note-taking, outlining, indexing, alphabetical sorting, key-word searching, correction of spelling and many other facilities. Even after just a few hours spent learning the essentials of a word-processing system, some of the practical advantages will be apparent; soon the savings in time and efficiency will also be obvious.

This chapter will not attempt to describe any one or more programs in detail. Rather, it is intended as a pointer towards aspects of word processing which historians at any level will find useful: from basic writing, note-taking and dissertation-outlining, through more complex formatting in the style of desktop publishing, to searching and import/export of text files for analysis. Word processing is both a practical way of getting to know how computers work, and a means of looking more closely at textual data of the kind that historians might use as raw material.

Which program?

For simple writing and editing of text, one kind of word processor may appear as good as another. Before becoming too deeply

committed to any one system, however, it may be worthwhile, as
with all computer applications, considering one's precise needs.
What follows is based on the assumption that the historian will
wish to go beyond the limitations of a dedicated word processor
(a machine that will not do anything else).

The most commonly used word-processing systems have significant differences. For example, the popular Amstrad PCW,
launched some years ago with an early version of LocoScript, was
remarkable not just for its price, but also for its ability to cope
with foreign alphabets. Its footnoting system, however, was crude,
and the quality of printing on the standard cheap system not very
satisfactory. Moreover, large texts, in say 20,000-word sections,
were liable to catch the machine short of memory.

On a mid-range machine running packages like WordPerfect,
WordStar or Word (either on an Apple Macintosh or an IBM-
type machine) there will be a wide range of facilities: foot- or
endnotes that automatically rearrange and renumber themselves
when the text to which they belong is moved, a wide range of
typefaces and font sizes (depending on the printer used), facilities
for sorting lists and printing in columns, a page-preview before
printing, and many other extras.

But even here there are real drawbacks: the historian who uses
languages other than English, for example, will find the nearly
universal but antiquated American-designed ASCII sets of
characters (including the extended version) frustrating and crude.
Some packages, like Word for Windows, have made the extended
character set more accessible by means of natural key combi-
nations. Other word processors have adopted alternative keyboard
layouts or keyboard customisation facilities, but none of these is
fully satisfactory for regular multilingual use, let alone for different
alphabets. Solutions to the problem already exist, in the form
of new standards such as those of the International Standards
Organization (*ISO*) and of *UNICODE*, exploiting the full potential
of 16- and 32-bit processors;[1] but it is not yet clear how widely
these will be adopted in new generations of standard software.

Instead, the more specialist user may face some difficult choices.
One solution is to customise the keyboard to individual requirements, but this is a time-consuming task which may have to be re-
done every time new software releases are adopted, printers
replaced, or texts sent to other systems. Instead, a powerful and

genuinely academic-orientated application like Nota Bene might be the answer – and with it the user would then also have a text retrieval program of some power. The more specialised a package, however, the less interchangeable it is with other systems. For everyday use, therefore, one of the common mid-range word processors, with minimal modifications if necessary, might prove the least unsatisfactory.

Keying in the basic text

There are many excellent guides to the common word-processing programs, so this and the following sections will merely suggest some of the features of most obvious value.

As noted in Chapter 2, the keyboard of any computer will have a middle section similar to that of typewriters.[2] For word processing, it is used much like a typewriter, except for some specific features. Firstly, it is worth noticing that the computer always acts (and usually ONLY acts) on what is *highlighted* – this means it is possible to work on any part of a screen of existing text by moving the *cursor* (the highlighted area) to any particular point, word, line or section of text. Secondly, the ENTER or CARRIAGE RETURN key should never be used except where a new line is indispensable (as for a paragraph): the computer will determine its own line-breaks (*word-wrap*), depending on the paper and layout being used.

In addition, a number of keys have distinctive functions in word processing. The backspace key is a quick means of correcting errors: it deletes back from wherever the cursor is placed, and like most other keys on the computer is a repeating key if held down. The SHIFT key works just as on a typewriter, but the CAPITAL LOCK key usually only affects letters, not the numbers and symbols. The TAB key will work as on a big typewriter, but will be able to align columns either on the left, the right or on any decimal point used. Other keys, notably ESCape, the Function keys, CTRL, and so on, will also have specific functions, which will depend on the particular word processor, but may offer significant short-cuts for more advanced use. If a mouse is fitted, it is worth adopting it immediately as a quick alternative to the arrow-direction keys at one end of the keyboard: it will often be quicker to use the mouse to shift the cursor, highlight words and passages, exchange adjacent passages, scroll, and (especially in applications with pull-down menus) perform many other functions as well. The mouse may seem a little awkward at first, but most users find it an enormous help once they have become familiar with it.

To get started, type in a passage of text, and then experiment with the facilities available on the system to see which ones are likely to be of use. First of all correct minor errors, and swap words and sentences around. Experiment with the *cut-and-paste* facilities: the different ways of deleting a section to scrap, re-inserting it elsewhere, copying, or deleting permanently. Try typing in new sections in the middle of existing passages, to see how the machine moves the text round. Switch to over-typing if the new text is to replace what is there already. Then centre any titles, add italics and bold type, and standardise the basic typing so that there is always one space after a comma, two or three after semi-colons and full stops, equal indentation for paragraphs, and so on.

Experiment on something that is not irreplaceable: at first some unexpected things may happen, and text may even appear to get lost. Neither the machine nor the software, however, will be harmed. Learn from the mistakes by working out what happened. Most users (including the two authors of this book, who wrote it using Word on 386 machines) continue to discover new things either by accident or by deliberate experimentation: the latest systems are so complex that few users will try to take in everything first (or even second) time round. Whenever a feature is needed which does not come instinctively (say, one-and-a-half line spacing, right-hand justification, tabulations, or special symbols) it is easy to look for them via the manual or the on-line help facilities that most applications have.

Operating systems, files and saving

The techniques used for editing and handling files (texts or data) with a word processor are not fundamentally different from those required for other applications. In order to keep track of files, and not 'lose' anything, it will be worth gaining some familiarity with the basic principles of operating systems and file management.

In any kind of computing, and especially in word processing, it is essential to save edited work regularly and systematically. Saving takes only a moment, and can avoid a great deal of trouble if text is accidentally garbled or there is a power-cut. If a hard disk is available, save there for greatest speed, but make sure to back up on floppy disks regularly. Floppies are less likely than hard disks to cause really serious problems, and are so cheap that there is no reason not to have several copies in different locations for maximum security. Some word processors can be set to save automatically at pre-determined intervals; but in any case it is a good idea to save every time a significant section of text has been added, and at least once every half hour or so of working time. The program will most likely also create an automatic back-up file (in effect the previous saved version) which can be recalled if necessary.

Underneath the software visible to the user, every computer runs an operating system. Sometimes the presence of the operating system is not obvious: on Apple Macintosh computers, and on IBM-type ones running the Windows environment designed to imitate the Mac, it is hidden under a façade (user interface) where pull-down menus and small pictures (icons) allow the user to perform operations more or less intuitively, without knowing anything about what is actually happening. Sooner or later, however, and especially if something unexpected happens, the user will come into contact with what lies underneath.

Different types of machines have different operating systems (or newer releases of the same system), and any one operating system may not behave identically on different makes of computer because it may be adapted ('tweaked') for particular purposes. However, the overall syntax will be largely the same for any one version of a standard operating system.

Any version of MS-DOS (Microsoft Disk Operating System), for example, will identify the computer's storage devices by means of letters: often a C: for the hard disk, A: for the first floppy disk drive, and so on. At any given time there is always what is known as the *default drive* – the current drive (hard disk, floppy or virtual drive) where the computer will act when the user gives a command.

To save a newly created file, any word processor will prompt the user for a *filename*. This will normally consist of three elements:

(1) The drive to which the file will be sent. If a drive name

(like 'A:') is not included, the text will automatically be saved in whatever the default drive is at the time of saving. Files rarely disappear without good cause: but the default drive may not at first be intuitive, so a little checking may avoid later anxiety.

(2) The name chosen for the file by the user. In DOS this may not be more than 8 characters long, must start with a letter, and cannot include either a blank space or certain reserved characters like * or \.

(3) A suffix which may be allocated automatically by the system. It is no more than three characters long, and is preceded by a full stop. In Word, the suffix .DOC is the normal one for a word-processed file, and .BAK for the back-up created during the last saving.

A typical response to a saving-prompt would therefore be to type in A:MYFILE. In a listing of what is on the floppy disk (called up in DOS by means of the DIRectory command, on a Mac or Windows system by selecting an appropriate menu) this file might then appear as MYFILE.DOC.

The larger UNIX operating system now common on some bigger workstations has a far more complex (and at times nearly impenetrable) syntax, but similar basic commands exist. The command **ls** produces a listing of files, **rm** deletes files, **man** gives on-line help information, and so on. In an ideal world the user should not need to worry much about the operating system: in the recent version of Microsoft Windows, for example, not even a salvage operation from a software crash requires DOS knowledge on the part of the user. However, to be on the safe side it is as well to be familiar with at least the basic commands.

As we noted in Chapter 2, each letter, space or other key-stroke of a file normally takes up one *byte*, so a 2,000-word essay may take around 15 kilobytes (Kb) of storage space. Each file of text can, on a middle-range machine, be of virtually any size, subject to the availability of sufficient *RAM* and sufficient storage space on the disks used. However, although there may be room for very large files, scrolling and searching will naturally become slower and less efficient, so it may often be best to allocate individual chapters of a dissertation or book to separate files. Such separate files can always be appended to each other (or in some programs treated in sequence without being joined) to allow easier searching or indexing.

In order not to clutter disks with large numbers of files, it will often be sensible to divide disks into directories and sub-directories, which, like sections in a filing cabinet, can each be labelled. In DOS, the command MKDIR DISS1 (make a new directory called 'diss1' for dissertation drafts) will mark off a section of the default drive (floppy or hard disk) under that name. That directory can be accessed through the change directory command (CD DISS1 will make that directory the current default directory). As a rule, always keep software applications in separate directories from personal text and other work files; and consider separating the latter into a logical hierarchy of directories and sub-directories, for ease of use. Sooner or later time will be saved if files and directories are given names which are as obvious and intuitive as possible.

If the machine does not have its own clock, make sure to adopt the habit, whenever starting up, of always entering at least the current date. This will ensure that each saved file will be dated, and thereby help avoid confusion later if several copies are made for safety. In most operating systems a list of all files on disk or in a directory can be called up in such a way as to show, with each filename, information on its size (in Kb), and the date and time of saving. This information is also vital in the unlikely event of file-reconstitution from the scraps left behind after a system crash.

Printing and WYSIWYG

Printing is the most obvious form of output for a word processed file: a *hard copy* (paper print-out) will probably be required even at an early stage, for checking. Most systems have a 'default' setting for printing which, with luck, may match the hardware used. Such default settings may select an appropriate *printer driver* (the part of the software which allows communication with the printing device itself),[3] the size of paper to be used, the width of margins all round, the presence and location of page-numbers, running heads, and footnotes, and the font to be employed. Most systems will also allow changes to these settings to be saved permanently as new default settings or as separate instructions in a 'style sheet'.

When printing, some experimentation will often be necessary at first in order to arrive at a visually satisfactory layout for a particular software–printer combination. It will probably be necessary to experiment with fonts, indentations, and margins; to check page-breaks to ensure that the last line of a paragraph is not printed as a 'widow' at the top of a new page or a title left at the bottom as an 'orphan'; and to examine the alignment of difficult sections such as complex tables – not to mention graphs and diagrams of the kind that bigger word processors will allow the user to import from statistics and spreadsheet software. Once saved, the text will reproduce in identical form at a subsequent printing on the same hardware. But, as in conventional printing, editorial changes may affect the overall layout, and a change of printer (say to a laser printer for the final copy) may also alter the layout.

Word processors will, to varying degrees, give an impression on screen of what the printed text will be like. No program is fully *WYSIWYG* (such that 'what you see is what you get')[4] – at the very best there will be only minor discrepancies (dependent on the printer), but more likely the screen will give only a rough approximation. It may reflect italics, bold, underlining and superscript in the extended ASCII character set. But unless it is a large windows-type program it is unlikely to show differences between fonts, non-standard line-spacing, double-column printing – or even the exact line breaks if printed in anything other than the often ungainly default font (Pica 12 on many DOS machines, an even larger typeface on older Macs).

Most significantly, however, the user will rarely see a full page in one screen: normal word-processing screens give a maximum of 80 characters across and 24 lines down, neither of which corresponds to common printing standards. Even if one can compensate by calling up a preview of the whole page, the resolution on the screen is unlikely to be good enough to get more than a general impression of the diminutive-looking type.

Some writers find the restriction to a maximum of 24 lines of text at a time a real limitation when editing and re-writing. It is possible to compensate a little for this drawback. For example, by splitting the working area into two or more concurrent windows, two separate sections can be displayed at once (or the text and its attendant footnotes). This will of course reduce the size of each, and may need some care when it comes to saving, but can reduce the need for cumbersome scrolling. Screen-splitting is of course also used for editing parallel texts. Sooner or later, however, a draft *printout* will be indispensable for final checking.

Taking word processing further

There is more to a word-processed text file than just the words of the text. All key-strokes on a computer produce characters in the file. Some, like new-line markers or the space produced by the space-bar, can be made visible on the screen by changing the display. Others, like some control characters (sequences of instructions used by the program), may be beyond recall on the screen. It is worth experimenting with the display to see what is available: observe, for example, the difference between genuine keyed spaces and 'empty' space (for example at the end of a paragraph), since such matters may be of importance in explaining otherwise puzzling results in a print-out. Occasionally, for example when doing complicated tabulations, it may also be helpful to change the display so that markers for tab stops and new lines become visible on screen for correction.

Some word processors can also be made to incorporate additional codes for index-marked words, title-words to be used for automatic content-listing and outlining, and other special features. Once the user begins to explore the potential of such mark-up, however, it soon becomes apparent that word-processors are much more than just 'smart typewriters'. The following sections will explore some of this potential.

Rough notes and outlines

One of the great advantages of a word processor is that there is no need to worry about textual detail during initial stages of drafting. A nearly random approach at first may help to get over writer's block, and it is often a good idea to enter notes, rough ideas and even reminders as they occur. What in a manuscript would be marginal notes can in some more complex word processors be entered as such, along with outlines and other jottings not intended for inclusion in the final text. But even if such facilities are not explicitly available, it is easy to mark out jottings and reminders by, for example, enclosing them in curly brackets, indenting them on a separate line, scoring them through without deleting, or highlighting them in some way for easy location later on. The ability to move around text in any case ensures that nothing need be lost, and nothing need be retyped unnecessarily.

If note-taking is an important part of your writing process, it is worth using some special features available in most packages. These include glossaries, whereby a short code is used to represent longer, more awkward phrases: if for example a text often includes the phrase 'the Imperial Free Cities of the Holy Roman Empire', one might assign the glossary code 'fc' to the whole phrase, and thereby reduce it to just two key strokes plus a Function Key every time it occurs. Alternatively, a consistent author might adopt a whole set of personal shorthand abbreviations, which can later be expanded into the full text by means of the 'Search and Replace' facility available on even small word processors. For more sophisticated mark-up, the rarely used characters on the keyboard (like the @ or the | signs) can be adopted as specific personal search codes to help locate particular types of annotations, phrases or indexable keywords at a later stage. It is worth remembering that, even if the application itself does not allow for unprinted marginal annotations, outlining, automatic indexing, or content-listing, a personal set of conventions can always be designed using distinct text-markers, which are easily removed before final printing by means of the 'Search and Replace' facility.

Footnotes and bibliographies

To ensure full flexibility in editing, it is essential that footnotes are entered in the way required by the integral facilities of the program, otherwise they may be garbled or misplaced during subsequent editing. Never attempt to enter footnotes at the bottom of the page as if using a typewriter: total confusion will sooner or later be the result. Most programs allow footnotes to be edited like any other part of the text, and material copied to or from the main text. This may happen via a separate footnote screen, or on the same screen via a separate section at the very end of the text file (regardless of whether bottom of the page printing has been selected). To avoid tedious scrolling or switching, a separate footnote window (allowing simultaneous viewing) can usually be opened.

Bibliographies can be treated like any other part of the word-processed text. To save time and facilitate last-minute editing, however, it may be worth considering storing a large bibliography not as a normal text but as a structured database. It is now increasingly easy to copy information from one application to another, even if the two are not directly linked within a single environment (such as Microsoft Windows). A bibliography entered as a structured database in a DBMS (database managing system) can be coded and sorted like any other data, and its fields (for example the year of publication) edited more quickly than would be the case if the information were held in a word processor. When ready, the data can then be listed into ASCII format (with, for example, commas separating the fields), saved as a text file, if necessary renamed, and then loaded into the word processor for final printing.

Many types of files can in fact be loaded into and out of word processors with more ease than the beginner might suspect. There is, for example, no problem about dumping blocks of data even out of the mainframe relational database manager Ingres, renaming them, and loading them into Word for editing and printing. Provided the Word text is saved unformatted and with delimiters, the process can just as readily be reversed. Some experimentation may be necessary for exchanges between unrelated applications, but provided back-up copies are kept there is no reason not to try.

Checking spelling and syntax

There are many additional features available to the user of a mid-range word-processing package. A spelling-checker facility, for example, may save time by locating typing errors. Provided the system can distinguish correct British and American spellings, it will pick up only unrecognisable words (including proper names), and will allow the user to correct these if appropriate – or indeed to revise (customise) the 'dictionary' itself. Spelling-checkers should never, however, be trusted fully: after all, the computer will not know whether 'there' is intended instead of 'their'.

Often a thesaurus can be called up on-line, to assist with problems. If you are working under contractual restraints of space, an automatic word-count will also be useful. In addition, there are a great variety of more complex applications which can

be used alongside existing word-processing software to help check
syntax and grammar (either for British or for American users).

Page layout

There is more to word processing than just getting the words
right. A clear sense of the structure of a text, its headings,
paragraphing, and logic, are all crucial skills which the computer
can help to make explicit. At the most basic level, a footnote laid
out in a standard scholarly way (for example with full name of
author, italicised title, place and date of publication, and page
references) will be much quicker to absorb. Similarly, a long
quotation, if indented, separated from the main text by a blank
line, and suitably noted, will not be mistaken. It may be desirable
to change the spacing of the lines themselves: a good word
processor will allow a wide variety of spacing, including the
neat 1½-line spacing commonly used on typewriters. If, as in
Word, formatting and layout can be standardised into a separate
style sheet, which can then be used on other files, uniformity of
presentation will be much easier to achieve.

No less important, however, is the logical structure within
the body of the text. Every text has a structure underlying its
apparently fluent prose; it is often instructive to identify that
structure explicitly by means of editorial mark-up, and to learn
how to use an implicit structure to best effect. These are skills
that should be central to any educational system, and which
deserve attention even after formal training is over.

For a more professional appearance, some care should be
taken over the justification of both margins, and over *microspacing*
(typesetting in units other than the fixed space by which a typewriter always moves its carriage). Right-hand justification may
not look right (and will certainly not make for easy reading) if the
software or the printer is unable to cope either with proportionally
spaced letters or with the microjustification of gaps between
words. Proportionally spaced fonts allocate noticeably different
widths to different letters across the page (the letter 'm' being
wider than 'i', for example); microjustification is when all the
gaps between words on a given line are of identical size (rather
than, say, a mixture of the single and double standard space-bar
strokes that might be required to make up the correct length of

```
This    is  the  kind  of  typeface  you  would  expect  from  a
conventional  typewriter.   Such a  machine is  not capable  of
spacing  letters proportionally  according to their  true width,
so  regardless of  the font  used it  will never  look  like  a
proper  typeset text.   Nor  can it microspace the gaps between
words:   since  this text  is justified at both  margins,  the
spaces  between some  words on  a single  line is  larger  than
between  others, destroying  the visual effect and slowing down
effective reading speed by "tripping" the eye.

If we now switch to microspacing, you will instantly recognise that
the visual effect is far better.  The font still looks much like
that on a typewriter, and is in fact the same size in printer's
points, but it looks more compact.  This is because the letters are
spaced more accurately.  As a result, reading is easier even
without right-hand justification.

If we now justify the right hand margin as well, you will notice
that what really makes a difference is the fact that full mi-
crospacing is incorporated:  all gaps between words in any one line
are the same.  Gaps between words on different lines have also
been brought nearer one another by using the automatic hyphen-
ation facility available on most machines.  As a result, the text
not only makes a more pleasing visual effect, but is also faster to
read.
```

Figure 3.1 Microspacing text on the page

line). These details do not usually show up on screen, but will be readily apparent on the page (see Figure 3.1). If the system is not set up to give microspacing of both letters and gaps, a more satisfactory visual effect is arguably achieved by not adopting right-hand justification at all.

Whichever solution is adopted, greater uniformity from line to line can be achieved by allowing hyphenation of long words at the end of the lines as appropriate. This should be done as the last stage before printing, since changes (including changes of font or of printer) may entail alterations in line-breaks. If an automatic hyphenation facility is available, it will normally be possible to set it such that each instance can be verified in turn: unsatisfactory hyphenations can thereby be avoided.

Desktop publishing and commercial publishers

Sophisticated use of the facilites summarised in the previous sections will, in combination with a high-quality printer, produce results indistinguishable from some commercial printing. With powerful facilities like those of Word for Windows (version 2), Pagemaker or Ventura Publisher, an impressive range of styles, fonts and layouts is attainable. MacPaint on an Apple Macintosh, or IBM imitations, will add attractive graphics and illustrations. This is ideal for student newspapers, broadsheets, journals or other publications with limited circulation, where a full-scale commercial production may not be viable.

With a system capable of controlling all aspects of page layout and typesetting, we have reached what is loosely called *desktop publishing*. It is very exciting to produce high-quality output from one's own computer; but a word of caution may yet be in order. For a start, the purist would point out that desktop publishing applications have no hope of living up to the name: they can neither market a book, nor even duplicate and bind it! However, there are less obvious problems as well. A large degree of authorial control may, at least for perfectionists, slow down completion rather than speed it up. Desktop publishing is in any case time-consuming and at times frustrating. Whilst electronic manuscripts and greater involvement of the author in the actual production process could ensure less frustration when it comes to proof-reading, the intermediary stages may entail the acquisition of skills not really relevant to the author. If these skills are not mastered, the result may be visually distracting or messy. Worse, such a text will also lack the visual guide to structure which a well-produced typeset book will offer. Since it is at times notoriously difficult to see even the substantive weaknesses in one's own writing, it may in any case be of benefit to have a professional editorial publishing staff sharing all the responsibilities from manuscript editing to final production.

In practice, anyone contemplating writing for commercial pub-lication will for some time yet have to adopt a compromise: submitting both hard copy and electronic manuscript, and in effect surrendering control over the details of production to the editorial staff of the publisher. If that is the case, it is essential to agree with the publisher exactly what should be in the electronic manuscript. Many publishers do not yet welcome complex embed-ded codes and formattings of text, for the simple reason that their printer's phototypesetting equipment will not recognise them. Often only the basic ASCII text is wanted, with nothing more than the most elementary styling such as paragraphing, italics, bold and underlining. Few publishers will want such frills as software-controlled footnotes or electronically derived indices and lists of contents, since these will not correspond to those of the final printing.[5]

The problems of compatibility between different word-processing applications in fact raise fundamental issues which are already being addressed. A case can be made for separating text-editing proper from the visual formatting of the output.[6] Word-processing applications are in fact all derivatives of much older mainframe text editors 'bundled' together with text formatting facilities, screen–image formatters (controlling what appears on screen) and printer drivers. Many word processors allow the user the option of saving a text unformatted (that is, without all the embedded codes of styling and layout), and it is essential to do so if a standard ASCII file is needed for transmission over a network or for transfer to an independent application. In the process, however, what will be lost is not only stylistic formatting but also in some cases the special characters in the extended ASCII set, including foreign letters and diacriticals. Consequently, transfers of text between different systems invariably at present entail some editing by the recipient.

If the text-editing and text-formatting functions are separated (or at least made distinct in the mind of the user), the opportunity arises for adopting a generic mark-up scheme such as that defined by the *Text Encoding Initiative* (*TEI*), within the parameters of *Standard Generalised Markup Language* (*SGML* – a set of internationally agreed rules regarding the principles of mark-up and formatting). A file with such mark-up codes could more readily be reconstituted within a variety of different applications: the explanation of the codes would be determined by a generic standard independent of the particular environment. Such an approach will sooner or later help overcome the barriers between different word processors, and between any one of these and commercial phototypesetters or mainframe academic text-handling systems. Not only will this make desktop publishing itself much more versatile; it will also allow, for example, the text of a biographical dictionary to serve both as the basis for printing and as the basis for a machine-readable database.[7]

This chapter has outlined some of the enormous range of facilities which ordinary word processors offer. After using a word processor, few will ever want to revert to typewriters. At the very least, the ability to clarify a line of argument by moving around sections of text will be appreciated by anyone other than the legendary writer who gets everything right first time. For bigger writing tasks the word processor also offers dramatic possibilities for rough outlining, note-taking, footnoting, import and export of both data and analysis-reports from other software, controlled editing and revising, as well as real flexibility in terms of presentation.

However, the historian will also be interested in the potential of moving text from a word processor into an application that can do some textual analysis. This is an area where considerable development can be expected over the next few years: Chapter 12 will provide some pointers in that direction.

Notes

1 The original ASCII set of characters was finalised in 1967. It used 7 of the 8 bits in the standard byte, producing altogether 128 (2 raised to the power of 7) different characters. Subsequently, the International Standards Organization produced agreement to incorporate the eighth bit, thereby doubling the number of characters to 256 (2 to the power of 8), and creating the extended ASCII character set which is still widely used at present. This eighth bit, however, has to be used for parity check during transmission over communication lines, so any characters from the extended character set are liable to be distorted during such transmission: that is why only the original 128 characters can be used reliably for data exchange. Already in 1984, however, the ISO also envisaged standard 16- and 32-bit character sets for all world languages. UNICODE developed from this in 1987, as a project to map and organise all the necessary character sets, including those required for Far Eastern languages. Much of this has now been achieved.

2 The layout of the standard typewriter keyboard, known in English as the QWERTY keyboard from the sequence of its first letters, may in itself take some getting used to: if necessary, one of the touch-typing tutorials available with many word processors may prove helpful.

3 When a new word processor is installed, some experimentation with its alternative printer drivers will often be necessary. Some systems also allow the user to modify the printer driver itself, for example to alter the typeface or to move symbols to different keys.

4 No less appropriate might be the variants proposed by Lou Burnard: WYSMSY ('what you see may surprise you'), or GOKWYG ('God

only knows what you get') – cited in S. Rahtz, 'The processing of words', in *Information Technology in the Humanities*, ed. S. Rahtz, Chichester, 1987, p. 75.

5 A useful short guide is to be found in *Word Processing and Publishing: Some Guidelines for Authors*, compiled by P. Denley for The British Academy and the Office for Humanities Communication, Leicester, 1985.

6 The case for this is well argued in D. Andrews and M. Greenhalgh, *Computing for non-Scientific Applications*, Leicester, 1987, pp. 210–36. See also S. Rahtz, 'The processing of words', in *Information Technology in the Humanities*, ed. S. Rahtz, Chichester, 1987, pp. 69–79.

7 Some word processors, including WordPerfect, now include an SGML option. For further discussion of SGML, see below, p. 177–9.

Part II

CENSUS: an introductory historical database

Chapter 4
Structured sources

Part II of this book is a case study of how to create, modify, and analyse a database created from an historical source. This chapter is about how the source can be put into the database.

A useful concrete example of a source is the nineteenth-century British population census. The census has a number of attractions. It gives unique insights into practically any part of British society. Because similar questions were asked of the population every ten years it is possible to get a sense of change over time. Although the example used here comes from Glasgow in 1851, historians with an interest in any part of the British Isles in the late nineteenth century can apply the same techniques to their own place and time. Raw census data is readily available in libraries and record offices, and often local historians and genealogists will already be familiar with it.

The census is not only of general interest as an historical source, but is highly structured and therefore well suited to computerisation. Indeed, one of the first uses of primitive computers at the end of the nineteenth century was in national censuses in the United States, Austria–Hungary, and elsewhere. Later, in the 1940s, the census was an area where the modern electronic computer (UNIVAC) was pioneered.

Appendix I contains census information for 100 people from the Gorbals district of Glasgow. One way to use this chapter and the three that follow it is actually to key those records into a computer database and then to ask some historical questions about them.[1] The idea is to give a small practical example of what can be done.

The British census

Censuses are held in Britain every ten years. The results are available as printed volumes soon after the census is taken. In these books the information gathered in the census is lumped together (aggregated) to give an overall picture of the society – based on *aggregate data*, e.g. there are 100 bakers in the Gorbals census district. In contrast, the census information on individuals (the *nominal* data), e.g. John Smith is a baker, is confidential. This information is generally not released to historical researchers until a hundred years after the census; the 1891 census is the last that is available for most census districts.[2]

Although the aggregate census data is a most important source, there are a number of reasons why historians would want to get back to the data on individuals. Modern historians often have different or more precise or more complex questions than the original census-takers. They may want to link census information with non-census information, and for effective linkage aggregate data will not do. To get individual data it is necessary to refer to the original records produced by the census-takers. After the designated night of the census, census-takers ('enumerators') visited every household in the country and collected the forms ('schedules') which people were required to fill in. The census-takers then transferred this data to enumerator's books. Microfilms of the returns in these books, at least for 1851–91, are available in regional libraries. Figure 4.1 is a facsimile of census-taker's book, showing information about 20 people living in Malta Street, Glasgow, in 1851 (Appendix I reprints these 20, plus another 80).

This document makes it clear that structured data was not something thought up in the computer era, or even in the twentieth century. A great deal of the data which historians work with is already structured. The idea of structure can mean different things at different times, but it might be defined here as information about a number of different things (in the case of the census, of people) about whom several items of information are always known (name, age, etc.).

In the case of the census data the government wanted information about the people of the UK. In the census-taker's book each row (horizontal line) related to one individual, and the ten

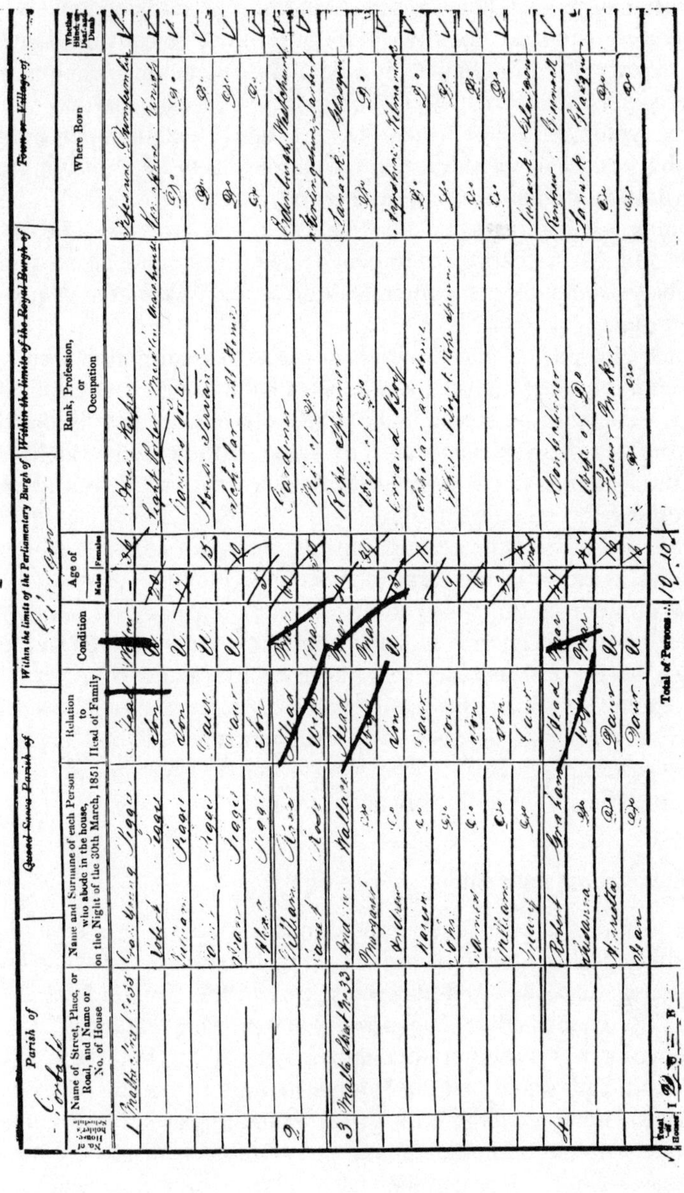

Figure 4.1 Specimen of a page from a census-taker's book

columns provided uniform categories which could be applied to any individual in the country. This layout from the mid-nineteenth century can be of a help in understanding the fundamentals of a structured database. The rows of the return can be converted into the *records* (the basic units) of a database. Sometimes computer records are called *rows*, *observations*, *cases*, or even *entities*.

The columns in the census-taker's book include household number, address, name/surname, relationship to head of family, [marital] condition, age/sex, occupation, and place of birth.[3] The columns are categories of information which are the same for each and every record; they can be made into the *fields* of a database. Sometimes computer fields are called *variables*, *columns*, or *attributes*.

Each box on the page contains a piece of information which, once put into the database, would be called a *value*. The technical term 'value' can be misleading. Values are not necessarily to do with money or even numbers. The value of the database field is the information that is in it; if 'Marital Condition' were a field, then the value might be 'Widow'.

The structure of the census information is not confined to the fact that it exists in the form of rows and columns, i.e. that the same number of things are known about each person. Another aspect of the structure is that the information was entered in the return by the census-taker in a more or less standardised way. For example, the census-takers had instructions about how to describe particular occupations – although they did not always follow these instructions. The same kind of standardisation is extremely useful in an historical database.

Thinking about data entry

The next step is actually to transform the source in Appendix I, the 100 residents of the Gorbals, into a database. (The terms 'database', 'datafile', and 'databank' can, at this general level, be used interchangeably.) The process of entering data will vary from computer program to computer program, but there are basic principles that will be found in most programs. Before trying to create a database for the first time it is useful to become familiar with an existing database on any subject, just to see how databases work. Most commercial database programs include in the instruction manual some whimsical small-business database as an example of what can be done.

The database will exist as a computer file and will have some sort of name (or filename). This is exactly like the filenames for word-processor files mentioned in Chapter 3. Any word of eight letters or less can be chosen as a filename: the file being created from the Appendix I data will be referred to as *CENSUS*. The file can be saved under this name to a storage device like a floppy disk at each stage of its development – just like a word-processor file. Once the database structure has been created in one session and a number of records have been entered, the process can be stopped; it is always possible to come back to the computer later, load the database using its filename, and continue data entry or data analysis from where it ended in the previous session. The file will also be re-loaded under this name when the user wants to begin analysing the data.

Having assigned a name, a much more complex task begins. Exactly what information is to be taken from the paper source, and how is it to be recorded? These questions should be sorted out before data entry begins; a thoughtful session with pencil and paper is essential and will save much more time later on. The next step is to create a small pilot version of the database, with five to ten records; simple questions can be tried out with the model to see how it should be altered. It should be possible to modify the database structure even after some records have been entered, but it is better to start with a solid foundation.

The database software will allow the user to create some kind of uniform structure (e.g. eight categories of information for which data will later be provided). An example of a paper version of this is a blank census-taker's return, before the data was filled in. In computing terms this blank form is sometimes called a *template*. The data can then be filled in, following the template, record by record.

The categories of information are the fields (or variables). Each field needs to be given a *fieldname*. Long fieldnames are unsuitable; database software usually demands short names, and a long name is inconvenient when questions are being asked. 'Relation to Head of Family' is, in effect, the fieldname in the census-taker's book, but in the database some kind of abbreviation will be used – like RELN. The fieldname also should not be too short, as it has to be easily remembered; four to eight characters is about right.

Aside from deciding on fieldnames, some other decisions may have to be made about what form the database will take. It will probably have to be decided whether a particular field is going to be one of numbers or words (*alphanumeric*). A decision is not necessarily final here – it may be possible later to change the characteristics of a field – but it is easier to make changes at an early stage. As a simple rule of thumb the values in a number field are ones on which mathematical operations can be performed. To take an example, suppose there is a field for 'year of birth' and it is decided that this is to be a numerical field. The value '1910 or 1911' (i.e. including the word 'or') cannot appear in this field; the database will treat this as words rather than numbers. A mathematical operation (e.g. finding the average year of birth) could not be carried out on '1910 or 1911'; it has to be either '1910' or '1911'. Many systems also have a special information type for dates (day-month-year).

Whether a field is numerical or alpha, the computer will also normally have to be told at this stage the maximum number of characters that any field can contain. This decision is important for two reasons. File storage space may be limited. Many database managers count blank spaces as characters; if 80 characters were allotted to a field, and there was never a value in the field of more than 20 characters in length, 60 characters per record would be wasted. One character takes up one byte of file space; if there were 1,000 records that would be a wastage of 60,000 bytes, for just that field. A second reason for keeping fields compact relates to possible display: it must be remembered that only about 80 characters of text can be fitted across the screen (or printed on an A4 page).

Standardisation and coding: introduction

A fundamental question is whether the data should go into the database exactly as it appears in the source, for example in Figure 4.1 or Appendix I. Altering the data means that to a greater or lesser extent the source is being tampered with; how important is this? Coding will be discussed more in Chapter 6, but for the moment it can be said that altering the sources at the data-entry stage has a number of advantages and a number of disadvantages.

A quick examination of a real historical source, Figure 4.1, shows that it would be foolish simply to replicate it mechanically (Appendix I is just such a replication). This is the case even though the census-taker's book is better than many other sources: it is highly structured and has been filled in in a legible and fairly consistent way.

How should the anomalies in the original be dealt with? Should the 'dittos' ('Do') used (inconsistently) by the census-taker be repeated exactly, or should the data entry assume Margaret 'Do' is really Margaret Wallace? Should the full version of little Alexander Piggie's name be used, or Alex^r as in the source? Should it be assumed that those for whom there is no entry in the 'Condition' column are in fact unmarried? (Most of these are children under 10, but there are two adults without a 'Condition' in Household 18 – Mary and Peter Heron.)

Assuming the anomalies can be cleared up, should the form of the original be maintained? For purposes of sorting, for example, it would be sensible to put the name and surname in directory order, e.g. 'Piggie, Grace Young', so that the people can be sorted alphabetically. It might be better to put surname and (fore)name in different fields in order to quickly find people with the same surname. In the same way, 'Where Born' might well be divided into two fields, one for town and one for county.

It may be desirable to abbreviate some entries, which is related to field length. Should the census-taker's abbreviations be used, such as 'Daur' for 'daughter', or 'U' for 'unmarried'? Should the process be taken further? Is it necessary to write in 'Son-in-Law' (10 characters) or could some abbreviation ('sl') be used? 'Malta Street, No 35' could become 'Malta St, 35'.

Are any new fields needed? Leaving aside the question of whether coded fields might be inserted alongside the original one, there is a case for giving each record a unique number, and for putting that number in its own field; after all, two people might have the same name and surname.

Alterations within fields might be given the general name *coding*. On the positive side, coding will make the data more compact, and it may be that nothing of any importance will be lost. It would also be necessary to have standard codes for all possible kinds of relationship to the head of household, all possible marital conditions, and both sexes. The greatest potential difficulty – and greatest possible benefit – concerns 'Rank, Profession, or Occupation'. To avoid complications at this stage, however, it is probably best to enter the rank data exactly as found in Appendix I; suggestions for coding will be found in Chapter 6.

Having thought about the pros and cons of data structures, it would be useful – before looking at the structure laid out below in Table 4.1 – as a paper exercise to look at the data in Appendix I and write down a way it might be structured: how many fields, what fieldnames, type and length of each field, coding, etc. Added to it should be an unambiguous description of abbreviations or codes to be used.

The following is a suggested structure for the CENSUS data.

Table 4.1 One possible structure for the CENSUS database

Fieldname	Data type	Example
IDNUM	number (3 chars)	1
SURNAME	string (10 chars)	Piggie
FORENAME	string (10 chars)	Grace Young
ADDRESS	string (25 chars)	Malta St, 35
HOUSEHOLD	number (2 chars)	1
RELN	string (15 chars)	Head
COND	string (2 chars)	W
SEX	string (1 char)	F
AGE	number (3 chars)	36
RANK	string (80 chars)	Housekeeper
TOWNBORN	string (15 chars)	Dunfermline
REGBORN	string (15 chars)	Fife
MISC	string (20 chars)	na

Data entry

Once the data structure has been provisionally worked out the source can be typed in (transcribed), reading line by line from Appendix I. The labour of data entry may be reduced by assigning one key to a word or series of words; function key <F6> might produce 'Glasgow', which is a string frequently encountered in the CENSUS data. The program might even allow for checking (validating) the data as it is entered, for example not allowing the entry of an age greater than 110 or less than 0, or a sex other than 'M' or 'F'.

It may seem that entering data is not a very dignified task for an historian. After all, someone examining a source in a conventional way would just note the interesting bits. To exploit a source fully using a computer *all* the relevant information in the computer has to be entered. Transcribing a whole page of statistics is not a very edifying task nor one requiring a great deal of creativity (although it is a highly skilled job). One way around this is to get the data 'off the shelf'. Another is to get someone else to do the data entry. Yet another is to do the data entry collectively, which might be especially suitable for local history groups. It also may be possible to enter data electronically using an optical scanner – provided the data is printed or typed rather than a manuscript. Finally, it is possible that data for only a part of the group would be entered, on the assumption that conclusions reached with that group will correspond to all the group; this falls under the general heading of sampling, and will be introduced in Chapter 7.

You are now able to create a simple database. The next stage is to see what kind of questions can be asked. Remember that this is just the functional order; it is important – *before* data entry of a real historical database ever begins – to know what questions are important, how to ask them, and what forms they will take. More questions may suggest themselves as the job proceeds, but it is essential to have the basic approach from the beginning. In any event, interrogation of a database is the subject of Chapter 5.

Notes

1 This dataset was developed as part of the 'Gorbals Census Datafile' by Alison Gray under the auspices of Strathclyde Regional Archives and the Scottish Office Education Department. The original dataset was for the same street in both 1851 and 1881 and included over 750 people; the value of the dataset has been enhanced by coding. Information on the teaching package may be obtained from Alison Gray at Strathclyde Regional Archives, Mitchell Library, North St, Glasgow G3 7DN.

2 The nature of the census has changed since the first one was held in 1801; really useful questions relating to social conditions began to be asked in 1851, and there is a fair degree of consistency between that census and the later ones (1861–91) for which information about individuals is available.

   For the best and most up-to-date treatment of the subject of the census see E. Higgs, *Making Sense of the Census*, London, 1989.

3 The final column headed 'Whether Blind, or Deaf-and-Dumb' was evidently not used for that purpose by the Malta Street census-taker, and it is ignored here.

Chapter 5

Using a database: basic queries

Chapter 4 looked at how a source could be structured and put into a database. This chapter introduces basic ways of asking historical questions about such a database. It can be followed without 'hands-on' experience, but it will make more sense if the CENSUS source, printed in Appendix I, is typed into any database management program as suggested in Chapter 4. As an alternative any similar database could be used.

Analysing the census without a computer

Information on 20 people is given Figure 4.1, with a further 80 in Appendix I. How can this source be analysed?

A computer is not actually necessary; after all, the analysts in 1851 had to make calculations based on the census-taker's books. The census-taker's books could of course be studied exactly as they are. Looking at Appendix I it is possible, for example, to find the number of people recorded who were women by moving down the 'sex' column row by row, keeping a running count. There are only two categories, male and female, so this is a fairly simple operation. If, however, the people were to be divided into a substantially larger number of categories, say the various towns of birth (under 'Where Born'), then the book-keeping involved in maintaining a running total would be more complicated. Finding any one named individual in the list of 100 is also quite difficult, the listing in the census-taker's return is by order of their address; even for a small list of 100 this can be a time-consuming task.

To allow a researcher to lump individuals into groups (e.g. by town of birth) or to look at the information in another order (e.g.

alphabetically by surname) each individual might be put on an index card or a slip of paper. Anyone who does not have access to a computer might consider putting the first twenty records in Appendix I on to index cards to get a better grasp of the principles involved. These cards could now be sorted into any order. If they were sorted by last name it would be very easy to pick out the card with the information on any chosen individual. If they were sorted by county of birth it would be easier to examine one sub-group (those born in the county of Ayrshire).

Even with the small amount of information available and primitive index-card technology, there are many historical questions that could be asked and answered. Other characteristics of the group could be examined; cards could be put in piles corresponding to place of birth, and the number of cards in each pile could be counted. Two different attributes could be examined; after putting the cards in piles by county of birth, each pile could be subdivided into males and females. Another way of using the raw data (either from the list or cards) would be to add up all the ages in the 'Age' category, divide by the number of individuals, and find the average age.

All of these procedures, however, would be much easier, in fact nearly instantaneous, if the data were entered into a computer.

Choosing records from the database

The basic terminology is important. To repeat what was said in the last chapter: the *record* is the database unit; records have *fields* (also called variables), and fields contain *values*. CENSUS has 100 records; if organised as outlined in Chapter 4, each record would have 13 fields. Table 4.1 gives an example record for Grace Piggie; this record, like all the others in CENSUS, has a field called SURNAME; the value in this field for this particular record is 'Piggie'.

A *database management system* (*DBMS*) is a computer program that will provide a way of choosing certain information from a database. A few years ago powerful DBMSs were only available on mainframes, but now a range of powerful and easy-to-use packages are available for desktop computers. Some are self-contained, like Borland's dBase or Paradox, others are part of integrated packages.

The process of choosing information is sometimes called *filtering*, and that is a useful way of thinking about it; the software filters out what is needed from what is not needed. The basic operation in database interrogation, querying or searching is to find all the records that have certain characteristics specified by the user. Let us assume that the source in Appendix I has been put into a database called CENSUS and that the first question concerns small children, those under ten years of age. This means that all the records (individuals) in the database will be examined to find those where the value in the AGE field is a number less than 10. In purely mechanical terms, the computer is scanning through every record and looking at that part of the record which has been designated as the AGE field. If the value in that field is between 0 and 9 the computer puts that record to one side (i.e. chooses the record); if the value is 10 or more the computer ignores the record. It then looks at the next record and repeats the process – until it gets to the end of the database.

One other aspect of database interrogation is subtly, but importantly, different: *choosing* records is not the same as *displaying* certain fields from the chosen records. The computer could show (display) *all* the information (all the fields) in a record. It could be instructed to display the contents of only *certain* fields, and this is independent of the previous filtering process. For example, the criterion for choice might be children under ten, but the user might want to have displayed only information from three – rather than all 13 – fields: SURNAME, FORENAME, and AGE. The criteria for the records chosen need have no connection with the fields displayed. SURNAME, FORENAME and TOWNBORN might be the fields displayed – even if the filtering condition was that the records chosen should have an AGE less than 10. Finally, the computer could be instructed to display no fields at all, but simply to give a *count* of how many records matched the criteria (there were 35 such records). The more elaborate database managers will have tools for formatting the results of queries as *reports*, specifying not just which fields to display but how the results will be laid out on the page, what kinds of heading will be used, etc.

Different database software will allow the user to work on the data in different ways. Some software is *command driven*: a series of words are typed in as a command. Command-driven

software is very flexible but it does involve knowing what words
(commands) to type. Other software is *menu driven*: there are a
series of choices to be made from a list (menu) displayed by the
computer. In either a command-driven or a menu-driven system
the same thing is being done: the computer is receiving a clear
instruction. An example of such an instruction, in plain English,
is the following:

> *Choose* all the records from the CENSUS database where the
> value in the AGE field is less than 10.

> Now, from those records chosen, *display* what is in the
> SURNAME, FORENAME, and AGE fields.

In a command-driven system this will involve typing in the command in some unambiguous and special form understandable to
the computer. One widely-used form is *SQL* (*Standard Query
Language*). The form would be:

> Select SURNAME FORENAME AGE
> From CENSUS
> Where AGE < 10

The last element, '<10', means 'less than 10'. It is a useful
introductory exercise to go through this query and work out what
is the database name, what are the fieldnames, and what is a
value.[1]

The same instruction may be made in a menu-driven database
software by marking boxes, or typing in a number and symbol.
Whatever the system for giving commands, the computer will
produce a result looking something like Table 5.1.

All records where AGE is less than 10 have been found. In
much the same way it would have been possible to choose records
where AGE equalled 10 (sometimes given as AGE = 10), was
greater than 10 (AGE > 10), or was greater than or equal to 10
(AGE ≥ 10). Database managers will also have some way of
specifying negatives, e.g. where AGE is *not* equal to 10, *not* less
than 10, etc. A basic concept here is that of the *operator*, the
element in the query like 'equals' or 'is greater than'. Examples
of some of the most important operators are listed below:

> X = Y   X *equals* Y
> X > Y   X *is greater than* Y

Table 5.1 The result of a simple retrieval from the CENSUS database (first 9 of 35 records)

Surname	Forename	Age
PIGGIE	ALEXR	5
WALLACE	JOHN	9
WALLACE	JAMES	6
WALLACE	WILLIAM	3
WALLACE	MARY	0
GRAHAM	JAMES	7
HUSSEY	JOHN	5
HUSSEY	MARY	3
HUSSEY	JAMES	0
. . .		

$X < Y$ X *is less than* Y
$X \geq Y$ X *is greater than or equal to* Y
$X \leq Y$ X *is less than or equal to* Y

The queries looked at so far have concerned numbers, but filtering is not just about numbers. It is also possible to set as a criterion the words (technically called *strings*) which can be found in a given field; this is called *string matching*. The criterion will, in plain English, be something like the following:

Choose from the CENSUS database all those records where the value in the TOWNBORN field is the word 'Glasgow'.

In some command-driven database managers it may be necessary to put strings in quotation marks; in SQL the command might be:

Select SURNAME FORENAME AGE TOWNBORN
From CENSUS
Where TOWNBORN = 'Glasgow'

The form of the word may need to be exact, i.e. 'GLASGOW' is not the same as 'Glasgow' or 'glasgow', i.e. the database manager may well be *case-sensitive*.

String matching can take several forms. Records can be chosen for people born somewhere other than Glasgow (TOWNBORN is not equal to Glasgow). Most systems will also have some means of partial string matching. Every record can be found where the RANK contains the string 'weaver'. This is often done with some form of *wild card*, for which many systems use an asterisk: '*weaver' will match 'Steam Loom Weaver' (Ann Speirs in CENSUS) or 'Power Loom Weaver' (Elizabeth Wilson). Most database managers have ways of finding strings that begin with certain letters, or end with certain letters, or – for example – contain a certain letter as the third character in the string, etc. This can be very useful with coding systems.

The examples above each looked at just one field (AGE or TOWNBORN). Increasingly interesting historical questions can be asked if *several* fields are examined at the same time. Suppose what is of interest is: (a) the younger children who were (b) born in Glasgow. This question involves numbers and strings, and the command is essentially the following:

Choose from the CENSUS database all those records where the value in the AGE field is less than 10 *and* the value in the TOWNBORN field is 'Glasgow'.

This assumes that a record will meet *both* of two criteria. It is also possible to choose records which meet *one or other* of two criteria, some form of *either/or*, i.e. people who are *either* (a) younger than 10 *or* (b) of any age, but born in Glasgow:

Choose from the CENSUS database all those records where the value in the AGE field is *either* less than 10 or the value in the TOWNBORN field is 'Glasgow'.

Within any one field several criteria can be set. For example people who were born either in Glasgow or Edinburgh could be found, i.e. where the value in the TOWNBORN field is either 'Glasgow' or 'Edinburgh'.

Once *and/or* searches and pattern-matching have been mastered the possibilities become very varied. Different database systems will deal with these searches in different ways. Many will use standard means of presenting complex expressions. An SQL example is the following:

Select SURNAME FORENAME AGE TOWNBORN
From CENSUS
Where (AGE > 10) and (TOWNBORN = ('Glasgow' or 'Edinburgh'))

The last line is based on the convention in maths that operations in brackets are carried out first.

Another useful way of manipulating the data is to sort it and list it in some order. Most databases will allow a listing of the database (or the results of a query) in any order desired, based on one or more fields. The data could be sorted by surname to get a simple name list, or it could be sorted by county of birth. The records can be sorted and listed by age from youngest to oldest ('ascending' order) – and there will probably be the option of doing this from oldest to youngest ('descending' order). Sorting can also be carried out based on more than one field, for example first of all sorting the records by surname, and when two or more individuals have the same surname, sorting these records by forename: Graham Henrietta, Graham Jean, Graham Robert, Graham Susanna.

The filtering process can also be used to create what are in effect new databases. A new database might be needed with just the women in it; this simply involves asking the appropriate question – requesting all fields – and saving the result to a new file: the original file will be left intact.

Aggregates and simple graphics

What has been asked for so far are longer or shorter lists, e.g. those aged under 10, or those born in Glasgow. In many cases, however, historians do not want a list and are not interested in Grace Piggie or any other named individual. What they want is general information about the entire group, a *count* of children under ten, which for CENSUS is 35. All database managers should provide a way of getting such a count. It may also be possible to work out different information like the highest and lowest value and the averages (mean, median), etc; techniques for this are dealt with more fully in Chapter 7.

A count, for any chosen field, of the number of records which have a chosen value, is called a *frequency count*. The object might be to look at the CENSUS file to find what the distribution of marital condition was among adults. Taking just those over 18, the result would be as Table 5.2:

Table 5.2 A frequency count of the COND (marital condition) field from the CENSUS database (people aged over 18)

COND	Meaning	
M	Married	38
UM	Unmarried	9
W	Widowed	5

It is only a short jump from this kind of frequency count to simple graphics such as the bar chart in Figure 5.1.

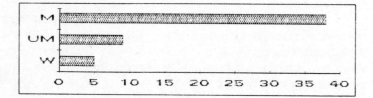

Figure 5.1   A simple bar chart based on Table 5.2

There are many cases where the ability to establish *ranges* is useful. Taking the example of AGE, a frequency count of every single possible age from 0 to 67 years (the extremes in CENSUS) might not be practical or – more to the point – historically useful. It would mean 67 different categories, most probably an unmanageable number. The analysis might be clearer if ages were lumped together into several ranges (0–15 years, 16–29, over 30); these ranges do not need to be of equal size. Good software will allow the user flexibly to establish ranges, and then to make a frequency count of the numbers of records in each range. Ranges can be set up by *recoding*. After using the database management software to create a new field called AGEBAND, the computer could be told to go through the database record by record. Every time it met the value between 0 and 15 in the AGE field of a record it could put the value '0–15' in the new AGEBAND field *of that record*; every time it met a value between 16 and 29 it could put '16–29' in AGEBAND. Note that in this case AGEBAND would be a string field rather than a number field, as the numbers in AGEBAND are not numbers on which mathematical operations can be carried out. A frequency count could then be carried out on the new field.

Table 5.3 A frequency count of the CENSUS database using ranges

AGEBAND	
0–15	44
16–29	24
30+	32

Mathematical calculations are also important. There is only one meaningful number field, AGE, in the CENSUS database, but there is little point in finding the total age of a whole community (2,103 years in the CENSUS group) for its own sake. A better example would come from another database on Victorian Scotland, *CONF1881*. This comprises information on all 5,307 people who left recorded estates in Scotland in 1881.[2]

Table 5.4 A typical record from the CONF1881 database

ID	2801
NAME	MENZIES,GRAHAM
ADDRESS	EDINBURGH
SEX	M
D_DEATH	1880/11/20
OCCUPATION	DISTILLER
D_CONF	1881/02/16
TOT_EST	432823.5

A frequency count could be made of all people with an estate (TOT_EST) over £300,000, which would yield the number 5 (out of 5,307 estates). Something different could also be found out, not the number of records but *the total of the values in those five records*: £432,824 + 1,000,000 + 350,000 + 886,497 + 362,467 = £3,031,788). This operation is different from a simple frequency

Table 5.5 A crosstabulation of COND (marital condition) field by the SEX field from the CENSUS database (people aged over 18)

	Married	Unmarried	Widowed
Male	19	5	1
Female	19	4	4

count, but may be even more meaningful to historians, and any but the most basic database software should be able to do it – although not all software could easily handle 5,307 records.

There is one final form of analysis to consider, which should be available in any relatively powerful database program. So far the analysis has involved one field at a time: CONDITION or AGE or TOWNBORN or ESTATE. *Two* fields could also be examined together. An example has already given about how the adults in the CENSUS records could be divided up by marital condition – so many married, so many unmarried, so many widowed. A second field, SEX, could then be brought in and a *contingency table* (*crosstabulation* or *crosstab*) set up, as Table 5.5.

There are three possible marital conditions (married, unmarried, and widowed) and two possible sexes; the result is a 3 × 2 contingency table contained in six cells. Each record could be placed in only one cell: William Ross was counted in the 'married and male' cell and only there; his wife, Janet Ross, was in the 'married and female' cell and only there; each of the remaining 50 adult records was also assigned to one of the six cells. Crosstabulations will be discussed in greater detail in Chapter 7.

The aim of this chapter has been to introduce the kinds of standard questions which can be asked of a source using a database manager. Many of the questions *could* be asked by simply working manually through the original paper source (e.g. the enumerator's returns), but it would be painstaking task even with simple questions. The job would be a little easier with the card index. The computer, however, can ask almost any question instantly, and moreover is so flexible that it can quickly follow up lines of enquiry and fully explore the source. As the questions become more complicated so the computer really comes into its own.

Notes

1 The structure of an SQL command has to be complete and unambiguous. A little confusingly, the criterion for choice of records is given in the final line, the fields for display in the first line. If the last line were left out of the command the computer would display information about the three fields from *all* CENSUS records. If the field names were left out of the first line, and it became 'Select/From Census/Where AGE < 10', then *all* fields would be displayed – but just for the under-tens.
2 The source is based on the *Calendar of Confirmations*; the project to create a machine-readable version was organised by Nicholas Morgan and Michael Moss at Glasgow University. For background see their article 'Listing the wealthy in Scotland', *Bulletin of the Institute of Historical Research*, LIX, 1986, pp. 189–95.

Chapter 6

Enriching the information: coding and structure

In Chapter 4 we looked at a simple structured source which could be entered into the computer virtually unchanged. We decided that some information in the original might be abbreviated (like marital condition), and that some information might be slightly edited (so deriving two fields, AGE and SEX, from the double-column entry of the original: see p. 49). We considered abbreviating or coding the information on birthplace, but recognised that it might be safest at first to enter something akin to what was in the source, and adopt coding schemes only later.

This chapter will consider more fully how one might enhance the usefulness of a database by extrapolating from the information transcribed from the original. A historian collecting information on filing cards is likely to make annotations on the cards to help sort the information into categories. Exactly the same can be done with a computer database, by adding new fields containing abbreviating and analytic codes. The advantage of using a computer, however, is that such coding can in part be implemented by means of the kinds of 'filters' discussed in the last chapter. This not only lightens the work, but ensures greater consistency and accuracy than even the most meticulous annotator could hope for.

Imposing coding fields on a database has to be done with some care, and the normal practice nowadays (when constraints of filestore space are no longer usually a problem) is to insert codes into newly added editorial fields (in effect *post-coding*). This means that the field containing the transcription of the original material is retained in a form as close to the source as possible. Since no information is lost, the coding scheme can be checked or modified later.

The techniques discussed here will have validity for a wide range of different types of historical sources, but we shall start with the data already discussed in Chapters 4–5. A historian might object that even what was done in Chapter 4 already destroyed useful historical information: no note was made, for example, of where the page-breaks occurred in the original enumerator's book – nor of corrections, changes in handwriting and other marks that might have significance for some kinds of research.[1] However, any research will always be guided by preliminary hypotheses, and thus entail a reading of the sources that is not absolutely (vacuously) open-minded. Given that our aim was to construct a consistent set of data to illuminate specific wider problems in nineteenth-century social history, we decided that we were more interested in the *substantive* information in the source (about household structure, occupational patterns, and so on), rather than in specific information regarding the compilation of any particular enumerator's report. Provided these decisions are properly written up during the data-entry and editing stages, it will always be easy to document exactly what procedures have been adopted.

Coding simple information in a single field

Coding (whether of the pre-coding or post-coding type) is normally done in one of four basic ways: (1) replacing information in a single field with a standard abbreviating code; (2) adding a new coded field which classifies or imposes a structure on information in another field; (3) adding a new field which contains information derived from the source but not explicitly stated in it; or (4) adding a coded field which groups together records according to information given in several of the fields in the original data (or even several sets of sources). The purpose is always to simplify and/or enhance search procedures. We shall discuss each of these kinds of coding briefly in this and the next sections.

The simplest is an abbreviating code (like that for marital condition in the 1851 census). Most database applications will allow the user to do a set of substitutions, replacing any one or more values in a particular field with another (usually simplified) value. If initially the information had been keyed in exactly as it appeared in the source, the program could produce a list of all the variants in order. Such a list, with a second column of standard codes added, could become a 'translation table' by means of which the program could standardise the information, thus:

Mar	– M
Married	– M
NK [Not known]	– X
U	– U
Unmar	– U
Wdr	– W
Wid	– W

If there were no further variants or complications in the data, it would be safe to substitute one-letter codes for the original information, arguably without losing anything significant. In use, such a code would ensure maximum speed and consistency in retrievals relating to marital condition.

Many DBMS have the facility *either* to modify the information in a particular column (for example changing 'Married' to 'M') *or* to place the code in a new column, without affecting the information on which it is based. The latter option is particularly appropriate for coding which summarises information intrinsically too diverse for general analysis. An obvious example is AGE, where in the census database all values between 0 and 80 or 90 are likely to be represented. Rather than using the actual individual ages of a census population, or the rough banding adopted above (p. 64), the historian might prefer finer subdivisions, and having added the column AGEBAND, instruct the computer to insert in that column a digit '0' for anyone whose value in AGE is less than 10, a digit '1' for anyone whose value in AGE is greater than 9 and less than 20, and so on. If the aim was to explore the relationship between age and marital condition, agebands narrower than 10 years might be adopted. In any case, such grouping codes can easily be modified (or altogether deleted from the database) once they have served their purpose.

A different approach might be adopted for the column RELN (the field containing relationship to the head of the household). This column will be central to any work on household structure, and any coding should be designed for maximum flexibility and clarity. It might be tempting to adopt a set of string (letter) abbreviations such as 'DA' for daughter, 'DAL' for daughter-in-law, and so on, on the grounds that it is easy to remember what they stand for. However, such letter codes are not likely to sort in a historically useful way during retrievals. Equally, it would be laborious to pick out, say, all male and female children and stepchildren, since their codes would be widely scattered through the alphabet. Rather than a letter-coding, therefore, it might be preferable to adopt a sequential 2-digit relationship-code: numbers up to 20 might be allocated for inner (nuclear) family relationships, with for example a son coded 11, a stepson 12, the head's son by previous marriage 13, a daughter 14, with a son-in-law separated at 21, and so forth. More distant relatives of head and spouse would be coded between 30 and 69, and non-related members above 70 – reserving 99 for records where no information is given, or where it is indicated as 'unknown' or similar. Such a numeric scheme would give great flexibility in retrieving not just individual relationships to the head. A single retrieval, say, of all individuals with a relationship greater than 20 but less than 70 would select all individuals living in a household to whose head they are related by ties other than those of the nuclear family.

If the relationship code is carefully designed and comprehensive, and the source itself consistent, replacing the original information with a code may be acceptable. Some inconsistently placed information, such as often occurs in a historical source, might also then be moved editorially: for example, the term 'apprentice', if entered by the enumerator occasionally under 'relation to head of household' but more usually under RANK, might legitimately be placed solely under RANK. However, most enumerator's reports will be vague (or inaccurate) in respect of certain relationships, notably in-laws, adopted or fostered children, distant relatives, and other groups. If that is the case, it may be better to add a new column for edited relationships, based on fuller scrutiny of this and other sources. One might then also build into the scheme a way of covering second families within the same household – for example where a married couple live-in as servants in a well-to-do household (see Malta Street no. 27½ in Appendix I). Such editorial columns, involving judgements which might prove less than absolutely reliable, should supplement, and not replace, the information taken directly from the original.

If there is uncertainty about the geographic information, a similar scheme might be adopted for the database fields

TOWNBORN and REGBORN (based on the single column
'where born' in the enumerator's report). Here, however, an
even more carefully designed coding scheme may well be required.
A single-character code would be insufficient for all but the
roughest analysis; a rational approach might be to create an
hierarchical scheme allowing retrieval at different geographic
levels. A six-digit geographic code could determine country in the
first two digits, region in the middle two (including perhaps a
distinction of Lowlands from Highlands), and perhaps parish in the
last two digits. If Scotland is coded 10, the Lowlands 1, Lanarkshire
3, and the parish of Gorbals 48, then all parishes in Lanarkshire
would have a code starting with the digits 1013, and all people
born in the parish of Gorbals would have the code 101348.
The number 9 might be reserved for unspecified values: anyone
described simply as being born in 'Lanarkshire' would be coded
101399. The advantage of such an hierarchical coding system
is that, with wildcards (a special symbol standing for any one
character or for a string), each geographic level can be picked out
separately during retrievals: the code 10* would pick anyone
born in Scotland, 101* anyone from the Lowlands, and so on.[2]

Such a scheme might be sufficient to replace all variants in
the original 'where born' column; alternatively, it might be
adopted as post-coding, and the original retained alongside. In
either case, the list of geographic names and allocated codes
will be equally suitable for other data, and can (with a relational
database manager) be used to convert between text and code
whenever necessary (see p. 162). Such a coding scheme could
also in itself be enhanced to allow for historic changes in the
boundaries of administrative regions: this is the approach which
we shall adopt for the deputies to the French National Convention (see p. 106).

Coding of a single more complex field: occupations

Coding schemes which classify information given in the original,
while also retaining the information on which it is based, are very
useful for more complex information such as that describing
'rank, profession or occupation' in the 1851 census. Whether a
computer is being used or not, however, this particular piece of
information is something of a hornet's nest for historians.

For a start, the enumerators relied primarily on information given by each head of household, so there are bound to be intentional or unintentional misrepresentations, variants or deficiencies. Should, for example, 'servants', 'maidservants', 'maids', 'house servants', 'house boy', or 'girl' be treated as a single category (servants) differentiated only by other fields (sex and age)? Do these labels mean the same in the countryside as they do in an urban environment? Would a person who remained in one occupation necessarily describe it in the same way at different times – or describe it on one particular occasion in the same way as others in the same occupation? How should one distinguish a blacksmith's apprentice or a blacksmith's journeyman from a 'labourer' or 'assistant' in a blacksmith's workshop? Should a housekeeper who is, say, the sister of the head, be classified in the same way as a waged housekeeper not related to her employer? And is the term 'housewife', explicitly ruled out from the older enumerator's reports, a sufficient label for, say, a church minister's wife, the (unpaid) parish assistant that she often really was? What about other euphemisms – not to mention the problem of individuals with several concurrent occupations, which should from 1851 have been listed in order of importance? All historical sources are full of these inconsistencies of nomenclature. Further complications are added if one wishes to compare occupations over time or between regions with different traditions: the official census instructions on nomenclature naturally changed from one census to the next, and not all these changes represent true shifts in the organisational and social realities of nineteenth-century economic life.

Even this is not the end of the difficulties. Clearly rank and occupation are two rather different concepts which contemporaries, like the General Register Office (and from 1855 the Registrar General in Scotland), were prone to blur even after the introduction of a new classification scheme in 1851. The role of the individual ('foreman', 'labourer', 'clerk') was not always distinguished either from the general sector in which the person was employed ('agriculture', 'heavy industry') or the specific branch ('machine-tool manufacturing', 'shipbuilding'). Depending on individual information, it may thus be possible to group by sector ('agriculture') or by social rank or class ('farm labourer', 'tenant', 'landowner'), but not necessarily both simultaneously and consist-

ently. Only from 1911 were clear instructions gradually introduced
to ensure that this was sorted out.

There are no simple answers to these and many related questions.[3] Decisions will in any case to some extent depend on what
the data is intended for. While a conventional note-taking approach
can take care of individual cases, any kind of aggregate quantitative
study (with or without a computer) would have to try to avoid
variants and ambiguity – almost invariably at the expense of
complete fidelity to the source. This, of course, was exactly what
the staff at the General Register Office did at the time in connection
with each census, compiling detailed word-lists with rules of classification by economic sector, for use in the published Census
Reports. The debate over the validity of adopting modified versions
of these classifications for a full-scale socio-occupational coding
of individuals is likely to continue. Given the nature of the
enumerators' work, however, one has to accept that social class
and economic sector cannot be disentangled on this basis alone.
Unless one is prepared to work in very generalised terms only,
there is no alternative to allocating a code to the information in
this column provisionally, pending work on other sources.

Coding on several fields

Coding is not just a matter of standardising information in individual fields. Coding may also be useful as an intermediary stage
in the analysis process itself, by helping to identify certain categories of records. A good database manager will allow the user to
introduce new coded fields based on information in several other
fields – so that if, for example, field 1 has a value of x, and field 2
is either less than y or greater than z, the program will insert
code AA into a new coding-field 3.

One may, for example, wish to make a special comparison of
the kind of ranking/occupational labels attached to women in
different age-groups (and perhaps over different censuses). For
that, it might be worth separating out women below the age of,
say, 15, and grouping those aged 15 or more into different categories depending on whether they have responsibility for a family
of their own (are married and/or have children), have co-resident
older relatives, have live-in servants or other domestic assistance,
or have husbands whose earnings are likely to be sufficient to

secure a reasonable level of financial security. The census on its own, of course, will not answer all these questions satisfactorily; but before we draw on other historical sources (as we shall in Chapter 11) we can still do a preliminary coding based on a series of 'filters' relating to the information in other fields of the same record. One of a sequence of such filterings, to add a code in a new field called ROLE1, might take the generic form of:

IF RECORD HAS
AGE > 14, SEX = 'F',
COND = 'M', RANK = <BLANK>
THEN INSERT VALUE XX IN ROLE1

For the time being, information on the size of family and (from other sources) on the husband's earning capacity would have to be edited manually into the resulting column of coded values. But such coding, even if based solely on evidence from several fields within the census itself, can produce far more flexible lines of enquiry than a manual search through the source material would normally allow.[4]

With the awesome speed and growing statistical power of modern software, there are few limits to the range of hypotheses that can be tested quickly and efficiently. In the process, it is sometimes worth reminding oneself of two obvious points. First, technique must not be allowed to give spurious validity to results that go beyond what the original sources can support: the function of coding is to simplify retrievals, and to add new search-potential to a given set of data, not to distort it. Secondly, all editorial operations and coding need to be carefully documented and covered by archived back-ups, so that if a particular stage proves invalid, for good historical reasons, it is possible to trace one's steps back to the uncoded data.

Further editorial fields

Most data has information within it which is not explicit but which can readily and often quite reliably be extracted. In the case of the 1851 census, for example, two kinds of enhancement are possible regarding 'household' information. Each depends of course on the reliability of the information given in the enumerators' books regarding what social historians usually call the co-residential unit or CRU – the group defined by their permanent sharing of meals and living quarters. There are major problems relating to the way in which CRUs were marked in the enumerators' books;[5] but provided a reasonable margin of error is accepted, some interesting results can still be reached.

If we regard, except in difficult cases, the person described as 'head' as the first person in each co-residential unit, and the person preceding the next head (or preceding the various indicators in the enumerators' books of the start of a new unit) as the last, it is a simple task to count up how many live in each household, and how many of these are related to the head. The result might be inserted in two new columns in the data, HSIZE (household size) and FSIZE (family size). This information in turn, within the limitations of the source, will allow not only the calculation of average family and household sizes for different types of household, but may also help with the coding scheme for the role of women suggested above.

As an additional step in this direction, another column might be added, HHCODE (household structure code), to take what is a variant on the numeric 'stem and leaf' code. This consists of a visual representation of each household unit in terms of its constituent elements: an A for each adult head and spouse present, a C for each child, a G for each grandchild, an R for each non-nuclear relative, an L for each lodger, an S for each servant, and so on. An entry for a household with two adults, three children, an aged relative, a lodger and a journeyman might thus be: AACCCRLJ. If entered once for each unit (for example against each head of household), such a system makes possible a graphic summary of the household structure of the entire community on file. Although slightly time-consuming, such a graphic code is likely to produce some striking insights into the patterns of household structure in the community.

Thinking about the data and its internal assumptions

So far, we have experimented by adding codes for relationship to the head, place of birth, occupation, family and 'household' size, with scope for more work on the women, and a graphic summary of CRU patterns. Such 'enhancement' of the original data clearly needs to be done cautiously, given the limitations of the sources.

But we might well go further, and think about the underlying structure of the data itself.

A source like the enumerators' reports actually gives information at different levels. Most obviously, it has details of each individual. But equally, there is information regarding bigger units: partly in terms of the household or CRU just discussed, but also in terms of the separate buildings, through the addresses given for each family or on each page. This last type of information is, especially for very densely populated urban areas, yet more uneven than other information in the census. Nevertheless, there is an obvious structure to the data: each person belongs to a co-residential unit, and every CRU inhabits a building of some kind.

To reflect this structure, and to avoid repeating information such as address, HSIZE and FSIZE unnecessarily for every record, one might with relational database software distribute the data hierarchically between several tables. Logically, there would be one table for each level: in this instance three, namely for the house, the CRU and the individual respectively.

Unfortunately, the information on each building is very unreliable in the early censuses, so to make any substantive progress in terms of historical analysis it would be necessary to locate other material on the buildings themselves. Assuming that research is to be extended in this area, a data model such as that shown in Figure 6.1 might be adopted, where the census information itself is distributed in three tables linked by unique identifiers, one for each building and one for each CRU. Links to other types of historical sources (containing data concerning the house, the household, and so on) could then be made at the appropriate level.

Splitting a single source into three different tables – turning it from a 'flat-file' database into a simple relational structure – may seem to constitute a distortion of the original. In reality, however, this approach may be truer to the source. The census did not evolve in a linear way as a simple piece of administrative fact-finding. As the early instructions and census reports clearly show, those pressing for a national census were concerned as much with poor relief, housing and family structure, community self-help, urban sanitation and even military potential: the census itself was meant to work at different levels. For nineteenth-century administrators the household unit, for example, had both economic and moral, as well as social, significance. As in the case of the occu-

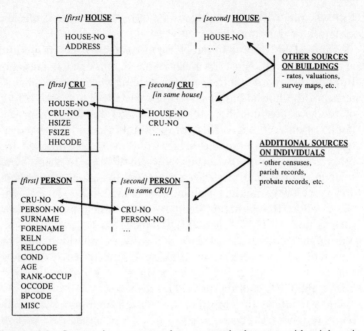

Figure 6.1 Structuring census data around the co-residential unit (CRU)

pational information, the central administration only gradually worked out reliable means of collecting the required information, but the trend is unmistakably there.

A relational or multi-table data-model can thus sometimes facilitate critical examination of even an apparently simple source. At a more practical level, relational database systems have other advantages. Since information can be held in different appropriately structured tables linked by a key (such as a unique identity number), it will be easier to do retrievals at distinct levels (that is, not just about the individuals, but also about the co-residential units as blocks, or about the houses themselves). It will certainly also be easier to draw in information from supplementary sources (as outlined in Figure 6.1, and described more fully in Chapter 11). The database manager can be used to avoid the internal self-contradictions that might occur if the information in one table were edited without its counterpart in another table; similarly, automatic validity checks can if desired be incorporated (to ensure, say, that no one is unwittingly given an age over 110, or recorded as married when under the age of 12).

Most database managers can be used at various levels of sophistication and complexity. For some types of work it may be quite unnecessary to go beyond a simple flat-file structure. But a database manager that allows the user to clarify and restructure the historical material according to need has obvious attractions.[6]

There are some important general principles underlying this discussion. All historical sources (and not just ones tabulated like the census) have some degree of structure, and that structure is worth examining both in terms of what it says about the way the source came into existence, and in terms of how the data might be used, and perhaps enhanced editorially, to maximise its legitimate potential. This in turn is likely to help in the identification of other types of source material relevant to each particular line of enquiry. We shall look at recent developments in history-orientated software in a later chapter; but it will be apparent even at this stage that a relational database system can, with some careful thought, go a long way to accommodate data from a wide range of sources. No historian, of course, would suggest that there is a simple or 'right' way of modelling data; in any case each project will be limited by the resources available. But any process of data-entry and computer analysis is likely to foster critical and systematic examination of the source in a way that might otherwise not have occurred.

Notes

1 It is worth emphasising that enumerator's books were normally themselves edited copies of information contained in the schedules (forms) issued to individual households. Partly as a result of a host of problems associated with so massive a statistical undertaking, these books are not flawless sources in themselves. See especially P. M. Tillott, 'Sources of inaccuracy in the 1851 and 1861 censuses', in *Nineteenth-century Society*, ed. E. A. Wrigley, Cambridge, 1972, pp. 82–133, with its summary p. 132f. See also the excellent survey by E. Higgs, *Making Sense of the Census*, London, 1989.

2 For a simple use of wildcards like this, many DBMS would require the code to be regarded as a string (letters and numbers) rather than as a genuine number. If the field is defined as being numeric, the

selection to include all parishes in Lanarkshire would be '>101299, <101400'.

3 For a full discussion of this very complex topic, see W. A. Armstrong, 'The use of information about occupation', in *Nineteenth-century Society*, ed. E. A. Wrigley, Cambridge, 1972, pp. 191–310; the more recent attempt to modify the social classificatory side of this, in D. and J. Mills, 'Occupation and social stratification revisited: the census enumerators' books of Victorian Britain', *Urban History Yearbook*, 1989, pp. 63–77; and E. Higgs, 'Structuring the past: the occupational and household classification of 19th-century census data', in *History and Computing III*, ed. E. Mawdsley *et al.*, Manchester, 1990, pp. 67–73. See also Armstrong's briefer comments in *The Census and Social Structure: an Interpretative Guide to Nineteenth-century Censuses for England and Wales*, ed. R. Lawton, London, 1978, pp. 28–81, which also reproduces some of the early instructions to the enumerators. For practical guidance see R. J. Morris, 'Occupational coding: principles and examples', *Historical Social Research*, XV, 1990, pp. 3–29.

4 On coding generally, see K. Schürer, 'The historical researcher and codes', in *History and Computing III*, ed. E. Mawdsley *et al.*, Manchester, 1990, pp. 74–82. See also K. H. Jarausch and K. A. Hardy, *Quantitative Methods for Historians*, Chapel Hill, 1991, pp. 37–41.

5 The identification of co-residential units is one of the biggest problems in nineteenth-century census material, especially for Scottish censuses before 1881: see M. Anderson, 'Standard tabulation procedures for the census enumerators' books 1851–1891', in *Nineteenth-century Society*, ed. E. A. Wrigley, Cambridge, 1972, pp. 134–45, esp. 138–44; and M. Anderson, 'Households, families and individuals: some preliminary results from the national sample from the 1851 census of Great Britain', *Continuity and Change*, III, 1988, pp. 421–38. In this chapter, household-unit and co-residential unit are used interchangeably. Other historians have used the term 'co-residing group' or 'commensal group' – all, of course, different from the term 'family' with its connotations of kinship links outside the household.

6 For a summary of suitable alternatives, see D. Spaeth, *A Guide to Software for Historians*, Glasgow, 1991. For the material in this book we have used primarily Borland's Paradox, but other good DBMS will perform similar operations.

Chapter 7

Simple statistics: description, correlation, and sampling

So far in this book historical sources have been looked at in what might be called common-sense terms. In Chapter 4 the 1851 census-taker's returns were discussed, and how they could be organised and entered into a database. Chapters 5 and 6 showed the kinds of standard questions that could be asked of such a database and how the original source could be enhanced. This chapter goes one step farther, and the same historical information will be used as part of a simple introduction to some uses of *statistical analysis*.

Historians and statistics

Historians and students of history are wary of statistics and even more of statistical analysis. This wariness is part of the controversy between traditional and quantitative history. It is still very unusual to find even moderately complex statistical techniques in mainstream historical journals – other than those devoted to economic history.

The limited use of statistics is not caused by the laziness or stupidity of historians, but reflects real problems. One anecdote, attributed to a British government official, would win general approval:

The Government are very keen on amassing statistics. They collect them, add them, raise them to the Nth power, take the cube root and prepare wonderful diagrams. But you must never forget that every one of these figures comes in the first instance from the village watchman, who just puts down what he damn pleases.[1]

Even when traditional historians agree with the findings of a quantitative study, they may argue that an elaborate statistical analysis has simply re-stated the obvious. The traditionalists are certainly right to feel that a statistical approach can get in the way of a stylishly presented argument. And there are other reasons to avoid too many statistics: special skills, not generally part of the historian's education, are required to carry out advanced statistical analysis, and even the results of such analysis are often meaningless without such skills.

On balance, however, historians can make greater use of statistical techniques, for political as well as social and economic history. Forty years ago extremely tedious calculations were required; ten years ago statistical programs required a mainframe computer; now powerful, easy-to-use, and well-documented programs like SPSS and Minitab are available for standard desktop machines. Different *statistics packages* operate in different ways, but in any event the object in this chapter is not to learn how to operate the software. The stress will be on basic statistical skills that can be useful in dealing with historical sources:

- describing the attributes (variables) of historical entities (e.g. what is the typical age of the members of a group);
- measuring the relationship between one attribute and another;
- reaching valid historical conclusions along the above lines about a large group while looking at just part of it.

Any serious use or understanding of statistical analysis requires reference to specialist works, some of which are listed in the bibliography; there are several statistics textbooks aimed at historians, and many more aimed at social scientists.[2] The manuals and supporting documentation of statistics software packages are also often useful.

Basic concepts

The basic vocabulary of statistics is closely related to the concepts used with databases. A *population* (or *universe*) is the group of things that are being studied. It should not be identified solely with the everyday use of population – as the number of people living in a particular place (Deadwood Gulch, pop. 33). In database terms a population might be called a database, a dataset or a table; the CENSUS database is a population.

Each thing (entity) in the population may be called a *case* or an *observation* (case + case + case = population). A case is the same as a database *record*; in the basic CENSUS database each person is a case. A selection of cases which is taken to be typical of the whole population is called a *sample*. Characteristics or attributes of entities in the population are called *variables* (e.g. age) and have *values* (e.g. the particular age, 65 years). Variables are the same as database fields or columns; in the CENSUS database the variables include SURNAME, SEX, AGE, TOWNBORN, etc. Values in statistics are the same as values in the database ('Piggie', 'F', '36', 'Dunfermline', etc.).

Table 7.1 Basic terminology for statistical analysis

Database	Statistics	Example from the CENSUS database
Database (File, Table)	Population	Part of Malta St
Record	Case (Observation)	Grace Piggie
Field (Column)	Variable	Age
Value	Value	36

The nature of each variable is important. One difference is between string (word) variables and numerical variables. It may in fact be necessary to code strings into numbers ('Dunfermline' = '221', 'male' = '1', etc.) if they are to be easily analysed by a statistics program. But even if all the strings have been coded into numbers there are still fundamental differences between nominal, ordinal and interval scale variables; for each type different kinds of statistical tools are used.

The *nominal* scale is a scale in which cases are simply divided (classified) into non-ordered categories (given names). An example of a nominal-scale variable in the CENSUS database would be REGBORN – region born. The people (cases) in the database (population) are divided into groups based on region of birth (with no logical numerical order of REGBORN). Regions of birth might be coded to appear as numbers, but meaningful mathematical operations – addition, subtraction, averaging – could not be performed on these numbers.

The *ordinal* scale divides items into groups that have some kind of order (i.e. are *ranked*), but which are not divided by equal intervals. There is no useful ordinal data in CENSUS.

In the *interval* scale the interval between the values is equal. In crude terms this is data that could be described as numbers, more specifically numbers on which mathematical operations can be performed. The only useful example of interval-scale data in the raw census-taker's books is AGE. If the data had been enriched – as described in Chapter 6 – by entering the number of people in each individual's family or household that would give another piece of interval data. Interval data can be converted into nominal data: those aged 0–15 years put in one group, those aged 16–29 in a second group, etc.

Describing variables

Descriptive statistics are used to describe variables. A simple and widely-used statistical operation is to produce one or more numbers that summarise a group. A simple example is a frequency count on the nominal-scale variable COND (marital condition): see Table 5.2. This simply shows how many married, unmarried and widowed people there were; giving the percentage of each type might make the figures more useful. With interval-scale data the distribution of values can be described in more interesting ways.

It is very useful to have one number which gives important information about the whole group. A much-used example of this is the *average*. The term is a common one, and is often used to refer to the statistical *mean*: the total of all the values (of one variable) added together and divided by the number of cases. The mean is one *measure of central tendency*; another is the *mode*, which is that value which appears most often. A third figure is the *median*: if all the values are listed in order from highest to lowest the median will be the one in the middle of the list.

The median need not be the same as the mean, as in the imaginary list of seven medieval estates given in Table 7.2. To find the median, all the values of the 'Number of Serfs' variable would be listed in order (10, 13, 13, 18, 33, 34, 99); the value in the middle of the list is the median, in this case 18. The mean is

Table 7.2 A hypothetical group of medieval estates

Estate	Number of serfs
Estate A	10
Estate B	99
Estate C	13
Estate D	34
Estate E	13
Estate F	33
Estate G	18
Total	220

about 31 (220/7), which is higher than the median because one unusually high value (Estate B) is 'pulling' it up. The mode is the value that occurs most frequently, in this instance 13. The historian really wants to know whether 31, 18 or 13 serfs is more *typical* of these seven estates.

Measures of dispersion complement measures of centrality; they show not what is most typical but how big the *variation* is. The *range* should give the highest and lowest values – 10 and 99 in the example in Figure 7.2. As with centrality, it is useful to have one number that sums up the dispersion. The most commonly met example of this is *standard deviation (s.d.)*. An imaginary example of the usefulness of s.d. would be comparing 1,000 inhabitants of a medieval town and 1,000 university students. Both groups might have the same mean age of 20 years (and they might even have the same median age), but the university students might have a narrow range, all being between 17 and 23 years of age, while the medieval town might have a range from age 0 to 70 (but relatively few aged over 30 years). As a result the s.d. of the medieval town would be much higher.

The software demands of descriptive statistics are not high. To take the example of the CENSUS database, most middle-range database programs should be able to give average age for any sub-group of people, or to break them into a number of different age sub-groups.

From description to explanation

Cases usually have several variables, for example: age, place of birth, etc. One obvious question to ask would be whether two variables are linked: did individuals with a higher age tend to have a higher income, etc? *Multivariate statistics* are concerned with showing the relationship between variables.

How can a relationship between two variables be tested? One basic statistical technique is *hypothesis testing*, which requires thinking in a particular way. The approach has been compared to the Anglo-Saxon legal system, in which the defendant is presumed innocent until proven guilty.[3] A hypothesis (the charge) might be that two variables are related. A null hypothesis makes the opposite case, and this null hypothesis has to be disproved before the original hypothesis can be accepted. A statistical test examines the evidence, and if the evidence is overwhelming then the null hypothesis is rejected and the hypotheses (usually labelled the 'alternative hypothesis') is accepted. Deciding when the evidence is convincing leads to the notion of *significance*. The significance level is the probability of incorrectly rejecting the null hypothesis; the lower the significance level the better.

This general approach can be used with different types of variable, but for each type particular statistical tests are employed.

Nominal variables: contingency tables and chi squared

For nominal-scale data the *contingency table* (*crosstabulation*, or *crosstab*) is a basic method of showing the relationship between variables. A simple contingency table was shown in Chapter 5, for sex and marital condition (Table 5.5). Another, also from the

Table 7.3 A crosstabulation of BIRTHPLACE by AGEBAND from the CENSUS database

	0–15	16–29	30+	Total
Glasgow	33	9	14	56
Outside Glasgow	11	15	18	44
Total	44	24	32	100

CENSUS database, is shown in Figure 7.3. BPLACE, birthplace, is a new nominal-scale variable created by simplifying the nominal-scale TOWNBORN and REGBORN variables to show those people born either inside the city of Glasgow or outside it. AGEBAND is a nominal-scale variable created from the interval-scale variable AGE; in effect AGEBAND breaks the population into three categories: children, young adults, and older adults.[4] Common sense would suggest some link between the two new variables: older people were more likely to have migrated into Glasgow, while children would tend to live near where they were born.

The hypothesis testing approach can be used here: the (alternative) hypothesis is that AGEBAND and BPLACE are related, the null hypothesis is that they are independent. This can be considered first in a general way. How would the table look if AGEBAND and BPLACE were independent? The total number for all three AGEBANDs born in Glasgow (56 people) is roughly the same as that for all three AGEBANDs born outside (44). So if AGEBAND and BPLACE were independent, the number in each AGEBAND group should be about the same for either the Glasgow or the outside-Glasgow categories: there are 44 children (0–15 years), of these a few more than half should be born in Glasgow, and a few less than half outside – say 25 and 19 (matching the total proportion of 56:44). In fact the number of children born in Glasgow is higher than expected (33 rather than 25), and this suggests that the two variables are *not* independent, and that they may be related (that the alternative hypothesis is true).

The hypothesis can be tested in a more precise way. The crosstabulation in Figure 7.1 was created by the statistics program SPSS.

Although this looks much more complicated, all that has happened is that the same information has been supported by interpretive calculations. Each of the closed boxes (cells) contains two pieces of information. *Count* is how many cases fall in each cell; the count for those born in Glasgow and aged 0–15 years is 33 people and is exactly the same as in the simple contingency table. *Exp val* (expected value) is what the count would be if the variables were independent.

A standard statistical tool used to show more precisely the

```
Crosstabulation:        BPLACE    Birthplace
                     By AGEBAND

              Count  |0-15    |16-29   |30+
AGEBAND->     Exp Val|        |        |          Row
                     |    1.0 |    2.0 |    3.0   Total
BPLACE        -------|--------|--------|--------
                1.0  |   33   |    9   |   14      56
   GLASGOW          |  24.6  |  13.4  |  17.9    56.0%
                     |--------|--------|--------
                2.0  |   11   |   15   |   18      44
   OUTSIDE          |  19.4  |  10.6  |  14.1    44.0%
                     |--------|--------|--------
              Column     44       24       32      100
              Total    44.0%    24.0%    32.0%   100.0%


Chi-Square    D.F.      Significance      Min E.F.      Cells with E.F.< 5
---------     ----      ------------      --------      -------------------

 11.72890      2          .0028            10.560            None

Number of Missing Observations =      0
```

Figure 7.1   SPSS crosstab based on the data in Table 7.3

possibility of a relationship between two variables in a contingency table is called *chi squared* (χ^2). 'Chi' (pronounced 'kye') is the Greek letter χ; statistical programs that generate a contingency table will also produce a chi-squared figure and other statistics for it. The details of how chi squared is calculated are not important here: it just represents the cumulative difference between the actual count and the expected value.

The size of the chi-squared figure – in this case 11.72890 – is not so important, because the more cells there are, the higher the chi squared will be. What is important is *significance*, which returns to the basic concept of hypothesis testing. What significance shows is the probability that the null hypothesis is correct, that the variables are independent, and that the difference between count and expected value (the chi-squared figure) could have occurred by chance. The computer calculates that there are 0.28 chances in 100 (28 in 10,000) that the null hypothesis is true. This is less than 1 chance in 100; one chance in 100 is expressed as .01, and the corresponding probability (*p*) or *confidence level* is p < .01. A common standard is actually looser, p < .05, less than five chances in 100.[5]

Table 7.4 is a 'real' example of a contingency table using census data, from Michael Anderson's *Family Structure in Nineteenth-Century Lancashire*. The example is taken from a rural sample from the 1851 census and contains information on

Table 7.4 Co-residence patterns of married men aged 55 and over engaged in agriculture (family of procreation only): agricultural village sample, 1851 [Anderson, Table 28, p. 95]

	Farmers of			
	50 acres and over %	*20–49 acres* %	*under 20 acres* %	*Agricultural labourers* %
Living with:				
spouse only	17	31	38	36
unmarried children only	62	58	58	64
married children	21	10	4	–
All: %	100	99	100	100
N	52	29	24	25

The difference between the residence patterns of these three groups of farmers are significant $p < 0.01$ (chi^2 = 13.40) at 4 d.f.

105 farmers aged 55 years and over. It is used to support an important part of Anderson's argument about how close-knit families were: 'Farmers with larger farms do seem to have been much more able to keep their children at home and thus keep support for their old age.'[6] The statistical analysis shows that this pattern is unlikely to have appeared by accident; the probability that farm size and extent of family are not related is less than 1 in 100.

Interval data: scattergrams

Interval-scale data allows different tests and easy use of graphics. A simple example can be created by reforming CENSUS into a database called COUPLES, where the record (case) is not an individual but a married couple[7] (see Table 7.5).

This gives two interval scale variables, husband's age (HAGE) and wife's age (WAGE), that can be compared to one another and plotted as a scattergram.

The actual operation of the software can be very simple, just telling the computer which two variables to plot in the scattergram and requesting supporting statistics. Each point on the resulting

Table 7.5 Variables in the COUPLES database

Variable	Meaning	Example	Scale
RID	Record id number	1	interval
HID	Husband's id	7	interval
HSURN	Husband's surname	Ross	nominal
HFORE	Husband's forename	William	nominal
HAGE	Husband's age	60	interval
WID	Wife's id	8	interval
WFORE	Wife's forename	Janet	nominal
WAGE	Wife's age	50	interval

scattergram represents one record, i.e. one married couple. There were 18 married couples in the CENSUS database, so there are 18 couple-records in COUPLES, and 18 points on the scattergram. The husband's age is measured on the y (vertical) axis, and his wife's age on the x (horizontal) axis. For example, the point in the bottom left corresponds to Joseph and Mary Gibb; he was 24, she was 22.[8] The example in Figure 7.2 produces a scattergram with points in a line which slopes up from left to right, and that line indicates a positive association between the variable for 'husband's

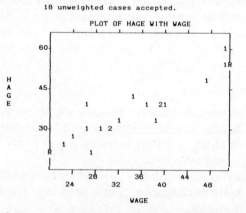

Figure 7.2 A scattergram of the COUPLES database

age' and the variable for 'wife's age'; if WAGE (x axis) is higher HAGE (y axis) will also tend to be higher.

Aside from giving the shape of the data in any particular example, scattergrams also help understand the general statistics involved. A common form of statistical analysis provides numbers which in effect sum up the scattergram; non-graphical statistical techniques can be applied to suggest the strength of the association between wife's age and husband's age.

The software generates various statistics which are shown at the bottom of the graph. The most important of these is *correlation*: for wife's age with husband's age in COUPLES the correlation is 0.89503. This is the *correlation coefficient* (*r*, or *Pearson's r*), which is a standard statistical tool; its value ranges from +1 to −1. A coefficient approaching +1, as in this case, means a high correlation and of a positive kind (e.g. higher husband's age, higher wife's age). A figure approaching −1 would have indicated a high correlation but of a negative kind (it might be reached, with different data, by correlating years left to live with age). Figures near 0, either positive or negative, mean a low correlation.

The correlation coefficient could be described as indicating how closely a pair of variables, if plotted on a scattergram, would correspond to a straight line. The line that could be plotted that was closest to all 18 points on the scattergram would be called the *line of best fit* or the *regression line*.[9]

Significance can be computed for a scattergram much as it is calculated for a crosstab. The Sig. .0000 statistic means that there is less that one chance in 10,000 that the pattern could have been as close as this by chance and that the variables were actually independent.

A typical example of the 'real' use of correlation coefficients for interval-scale historical variables appeared in an article by Robert Dykstra and Harlan Hahn.[10] In 1868 – immediately after the American Civil War – a referendum was held in the midwestern state of Iowa on extending the vote to blacks. Dykstra and Hahn's calculations show the relationship between the votes in the referendum to other pieces of data. The cases (records) were not individuals but counties; there were 97 cases, one for each county. For each county there are nine variables: percentage of the vote for black suffrage, percentage of thc vote for the Republican Party's candidate for Secretary of State, governor, etc. This

Table 7.6 Correlation between vote for negro suffrage in 1868 and political, social, and economic characteristics, by county [Dykstra and Hahn, p. 232]

Political, social, and economic characteristics	Correlations with vote for negro suffrage	p
Per cent of vote for Republican candidate for Secretary of State (1867)	+.92	.001
Per cent of vote for Republican candidate for Governor (1867)	+.84	.001
Per cent of vote for Republican candidate for President (1868)	+.86	.001
Per cent of eligible voters in incorporated towns (1876)	−.32	.01
Per cent of population Negro (1867)	−.23	.05
Per capita value of manufactures (1868)	−.26	.05
Value of farm produce sold per unit of production (1868)	+.31	.01
Average value of land per acre (1868)	−.30	.01

is one common function of the correlation coefficient, to compare the degree of relationship between one variable and several others.

The Republicans were the party in favour of extending the vote to the blacks; the figures show high positive correlations (+.92, +.84, +.86) across the 97 counties between percentage of the vote in favour of black suffrage (the dependent variable) and three indicators of the Republican vote (percentage of the vote for Secretary of State, Governor, and President, each an independent variable). Cases (counties) that had a high vote for Republican candidates tended to have a high vote for black suffrage. In each correlation there was less than one chance in 1,000 (p < .001) that the variables were independent. Other figures suggest that counties where support for black enfranchisement was high tended to be rural, and those that opposed it were more urban: there is a positive correlation (+.31) between value of farm produce sold (a measure of the relative weight of farmers in the local economy) and the percentage of the black suffrage vote, and a negative correlation $(-.32)$ between town voters and the suffrage vote.

Sampling

Sampling is a process of making generalisations about a large group (a population) by looking at a small part of it (a sample). This is part of *inductive* or *inferential* statistics. Sampling techniques were originally developed for market research and are generally most familiar through political opinion polls; in both cases the goal was to learn about mass opinion while minimising the number of expensive interviews. For computer-based historical research the object is to study a large group of people (or other types of historical case) while minimising the tedium and/or expense of data entry.

The starting point is that in an ideal world the sample should be truly *random*, i.e. that there is as much chance of one case in the larger 'population' being picked as another case. In reality there are different kinds of sample. The CENSUS database introduced in Chapter 4 is a 'sample' that is useful for getting an intuitive feel for the data and showing what the inhabitants of one street were like. It would not, however, be statistically useful if firm conclusions were wanted about all the people of Scotland or all the people of Glasgow: it is not random and with only 100 cases it is too small even as a statistical sample of Gorbals Parish (59,408 people in 1851). At the other extreme is a *pure random sample*, which involves using a table of random numbers to select the required number of cases. A *systematic random sample* is not quite so pure, but easier to carry out; for the whole parish of the Gorbals every tenth person or every tenth household from the census-taker's books might be selected. Another kind of sample would take in all people whose surnames began with a certain letter of the alphabet; this could create problems if there were more Scots among the 'M's and more Irish among the 'O's, but it might make research easier in alphabetically-ordered directories, where linkage of information with different historical sources was required.

Assuming that a researcher can create a suitably random sample, three related elements must be kept in mind:
- the *sampling error* to be tolerated;

■ the *confidence level* desired;
■ the *size* of the sample.

Sampling error is a standard of precision which is decided in advance by the researchers. It indicates how far the researchers decide to allow the proportion of a particular characteristic in the whole population to differ (err) from the proportion in the sample. If, for example, a sampling error of ±3% is assumed and a sample comes out with 40%, then the actual percentage in the population will be between 37% and 43%.

Confidence level is also decided in advance by the researchers; normal levels are .95 or .99. In theory any number of samples could be taken. Most samples would be fairly representative of the population. A small number of samples might be quite unusual, e.g. outwith – for example – a ±3% sampling error. A .95 level of confidence means that the researchers could be confident that 95 samples out of 100 would meet a particular standard of precision; 5 out of 100 would be outside that limit. The researcher never knows for sure whether his or her sample is within the accepted bounds or is a rogue one.

Statisticians have worked out tables to show the relationship between confidence levels and sampling error. The higher the confidence level is set the bigger the sampling error that has to be accepted. And to reduce the sampling error (±1% rather than ±3%) an inferior confidence level has to be accepted (only 90 samples out of 100 being to this more precise standard).

Once researchers have chosen a sampling error and a confidence interval they must accept a particular *size of the sample*. The size of the overall population is not the most critical thing. Meaningful results can be obtained about a large population from a fairly small sample, and beyond a certain point great increases in the size of the sample do not make it correspondingly more accurate. To determine the sample size for a serious project one of the specialist statistical sources listed in the bibliography should be consulted – or even better, a statistician. For a small project, however, on a population of 10,000 cases, with a pre-decided sampling error of ±5% and a confidence level of .95 an adequate sample would be about 400 cases. If a sampling error of ±1% were required the sample would have to be 5,000.[11]

The research on the Scottish medical profession by Marguerite Dupree and Anne Crowther is a good concrete example of an historical sample. A database called SCOTDOC was created from *The Medical Directory 1911*, which printed information on all 4,000 doctors then practising in Scotland.[12] Rather than keying in every single entry from the *Directory* a sample of 1,000 was taken by selecting a random starting point and then putting every fourth entry into the database. This was a systematic random sample.

Given the size of the SCOTDOC sample and its relation to the 'population' (all those doctors listed in the *Directory*), and opting for a confidence level of 95% (i.e. $p < .05$), there would be a sampling error of ±2%. Applying this sampling error to the finding that 38.7% of the SCOTDOC sample had addresses in a particular geographical area, the Western Lowlands, this would indicate that the actual range in the *Directory* could be estimated as between 36.7% and 40.7% (for 95 samples out of 100).[13] In fact the sample could have been as small as 400 (one in ten rather than one in four) had a looser ±5% sampling error been accepted (with the same 95% confidence level). This would have indicated that the actual range for those with addresses in the Western Lowlands was between 33.7% and 43.7% (again, for 95 samples out of 100).

Sampling should not be seen as cutting corners or lowering standards. It can actually let an historian be more ambitious, study a larger group, or compare different groups. Without sampling the SCOTDOC project might not have been practical. Looking at it in another way, in the time required to key in all the entries from the 1911 *Directory* good samples of the *Directory* for 1891 and 1931 could have been taken in order to extend the study to different periods.

Two further examples of historical sampling might be given; they are quite different in their subject matter, but both use sampling to draw conclusions from large historical sources. A major part in Michael Anderson's important computer-based study, *Family Structure in Nineteenth-Century Lancashire*, was based on a one-in-ten sample of occupied residences in the cotton town of Preston, based on the census-taker's books for the 1851 census.[14] The total population was 69,542; Anderson's sample included 1,128 houses occupied by 1,241 households and 6,741 resident persons. Herbert F. Ziegler's recent study of the SS leadership, *Nazi Germany's New Aristocracy* (1989), was based in part on a systematic random sample of 900 individuals from a total population of the 'general SS' (*Allgemeine SS*) category of 12,669; two smaller categories of SS leader, comprising 437 and 766 people, were discussed without a sample.[15]

A good statistics program can make a real contribution to the interpretation of an historical source. Within the last decade the computer and new software have unlocked statistical analysis for a wide range of researchers. The problem is now understanding the principles behind the methods; there is no denying that advanced statistics is a very substantial challenge. On the other hand basic descriptive statistics can easily enhance many historical projects, and the computer is an essential tool for creating them. The technique of sampling, too, is one which is particularly suited to a range of historical projects using computers.

Notes

1 Cited in Richard E. Beringer, *Historical Analysis*, New York, 1978, p. 198.
2 Particularly useful are: K. Jarausch and K. Hardy, *Quantitative Methods for Historians*, Chapel Hill, 1991; J. Manheim and R. Rich, *Empirical Political Analysis*, New York, 1991, and R. Floud, *An Introduction to Quantitative Methods for Historians*, London, 1979.
3 We are indebted for this insight to James Currall of the Glasgow University Computing Service.
4 In a contingency table the *independent variable* (*IV*) is often written first and forms the rows (horizontal axis, x axis); the *dependent variable* (*DV*) is written second and forms the columns (vertical axis, y axis). There is not, however, always a clear independent/dependent relationship and many conventional historical skills are involved in clarifying this.
5 The other information in Figure 7.4 is not important in the present discussion. *D.F.* is a technical term, *degrees of freedom*, which is based on the number of cells. *Min E.F.* means *minimum expected frequency*.
6 Anderson (1971), pp. 79f, 95f.
7 Separate id numbers for husband and wife were not necessary for the process of correlation. They are included here as an example of good practice; at some future stage it might be desired to link COUPLES to the CENSUS database, and the unique personal id would be the link.

8 By convention the *x* axis is the independent variable and the *y* axis the dependent one. In this case the wife's age has rather arbitrarily been made the independent variable and the husband's age the dependent variable.

9 Related to r is r^2, called the *coefficient of determination*. This is *r* times r, in the case of this example +0.89503 times +0.89503, equalling 0.80108. What this means is that 80.1% of the variability of husbands' ages is associated with differences in wives' ages.

10 'Northern Voters and Negro Suffrage', in *Quantification in American History*, ed. R. Swierenga, New York, 1970, p. 231f.

11 Manheim and Rich, p. 369f.

12 Marguerite Dupree, 'The Medical Profession in Scotland, 1911', in *History and Computing III*, ed. E. Mawdsley *et al.*, Manchester, 1990, pp. 195–201; Marguerite W. Dupree and M. Anne Crowther, 'A profile of the medical profession in Scotland in the early twentieth century', *Bulletin of the History of Medicine*, 1991, pp. 209–33. The source is *The Medical Directory 1911*, London, n.d.; the precise number of doctors was 3,958.

13 These calculations are not explicit in the SCOTDOC background articles. Geographical distribution is chosen as an example here because quite full information is available; it is not, however, the main point of the SCOTDOC research.

14 Anderson, pp. 19, 24, 43.

15 Ziegler (1989), pp. 19f.

Part III

Sources, resources, and approaches

Chapter 8

More advanced database techniques: collective biography

Collective biography or *prosopography* – the systematic study of all individuals within a defined group in order to try to understand any common characteristics of that group – is an area of research where there is obvious scope for the application of computing techniques.[1] At a practical level, the computer may help eliminate intermediary copying and possible errors if data is entered direct from the source. While still at the data-collection stage, it is easy to check for consistency and even build in validity checks – for example by ensuring that data in certain fields can only be entered in a prescribed form. If, as is often the case, a great deal of information is available on some individuals in the chosen group, and much less on others, it is easy to maximise flexibility by using a relational or hierarchical datastructure – placing into subsidiary tables detailed information relating to family background, education, career structure, and the like, which one may wish to simplify later for coding and analysis. Subsequently – and before too much time has been invested – it will be easy to do trial searches for key words, and start experimenting with coding, to see how well the collected data can support the intended analysis. If necessary, alterations to the structure and substance of the data can be made far more quickly than if working with a cardfile. And, not least, back-up copies and hard copies of the data can be made frequently, to protect against accidental loss of laboriously gathered information.

This chapter will discuss computer-based prosopography in the context of a particular example, a database of the French parliamentary Convention of 1792–95. Any revolutionary period, and not least that in France at the end of the eighteenth century,

generates a vast and complex historical literature. Whilst a full
discussion of the Convention period is beyond the scope of this
chapter, what follows will look at ways of making the database as
useful as possible, and will give some impression of how far a
database of this kind can in fact help clarify crucial historical
problems.[2]

Collective biography

Collective biography is a technique long used by historians for a
variety of purposes. At its simplest, it is based on selective and
consistently compiled biographical information for all individuals
in the study – for example all Scots who emigrated to Canada, all
women who graduated in medicine from one or more specific
institutions, or all deputies who sat in a parliament over a given
period. It has been used particularly for the study of social and
political elites, where more information is usually available, but is
equally valid for any definable social group. In contrast to
conventional biography, the real objective is not to illuminate the
life-cycle of an individual, but to establish collective characteristics
and patterns for the whole group. Prosopographical techniques
have been used at least since the late nineteenth century,[3] and
can yield considerable fruits.

The collection of biographical information for a group of people
can be at least as addictive as individual biography. It is also
fraught with obvious risks. At one extreme is antiquarianism –
collecting information simply because it is there, or perhaps
because of uncertainty over what information will eventually
actually be required for the analysis, or out of fear that the in any
case inevitable incompleteness may weaken the validity of any
eventual conclusions. Attendant on this problem is the ever-present
frustration in historical research of having to cope with 'fuzzy'
data – visibly incomplete or vague information – so conspicuous
when the researcher attempts to achieve some degree of consistency across the whole chosen group.

At the other extreme (though not always far away) are the
risks, when searching for common characteristics in a chosen
group, of making a choice of 'relevant' information which is
either too arbitrary, or else dangerously preconditioned by the
explicit or implicit working hypotheses adopted by the researcher.

Unless the chosen group is a very large one, and the preconceived objectives fairly loosely defined in terms of the social history of the period (like the Scots emigrating to Canada), the risks of unconscious bias are particularly obvious. In a study of an elite group, for example, one might be tempted to draw causal connections between economic and personal circumstances on the one hand, and political behaviour on the other – conclusions which might be correct in some cases, but inevitably might overlook no less potent but more obscure individual factors (including not readily identifiable ideological convictions) for others. Moreover, as the body of information increases to the extent that not all substantiating evidence and data-processing decisions can be fully documented in the analysis itself, it becomes less and less feasible for others to re-evaluate the original research-processes in a meaningful way. In the end, of course, there is no simple defence against these pitfalls; but collective biography is no more vulnerable in these respects than many other types of historical research.

Case study: the French National Convention

The example used in this chapter is typical of its kind. It is a database containing information on all the deputies who ever sat in the crucial French National Convention between its formal opening on 20 September 1792 and its last meeting on 26 October 1795. There is no decision to be made in regard of sampling, since every admitted deputy can be included – even those originally chosen as *suppléants* (standbys) who eventually took their seat because the first incumbent resigned or died. Although the Convention had a nominal membership of 749, this turnover in membership means that there are altogether 895 individuals to be included in the database.

The reason for creating such a database needs little explanation. Over the last thirty years, since Mark Sydenham's seminal work on the Girondins and Alison Patrick's detailed study of the deputies of the Convention,[4] there has been recurrent discussion of the rapid factionalisation of the revolutionary assemblies – and the extent to which these factions represent political 'parties' of the kind which Rousseau and others had specifically warned against. Even earlier, the revisionist work of A. Cobban on the National Constituent Assembly of 1789[5] had alerted historians to the need to identify the background and social classification of specific groups within the French political nation, in order to clarify the driving forces behind the Revolution. The Convention, the third of the major revolutionary assemblies after the National Constituent and the Legislative Assemblies (1789–91 and 1791–92 respectively), was in some respects the most critically decisive of the Revolution. It in effect presided over the process of radicalisation, from the trial and execution of the king through to the creation of a strong military Terror government, and indeed through the messy dismantling that followed the fall of Robespierre in July 1794.

Although the Convention has already been the subject of detailed analysis without a computer, Patrick's conclusions cannot readily be reassessed quantitatively. With a flexible machine-readable version of the data, however, fuzzy data can be taken into account more explicitly at crucial stages, so that it is possible to re-examine some of her conclusions. The relationship between the voting behaviour and affiliation of the deputies on the one hand, and their age, background and geographic base on the other can be tested without imposing as many pre-conceptions on the data. Going further, one might pursue questions of career pattern before and after the start of the Revolution, the actual role of each deputy in the Convention (in particular through the revealing speeches and roll-call votes between January and May 1793), not to mention each deputy's ability to survive either the Terror or the White Terror that followed Thermidor – all with reference not so much to individuals as to groups defined in a historically meaningful way (for example as 'Montagnards', 'moderates', and so on).

Most of the biographical information is readily derived from the standard and very thorough *Dictionnaire des Conventionnels* compiled by A. Kuscinski (1916). His information was supplemented from Patrick and Sydenham. For key votes in the Convention, contemporary roll-call lists and other records were also used for cross-checking.[6] In effect there was an ideal basis for collective biography: information could be culled from sources that in themselves treat the whole group as consistently as possible.

Any such study, however, has its problems. We know a great deal more, say, about someone like the notorious Claude Javogues, an over-zealous revolutionary from the upper Loire, than we do

JAVOGUES (Claude), born in Bellegarde (Loire) on 19 Aug. 1759; executed by firing squad in Paris on 19 vendémiaire year IV (10 Oct. 1796).

Belonging to an honourable family of several generations of practising *notaires* (lawyers), he was first trained in the military, then became *clerc de procureur* in Montbrison. There he made claims to nobility which were turned to ridicule even though they seemed more justifiable in his case than with the majority of those who composed the *bailliage* of Montbrison. Some biographers claim that he was prone to drunkeness; nothing proves it. What is more certain is that he was shunned by society; this caused him deep resentment, and he resolutely joined the revolutionaries. He succeeded in having himself nominated, first, administrator of the district of Montbrison, then in 1792 deputy to the Convention for Rhône et Loire.

In the trial of Louis XVI, he voted against the referendum, for death and against a reprieve.

In the vote on the impeachment of Marat, he declared that Marat's behaviour merited commendation on account of the firmness with which he denounced all conspiracies, especially that of Dumouriez and his accomplices, and that accordingly he was not able to vote for impeachment.

On 20 July 1793 he was seconded with Reverchon and Laporte as representative on mission in the department of Saône et Loire, where these deputies were to organise the largest possible force to march on Lyon [...]

LITTEE (Janvier), born in Saint-Pierre de la Martinique around 1751; died in Paris on 15 March 1820.

Chosen as deputy to the Convention for the colony of Martinique, he was admitted to the chamber on 5 Sept.1793 and served without making himself noticed. After the end of the Convention, he was retained as ex-Conventionnel in the Council of Five Hundred, where he remained until 1 Prairial year V (20 May 1797). He settled in Paris, living off a small pension paid by successive governments.

Figure 8.1   Dictionary entries in translation

about an obscure deputy like Janvier Littée, sitting for the overseas possession of Martinique in the West Indies. The entries on them in the *Dictionnaire des Conventionnels* (Figure 8.1) illustrate the difficulty straight away. For Littée we have virtually no usable evidence; whilst for Javogues there are several columns of text, only the first portion of which is rendered here – to which would have to be added the outcome of further recent research. As for any collective biography where the source material is so uneven, the quality of the results is bound to be affected.

A flat-file version of the data

The exact structure of a database necessarily depends on at least three factors: what information is available in the sources, how that information might ideally be structured conceptually,[7] and how far such an ideal structure should or can be implemented given the constraints of time and resources. Above all, existing database technology, and especially statistical analysis, tend to favour clear-cut variables in each field, or at least information which is not too convoluted: but as we all know, politicians rarely

NO	494
FORENAME	CLAUDE
SURNAME	JAVOGUES
DESCR-89	L-AV/CLERC DE PROCUREUR (MONTBRISON)
NCA	-
LA	-
SEAT	RHONE-ET-LOIRE
GROUP	M
CONVX	MISSION VS. LYON (JUL.93) & AIN; DENOUNCED IN CONV. 8 FEB.94, AGAIN 1 JUNE 95
LOUIS1	X
LOUIS2	X
LOUIS34	XX
MARAT	X
COM12	X
DEATH	961010, FIRING SQUAD
CCODE	569
BPCODE	542
PLBIRTH	BELLEGARDE
FAM	L-NT
YRBIRTH	1759
AGE1792	33
DEATHYR	1796

NOTES to database schema:

DESCR: each deputy's occupation/title before 1789.

CONS = *conseiller*, titular councillor
LTRS = man of letters, writer, journalist
OFH = officeholder (often venal)
OFCR = officer in the army or navy
L-AV = lawyer (*avocat*), in *Parlement* etc.
L-PROC = lawyer (*procureur*)
L-NT = lawyer (*notaire*)

NCA and **LA**: Constituency name of any deputy who had sat in Constituent or Legislative assembly. If in the NCA, code C is added for those chosen for the first (clerical) estate, N for the second (noble) estate, and T for the third estate. A *suppléant* might be indicated with the prefix S:.

GROUP: Provisional groupings might include:
  J = member of later Paris Jacobin club 1793-94, and also "sitting with Mountain"
  M = "sat with the Mountain"
  P = explicit protester against the expulsion of the anti-radical deputies from the Convention 2 June 1793
  G = reliably identified as member of inner Girondin circle (Sydenham, Kucsinski)
  F = a "federalist", actively involved in generating provincial resistance to Parisian dominance
  O = independent of any of the above categories
  E = deputy *à l'écart*, taking little active part

CONVX: Additional information on each deputy's role in the Convention, including:
  R/ = date of resignation
  SF/ = sat from <date>
  ARST = arrested on <date>
  PR-dd/mm/yy = was speaker of the Convention for a fortnight starting from <day/month/year>

LOUIS1, LOUIS2, LOUIS34, MARAT, COM12: Summary of votes cast by each deputy:
  O = moderate/conservative vote
  X = radical/uncompromising vote
  A = abstention
  - = absent
  S = away as Conv. representative *en mission* in province
  Q = important qualification (see source)
For the third of the LOUIS votes, M = acceptance of the Mailhe amendment, R = vote for a reprieve.

DEATH, DEATHYR: The year of death is given in DEATHYR. The field DEATH is used only for deputies who died prematurely, as result of political activity. Notice the date of death is given first, in the form yymmdd, to facilitate sorting.

CCODE, BPCODE: Three-digit code for constituency and birth-place respectively: first digit represents the pre-1789 region, the last two the number of the *département* after the regional re-organisation of 1790.

Figure 8.2 One record of the flat-file version of the French Convention database

speak plainly, and for some categories of information substantial textual analysis is required to produce fully sustainable results.

These reservations notwithstanding, a flat-file (single-table) version of the data might start off simply as a selective summary of the dictionary entry, as illustrated in Figure 8.2. Generally speaking, the data available for each deputy readily falls into distinct categories. First of all there is basic *biographical* data, including place and data of birth, parentage and family background, and education. Since election to the Convention was, unprecedentedly, by universal male franchise, it is of obvious interest to try to establish the background of those chosen as deputies. This biographical data can be used to supplement what is known of the *status*, occupation(s), or rank of each person both before and after the outbreak of the Revolution in 1789. To that one would naturally add details of earlier *parliamentary experience* – if the deputy had sat either in the Estates General (and the National Constituent Assembly which grew out of it, 1789–91), or in the Legislative Assembly (which took over in the autumn of 1791 and ended with the fall of the monarchy on 10 August 1792). Thirdly, the *département* (region) for which each deputy chose to sit is important both in establishing regional patterns and, in the many cases where deputies represented areas other than those of their own birth, in clarifying other geographic allegiances. Fourthly, it is natural to include information on the *political role* of each deputy in the assembly – for example as member of the various committees, or as deputy on mission helping to organise the war effort. The role of deputies who served for a fortnight at a time as presidents (speakers) of the Convention – an honour given to a deputy either in recognition of his leading role at the time, or as an indication that he represented, in the vacillating history of the Convention, the political trend at that particular time – is a useful indicator of overall mood. Conversely, some deputies did their best to keep out of trouble by taking as little active role as possible, and these were largely identified as such by Kuscinski – making a contrasting group to those who fell victim to various purges or attempted purges during the Terror period and in the reaction that followed.

Last but not least, there is information on how each deputy voted during the crucial divisions in the lead-up to the Terror government. The six *roll-call* votes are in many ways at the heart of the database. The votes on the fate of the deposed Louis XVI (LOUIS1-4, January 1793), coming after the formal hearings by the Convention of the case against him, concerned four crucial questions: (i) was he guilty of treason?; (ii) if so, should his fate be decided by a popular referendum?; (iii) what punishment should he suffer?; and (iv) should there be a reprieve on the death penalty? These votes need to be seen clearly in the context of the issues raised by the trial itself. Given the problems with some of the statements made by the deputies during the roll-calls, full content analysis of the speeches leading up to the votes would be a particularly valuable aid. Yet even in summarised form these votes give some indication of where each deputy stood.

The MARAT vote (13 April 1793) and the COMMITTEE OF 12 vote (25 May 1793) relate directly to the role of popular radicalism. Marat, the feared extremist journalist, had for long been notorious in the Convention, and the clumsy right-wing effort to have him impeached and expelled was thus not just a tactical move against a feared radical – which backfired – but also a deeper question of how the assembly saw itself. The COM12 vote was more technical, concerning the reinstatement of a committee originally appointed to examine allegations of a planned sans-culotte (crowd) insurrection against the moderates (Girondins) in the Convention itself (an insurrection which in fact occurred a week later, ending in the purge of the Convention). Both these votes serve to clarify the political orientation of each deputy in the spring of 1793.

The six roll-call votes, however, are in themselves not an adequate means of grouping the deputies into Jacobin (radical), Girondin (moderate) and other factions. The records clearly show that deputies took a highly independent view of the issues they were facing, in some cases explicitly making decisions according to their own conscience rather than in terms of pragmatic politics. This is particularly clear in the votes on the king; but to some extent also in the April and May 1793 votes, when pressure groups within the Convention had become more organised. Even then, however, actual votes do not always adequately summarise underlying reasoning. It is well known, for example, that a number of broadly moderate deputies protested against the purge of the Convention on 2 June 1793. The principle of parliamentary immunity, however, had been heatedly debated at various times since the autumn of 1792. Neither a moderate vote in the COM12 roll-call, nor support for a subsequent protest against the purge can therefore in itself be regarded as unequivocal evidence of Girondin leanings.[8] This is an example of the kind of complex historical question where the computer will *not* offer any help: its retrievals will as always only be as good as the data it uses.

Instead, other evidence for 'party' or group affiliation can be incorporated in the database for the GROUP field. Initially, in order not to prejudge any issues, it makes sense to adopt as many group codes as the known stances of all the deputies seem to require. We may therefore need distinct codes for those known to have signed a protest (listed as such by Sydenham), for those known to have had 'federalist' leanings (recorded as having supported provincial autonomy against the centralising tendencies of Paris), for those known to have occupied the middle ground in the Convention, and even for those who, wherever they sat, were by all accounts vociferously independent. On the left of the political spectrum the problems appear more manageable: those grouped as Jacobin and Mountain are more clearly identifiable from club membership lists and common contemporary attribution – though here again it is worth remembering that the Jacobin club network itself varied in the provinces, and in any case changed character as the Revolution proceeded.[9]

From flat-file to relational structure

It will already be apparent from the discussion so far that the French Convention database, like many prosopographical sets of data, in fact consists of different types of information which do not all fit equally well into the fairly rigid structure of a flat-file database. For a start, each deputy may well have several pre-revolutionary status-indications, a succession of different occupations, and a great variety of known functions within the Convention itself and its related committees. In a flat-file structure there can be only one row or record for each deputy, so for certain fields some of the entries will have a mass of different items of information, others nothing at all. Since each record will have to have the same field structure – usually with finite field lengths regardless of how little information there may be – the whole structure can soon become unwieldy. For the same reasons, the historian may have difficulty accommodating notes on the sources of his information for individual fields in each record: even the most cryptic coding scheme would soon lead to a bloated and inefficient data structure.

Take for example the pre-revolutionary career and status information. In the flat-file version, the field containing this information, DESCR-89, had to contain all the selected information. A keywords-count on that field produces a complex and cryptic table, part of which reads as follows:

LTRS, COMMERCE   1
LTRS, MEDIC   1
LTRS, TUTOR   2
LTRS: ACAD.SC. 1769, ACAD.FR. 1782, SGR,
   MARQUIS   1
MAGISTRATE   1
MANUFACTURER (SMALL SCALE)   1
MANUFACTURER/WOOL   1

Several problems are obvious from such a retrieval. There is no room for annotations (for example to explain whether the 'magistrate' was different in rank from the many lawyers and office-holders elsewhere in the list), nor is there an obvious way of ranking multiple descriptors in some kind of order. For the fourth individual on the list – in fact the philosopher Condorcet – the problems are acute. His combination of noble landownership and intellectual distinction is by no means unusual for the *ancien régime*, but this summary, given what recent research has contributed, is very inadequate.

At the present stage of software development there is no totally satisfactory yet simple solution to this problem. One could envisage using text-analysis software rather than a database to control some of the information, but there are as yet few single programs incorporating real power both over loosely structured text *and* over more structured data. Until the time when software is sufficiently flexible to allow the historian the luxury of treating all data through the same system, it may be simplest, for the kind of analysis proposed here, to adopt a relational database manager.

A relational system (as we saw in Chapter 6) will allow different hierarchical levels of information to go into separate tables: a unique numerical identifier for each record in the main table will provide the key to the corresponding rows in the subsidiary tables. In the case of the French Convention dataset, the pre-revolutionary career and status information can thus be separated into its own table (BACKGROUND), as can the data on subsequent career patterns from the Directory onwards (LATER-CAREER). To each of these can then be added coding and reference tables to help interpret the information in each. Similarly, for deputies who died prematurely before the end of the Convention, specific information on accusations, charges and defence procedures can be held in another table (EARLY-DEATH).

Each table can now be structured to suit more closely the data and types of analysis involved. And since each deputy can have one or more lines (or none at all) in a subsidiary table, no field there will need to contain more than one set of information per line. In the BACKGROUND table, for example, Condorcet's career as a man of letters (member of the Académie de Science and Académie Française) can be substantiated with reference to his publications, whilst his position as a nobleman and as a seigneur can be detailed on a separate line. Both lines will carry his identification number, 212, linking the information back to the main table, where he is identified by that number. This will of course not in itself 'classify' Condorcet, in terms of the kind of person he may have been in 1789 or 1792: but it will provide a clearer and more flexible framework for the kind of information that might be needed in order to allocate Condorcet provisionally to a particular category for purposes of overall analysis of the deputies' background. Such a categorisation can now in part be done reliably by filters (all individuals calling themselves *avocat* in 1789 will be in the law/office-holder category), but must necessarily be checked and supplemented by manual editing to take account of the complexities of the data. Deputy Littée (see Figure 8.1) will be no better off than in a flat-file structure, but at least the table will not have to include a run of empty fields for him.

So far, the relational database structure has simply been used to accommodate uneven and complex data in a flexible and more comprehensive way than was possible in the flat-file version. No less important, however, is the fact that a relational structure permits the incorporation of information which is not about each deputy as such. Most obviously, data on each *département* (for example population figures, estimates of the scale of terror executions, and emigration rates) can be summarised in a DEPT table linked to the main table by means of the constituency code (CCODE). This allows national parliamentary politics to be linked directly to the regional dimensions of the Revolution so crucial to our overall understanding of the period. It is now possible to explore, say, whether deputies who were particularly active in the

Convention tended to represent *départements* prone to high levels of revolutionary violence. More specifically, we know that the Rhône et Loire which Javogues (see Figure 8.2) represented was, like a few other areas, far more deeply torn by violence than most of France: a simple table join will now indicate whether deputies who gained notoriety in the Convention tended to come from similarly unsettled *départements*, or whether Javogues was unusual in this respect. If, as is likely, such a line of enquiry leads to a search for additional information on each *département* to help clarify the overall picture, such information can quickly and easily be added to the DEPT table.

It is easy to envisage how such a database could be extended even further, incorporating summaries of local government experience before and after 1790, a textbase of the major speeches of individual deputies, their publications, contemporary newspaper and pamphlet references, and so on. The schematic illustration of the database structure shown in Figure 8.3, using where possible the same field-names as in the flat-file version, incorporates only some of these types of information.

The relational approach, then, has some obvious advantages. Information can be accommodated in varying formats, reflecting

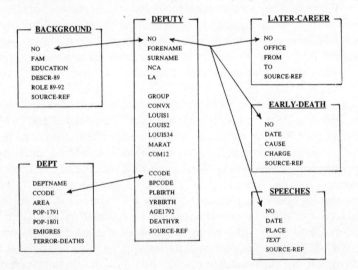

Figure 8.3 Relational model for the French Convention data (each box representing a separate table)

in different ways either the nature of the original sources or the chosen research framework, without cluttering the database too much. Complex material in separate tables can be used to generate simpler analytical codes, but in such a way that all the evidence is retained for subsequent revision or secondary analysis. Provided care is taken over the structure itself, data integrity (recording any item of information only once) can be preserved, making inconsistencies from subsequent editing less likely to occur.[10]

The particular example used here, the French Convention database, certainly has more potential than can readily be summarised in a chapter such as this – and more flexibility than the published tabulations which form the appendices to Patrick's pioneering work. In particular, the criteria for defining political affiliations (GROUP) in effect become open to experimentation and re-evaluation. Thus for example the elusive Girondins can be treated either with, or as distinct from, those deputies who protested against the political purge of 31 May–June 1793. Similarly, Jacobins and those who sat with the Mountain can be treated either separately or together; and patterns amongst the crucial but indistinct groupings in the middle ground of the Convention can be ascertained as far as the evidence allows. Other information (including that on previous political life) can be drawn in experimentally: in other words, the analytical potential is not fixed but adaptable. And most important of all, the structure allows considerable freedom both for complex data and for the extension of the information-framework itself through new research.

This is not the place to discuss fully some of the conclusions derived from the database described here. A few examples must suffice. At a simple level, one can immediately observe that the radical Jacobins were on average several years older than the moderate Girondins, but that, less surprisingly, those who kept a low profile were the oldest of all. With computer manipulation, an almost infinite number of permutations of questions and relationships of this kind can readily be tried.

To move on to major historical issues, one might note that the traditional image of south-western and western France as conservative and 'anti-Jacobin' is not reflected by the deputies themselves: radical and moderate deputies are distributed remarkably widely across virtually the whole of France, with only Paris itself showing a

E

clear radical dominance. No less significant is the fact that neither of the two sides in the Convention voted as consistently as traditional assumptions about Jacobins and Girondins might lead us to expect. Furthermore, the behaviour of the Protesters turned out to be noticeably different from that of the Girondins proper, whilst deputies who subsequently tried to keep a low profile (*à l'écart*) were on the whole much more moderate than the broad middle ground of active deputies who sat between left and right. Most interesting of all, however, is the fact that systematic analysis of voting behaviour in the Convention reveals a degree of independence and courage on the part of the deputies which makes the subsequent slide into authoritarian government appear even more tragic.

Prosopographical techniques such as these can readily be applied to a wide variety of historical data where the researcher wants to clarify group characteristics and dynamics on the basis of reasonably consistent biographical and/or demographic data. They have been applied with particular success in the study of elites, including social elites, deputies in elected assemblies, non-elected bureaucracies, and the like. With more sophisticated data, statistical *cluster analysis* might be attempted.[11] Although professional groups such as university graduates, doctors, clergymen, politicians and members of parliament may be the easiest to tackle – given readily available directories and biographical dictionaries – many different types of clearly defined historical groups are just as suitable: prisoners and criminals, migrant labour forces, factory populations, or military recruits will lend themselves just as well to such methods, provided sufficient material is available to justify such an approach.

For any one of these it is worth remembering that the computing techniques themselves, as described in this chapter, are not particularly complex or difficult to master. As is so often the case, the most difficult decisions have to be made away from the keyboard.

Notes

1 For a survey, see N. Bulst, 'Prosopography and the computer: problems and possibilities', in *History and Computing II*, ed. P. Denley *et al.*, Manchester, 1989, pp. 12–18.

2 The French Convention database was created from scratch, without any research grant. Much of the initial data was entered by employment trainees – several of whom showed an enthusiasm and level of accuracy (even for French-language material) well beyond the call of duty.

3 Amongst the best known examples are the works by Lewis B. Namier, *The Structure of Politics at the Accession of George III*, 2 vols., London, 1929, and *England in the Age of the American Revolution*, London, 1930. See also L. Stone, 'Prosopography', in his *The Past and the Present Revisited*, London, 1987, pp. 45–73.

4 M. J. Sydenham, *The Girondins*, London, 1961; A. Patrick, *The Men of the First French Republic*, Baltimore, 1972. See also C. J. Mitchell, *The French Legislative Assembly of 1791*, Leiden, 1988, and N. Hampson, *Prelude to Terror: the Constituent Assembly and the Failure of Consensus 1789–1791*, Oxford, 1988.

5 A. Cobban, 'The myth of the French Revolution', in his *Aspects of the French Revolution*, London, 1968, pp. 90–111.

6 These are not consistently recorded, even though the roll-call lists were published. The voting indicated here is based on the roll-calls as given in the Gazette Nationale from no. 18 of January 1793 onwards (reprinted as the *Ancien Moniteur*, vol. XV). This has been cross-checked with the listings given in P.-J.-B. Buchez and P.-C. Roux, *Histoire parlementaire de la Révolution française*, XXIII, Paris, 1836, and other material on the variants recorded at the time.

7 It needs hardly be emphasised that the design of a new database is so critical an operation that it is essential to experiment with different prototypes to ensure that the model will work. For a helpful discussion of the principles involved, see Lou Burnard, 'Principles of database design', in *Information Technology in the Humanities*, ed. S. Rahtz, Chichester, 1987, pp. 54–68.

8 Patrick, p. 15, assumes that anyone protesting against the purge can safely be ascribed to the Girondin group: this assumption is not self-evidently safe, but can be tested through the database.

9 Brissot, a leader of the moderate Girondins, himself remained a member of the Jacobin club until his expulsion on 10 October 1792: early membership of the club, therefore, is no proof of Jacobin leanings in the context of early 1793.

10 For a more detailed example, see D. I. Greenstein, 'Multi-sourced and integrated databases for the prosopographer', in *History and Computing III*, ed. E. Mawdsley *et al.*, Manchester, 1990, pp. 60–6.

11 For cluster analysis, see notably C. M. Dollar and R. J. Jensen, *Historian's Guide to Statistics*, New York, 1971, pp. 106–11, 214–23; and S. A. Rice, *Quantitative Methods in Politics*, New York, 1928.

For a recent example of complex analysis of European parliamentary elites, see the work of Heinrich Best and Ralph Ponemereo on the German Reichstag, described in H. Best, 'Computing the unmeasurable: estimating missing values in legislative roll-call analysis', *History and Computing II*, ed. P. Denley *et al.*, Manchester, 1989, pp. 104–16, and in his 'Elite structure and regime (dis)continuity in Germany 1867–1933: the case of parliamentary leadership groups', *German History*, VIII, 1990, pp. 1–27; see also E. Mawdsley, 'The Central Committee of the CPSU in perspective', *Soviet Studies*, XLIII, 1991, pp. 897–912.

Chapter 9

Tables and spreadsheets: voting and the census

This chapter will look at a common type of historical source – numerical information in tabular form. The computer is an excellent tool for handling tables and making sense of them. The main example in this chapter comprises the study of election behaviour, *psephology*, specifically the Russian national election held in 1917. Two main computer methods can be considered: the first is the database approach, which has been introduced in previous chapters; the second is an approach especially suited to tables, the *spreadsheet*.

The final part of the chapter will return briefly to the nineteenth-century census and show how a spreadsheet can be used to make sense of another aspect of the census – the tables of aggregate information.

Background and sources

Russia in 1917 was described as 'the freest country in the world' and it was in November of this year that the only nation-wide multi-party elections were held, for the *All-Russian Constituent Assembly*. The Assembly itself was closed by the Bolsheviks in January 1918 after a one-day session, so it was of no legislative importance. It was, however, a unique test of political opinion: 44,433,309 votes were recorded at a critical turning point in Russian history. In the confusion of the revolution and the ensuing civil war no full list of results was ever published. A survey of the returns was made by Oliver Radkey, in a classic work that has recently been updated. An even fuller report appeared in a 1968 Russian-language history of the early Soviet period by L. M. Spirin, and this is the basic source used.[1]

ИТОГИ ВЫБОРОВ ВО ВСЕРОССИЙСКОЕ УЧРЕДИТЕЛЬНОЕ СОБРАНИЕ ПО ОКРУГАМ

№№ п.п.	Округа	Большевики		Кадеты		Эсеры		Меньшевики		Националистическая мелкая буржуазия		Националистическая буржуазия		Прочие		Итого голосов	Примечание
		Кол-во голосов	%	Кол-во голосов	%	Кол-во голосов	%	Кол-во голосов	%	Кол-во голосов	%	Кол-во голосов	%	Кол-во голосов	%		
1	2	3	4	5	6	7	8	9	10	11	12	13	14	15	16	17	18
1	Алтайский	45 268	6,4	12 109	1,7	621 377	87,0	3 785	0,5	—	—	8 048	1,1	23 360	3,3	713 949	* Из них казаков 14 11 (7,3%)
2	Архангельский	36 322	21,6	12 084	7,2	100 570	63,2	7 333	4,3	—	—	20 412	10,5	6 192	3,7	186 105	
3	Астраханский	36 023	18,6	13 017	6,7	100 482	51,8	2 220	1,1	—	—	—	—	21 953*	11,3	194 107	
4	Бессарабский	Данных нет															
5	Витебский	287 101	51,2	8 132	1,5	150 279	26,8	12 471	2,2	26 990	4,8	53 364	9,9	20 201	3,6	560 538	
6	Владимирский	345 306	56,5	38 058	6,2	196 836	32,2	13 139	2,2	—	—	—	—	17 769	2,9	611 158	
7	Вологодский	74 358	18,0	25 337	5,4	348 239	74,1	—	—	—	—	—	—	11 945	2,5	469 900	
8	Волынский	35 612	4,4	22 397	2,8	27 575	3,4	9 658	0,8	570 988	71,0	—	—	147 636	18,3	804 308	
9	Воронежский	236 952	22,1	48 106	4,5	612 525	56,9	19 167	1,8	11 851	1,1	55 585	5,2	14 152	1,3	1 074 823	
10	Вятский	151 517	13,8	76 488	6,4	975 300	79,7	26 909	2,3	37 621	3,5	63 029	5,3	31 524	2,6	1 193 049	
11	Екатеринославский	213 163	17,9	27 551	2,3	231 717	19,4	4 581	1,3	579 176*	48,5	—	—	—	—		* Из них украинских эсеров, меньшевиков с.-д. 556 012 (40,6%)
12	Енисейский	96 133	27,0	12 263	3,4	233 345	65,4	6 899	2,9	—	—	—	—	10 452	2,9	356 779	* Из них левых эсеров 36,4 (1,0%)
13	Иркутский	33 576	14,3	9 393	4,0	127 834	54,4	4 293	0,5	39 248	16,7	—	—	18 202	7,7	235 152	* Из них левых эсеров 130 316 (21%)
14	Казанский	50 000	5,8	32 000	3,7	270 000	31,5	19 448	1,8	379 647	44,2	71 154	8,3	51 302	6,0	853 396	
15	Калужский	200 842	60,2	22 712	6,8	97 782	29,3	6 463	1,9	998	0,3	—	—	4 844	1,5	333 641	
16	Киевский	60 693	4,0	21 667	1,4	19 230	1,3	6 043	0,8	1 199 378	79,8	136 844	9,1	53 310	3,6	1 503 725	
17	Костромской	226 905	40,8	41 448	7,5	—	45,0	7 046	1,3	—	—	—	—	17 901	3,2	553 580	
18	Курский	120 794	11,3	47 221	4,3	869 497	82,0	—	—	—	—	—	—	17 306	1,6	1 060 161	
19	Лифляндский	Данных нет															
20	Минский	97 781	71,9	10 724	1,2	—	—	—	—	31 253	22,9	—	—	13 577	1,4	136 080	
21	Могилевский	579 087	63,2	44 478	6,7	181 873	19,8	16 277	1,8	14 054	1,5	101 928	11,1	13 577		917 520	* Из них членов крестьянского союза 14 556
22	Московский	368 264	55,8	—		172 229	26,2	27 928	4,2	—	—	—	—	46 872*	7,1	659 771	
23	г. Москва	370 256	50,1	265 136	35,9	62 725	8,5	21 627	2,9	—	—	—	—	19 149	2,6	738 904	

Figure 9.1 Spirin's district election returns

Spirin actually printed six pages of results in three tables: the first table gave the results for all 79 election districts (*okrugs*) into which the Russian Provisional Government divided the country. Most election districts, some 68, were large geographical areas, usually equivalent to a pre-revolutionary province; the majority of the remaining election districts were for army groups or fleets. The second table gave the results for the capital town of each election district (and occasionally for other important towns); and the third table gave the results for the garrison of each capital town. Figure 9.1 gives the first 23 rows of the table for the election districts; the other two tables had a similar layout.

A very large number of parties took part in the elections, reflecting the political, social, and ethnic diversity of revolutionary Russia. For purposes of fitting the data into tables some of the smaller groups were lumped together (aggregated) by Spirin, using Marxist–Leninist categories; this is a form of coding, or at least a Leninist approach (!) to 'collapsing' the data. The groups are given in Table 9.1, with the codes used in a database created from Spirin's tables. A full understanding of the various parties is not important here. The Kadets represented the middle class and the SRs the peasantry; the Mensheviks were moderate Marxists. LNAT and RNAT were parties from the national minorities, the former being peasant-based socialists; *petit bourgeois* and *bourgeois* are Marxist categories, used by Spirin.

Even though the text of Spirin's table is in Russian it is obvious that there is a structure here suitable for a database or a spreadsheet. The rows are geographical areas, in this case election

Table 9.1 Explanation of Spirin's columns (with RUSSCA-database abbreviations)

Column	Party
3	Bolsheviks (BOL)
5	Kadets (KD)
7	Socialist-revolutionaries (SR)
9	Mensheviks (MEN)
11	Petit-bourgeois nationalist (LNAT)
13	Bourgeois nationalist (RNAT)
15	Other (small or hard to categorise) (OTHER)

districts; row 2 is the Arkhangelsk election district. The columns give the vote; column 3 is the *absolute number* of votes received by the Bolsheviks in each district (36,522 in the case of Arkhangelsk), column 4 is the Bolshevik vote as a *percentage* of all the votes cast in that election district.

The geographical spread of the vote across the Russian Empire was one dimension, but Spirin's three tables make it possible to see the 'vertical divisions' within particular areas. For example, it becomes clear that within one province-sized election district the capital town often voted differently from the surrounding country-side, and the local garrison voted differently from both.

The elections and the computer

If a 'result' is taken to be the vote for one party in one district at one level, then Spirin gave nearly 1,500 results. The computer examines large amounts of data quickly; it can also enhance the data and, most important, make it easier to understand.

A computerised version of the election results was created called RUSSCA (*RUSS*ian Constituent *A*ssembly). There are several – equally sensible – ways that the data could have been structured, given Spirin's tables; the choice depends on exactly what kind of analysis is required and what software is available. The first approach is shown in Table 9.2; it is designed for

Table 9.2 A typical record from the RUSSCA database

Fieldname	Example value	Meaning
RNUM	88	unique record number
EAREA	ARKHANGELSK	election area
AREATYPE	P	(P = province election district, F = 'front' election district, C = capital, or G = garrison)
REGION	NORTH	code for geographical region where election area was located
PARTY	BOL	code for party; BOL = Bolshevik
VOTE	36522	number of votes, i.e. the 'result'
VOTEPC	21.6	vote as % of election area total
REM		remarks (if any)

maximum flexibility as a teaching tool and for suitability to the simplest database management software. The database *record*, the basic unit of the RUSSCA database, consists of details about how *one* party performed in *one* election area. The example in Table 9.2 corresponds to row 2, columns 3 and 4, of the Spirin table printed in Figure 9.1. (Note that in most previous examples in this book a record has corresponded to an entire row.) Eight records are needed to show the results in any one area (row); there are six political groups, an 'other' category, and a 'total' category. For all three tables there are, corresponding to Spirin's results, nearly 1,500 records.

All three of Spirin's tables (for election district, town, and garrison) are put together in RUSSCA into one database or 'table'. This presents no problem, as the structure of all three of Spirin's tables was the same (i.e. the same number of columns). The only slight complication is the coded '[election] AREATYPE' field; this is to distinguish Arkhangelsk *province* from Arkhangelsk *town* or the Arkhangelsk *town garrison*. A record with 'ARKHANGELSK' in the EAREA field and 'P' in the AREATYPE field, for example refers to the main province-level election district (*okrug*).

The one new piece of data added to Spirin's data when the database was created was the REGION field; each territorial election district (and the town and garrisons within it) was assigned to one of thirteen broad geographical regions of the Russian Empire. Arkhangelsk election district, for example, was in north European Russia, coded as NORTH.

Even with this simple structure there are a large number of questions that can be asked. The first step might be to explore the data, listing the election result for all parties by selecting one area (EAREA) and one type (AREATYPE). The command in SQL (the query language outlined in Chapter 5) for obtaining details of the garrison of Arkhangelsk would be:

Select EAREA AREATYPE PARTY VOTE
From RUSSCA
Where EAREA = 'ARKHANGELSK'
And AREATYPE = 'G'

The result is shown in Table 9.3. That can be done, of course, from Spirin's data by finding the right table and row. The machine-

Table 9.3 The vote in the Arkhangelsk town garrison (RUSSCA database)

AREA	AREATYPE	PARTY	VOTE
ARKHANGELSK	G	BOL	3,670
ARKHANGELSK	G	KD	406
ARKHANGELSK	G	LNAT	
ARKHANGELSK	G	MEN	240
ARKHANGELSK	G	OTHER	
ARKHANGELSK	G	RNAT	
ARKHANGELSK	G	SR	1,256
ARKHANGELSK	G	TOTAL	5,572

Table 9.4 The total vote for each level in Arkhangelsk (RUSSCA database)

EAREA	AREATYPE	PARTY	VOTE
ARKHANGELSK	P	TOTAL	168,705
ARKHANGELSK	C	TOTAL	19,459
ARKHANGELSK	G	TOTAL	5,572

readable version is, however, much more flexible. For example, the relative size of the vote at election district, town and town garrison level for any area can be shown instantly using the computer; to do the same task manually would involve looking at all three of Spirin's tables. The computer procedure is to select records that relate to one EAREA name and where the value in the PARTY field is 'TOTAL'; the result is shown in Table 9.4. The computer is *not* at this stage calculating this total vote. Because RUSSCA was designed for easy use the total vote calculated by Spirin was included beforehand as a separate 'result'; TOTAL is treated as a party, like SR. The city vote is included in the province-level electoral district vote, and the garrison vote is normally included in the city vote. There were a total of 168,705 votes cast in the Arkhangelsk province-level election district; of these 5,572 were cast by the garrison of Arkhangelsk town.

Table 9.5 The total vote in the three election districts in the Northern region (RUSSCA database)

REGION	EAREA	AREATYPE	PARTY	VOTE
NORTH	ARKHANGELSK	P	TOTAL	168,705
NORTH	OLONETS	P	TOTAL	150,211
NORTH	VOLOGDA	P	TOTAL	469,900

With the help of the new REGION field the total vote of all provinces in one region – or group of regions – can be found. For example the NORTH region is made up of three province-level election districts, Arkhangelsk, Olonets, and Vologda (see Table 9.5). What would be very helpful would be to get the regional *total* (168,705 + 150,211 + 469,900). Not all database software will do this, but most middle-range products will. (The exact parallel is the computation of the cash value of a group of estates in Chapter 5, p. 65ff.) If the available database software cannot do the job other tools can; these will be discussed later in this chapter.

The real analysis begins with the examination of how the different parties fared. The five province-level election districts where the Kadet (KD) vote was largest, both in absolute and percentage terms, might be listed, using some kind of 'sort' command.

Select EAREA AREATYPE VOTE
From RUSSCA
Where PARTY = 'KD' and AREATYPE = 'p'
Order by VOTE desc

This would list all the Kadet results in descending order, i.e. from the election area where they won the most votes to the one where they won the least. Another simple approach would be to set a threshold, i.e. those election districts where the Bolshevik Party won more than 75 per cent of the vote. This information is of vital importance for understanding the election, as the geographical strongholds (and weak points) of each party become clear. This operation could be repeated with other thresholds and other parties. Since the geographical distribution of the votes is an

important part of the analysis it would be most useful to be able
to link results to a map. It is in fact technically possible to create
a computerised map giving all election districts, with distinct
colours to show, for example, where the Bolshevik Party received
0–20% (purple), 21–40% (blue), 41–60% (yellow), 61–80%
(orange) and over 80% (red) of the vote, but that would not be
suitable in the present limited project; software of this type is
currently a few years from general use. However, the same effect
could be achieved for analytical purposes using a paper sketch
map.[2]

Table 9.6 The Bolshevik percentage of the vote at each level in
Arkhangelsk (RUSSCA database)

EAREA	AREATYPE	PARTY	VOTEPC
ARKHANGELSK	P	BOL	21.6
ARKHANGELSK	C	BOL	29.7
ARKHANGELSK	G	BOL	65.9

The relative strength of the Bolshevik party at province, garrison,
and city level is also a fruitful question. The interesting result
here, and one full of historical significance, is that the Bolsheviks
received 65.9% of the votes cast by soldiers in the Arkhangelsk
town garrison, but only 21.6% of the votes for the whole
province.

With a reasonable powerful database or spreadsheet (see below)
software *pie charts* could automatically be drawn showing the
share of all eight groups in one province, or in all the provinces
of a region (see Figure 9.2).

A number of interesting historical conclusions emerge from
this exploratory computer analysis of Spirin's data, and these
conclusions could not easily be reached without the computer.
The substantial regional variations become clearer, showing the
division of the country into political zones. It is also apparent that
there was important vertical differentiation; the Bolsheviks frequently held the capital towns, and even more often the garrisons,
while the rural hinterland was dominated by the SRs or nationalists. The Bolsheviks may have had less overall support, but they
controlled strategic points with the help of the war-weary garrisons.

ARKHANGELSK PROVINCE ELECTION DISTRICT

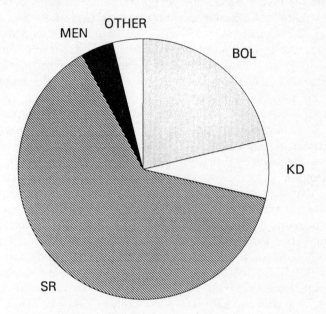

Figure 9.2 A pie chart for the vote in Arkhangelsk election district (RUSSCA database)

More advanced analysis

The analysis of the Russian 1917 election cannot be developed much further here. However, one of the key features of this data is that it consists of interval-scale variables (crudely, numbers), and that some of the simple statistical techniques discussed in Chapter 7 could be applied. Descriptive statistics could be worked out for the results comparing, for example, the mean and standard deviation of the Bolshevik vote in several different regions. A range of more complicated questions could be examined, such as the relationship between the vote of the capital cities and vote of the corresponding provincial election district. The relationship between winners and losers could be examined: to what extent was a high Bolshevik vote associated with a low SR vote? With some additional data a simple correlation could be attempted between the proportion of the Bolshevik vote and the distance from the revolutionary capitals (another interval scale variable).

A more sophisticated operation would be to test the hypothesis that the peasant-based SR party did better in election districts where the proportion of peasants was highest. Such an analysis would raise the *ecological fallacy*, which is an important issue for researchers. The ecological fallacy means the drawing of misleading conclusions about individual data from ecological data, i.e. data about a community. The basic units in the RUSSCA database here are not people, but geographical areas. A high correlation between the percentage of peasants and the percentage of SR votes in the voting districts of a constituency would not necessarily mean that peasants voted for the SRs. All that might be said – if the data supported the hypothesis – is that at election area level there was a strong association between areas with a high proportion of peasants and areas with a high proportion of SR voters. (A comprehensive statement about peasant voting behaviour could really be made only if the researcher had – say – individual data for each of the 168,705 voters in Arkhangelsk – or for a significant sample – showing their social class and who they voted for.)

All the above shows that a remarkably broad range of questions can be asked about a fairly simple-looking source; one of the key ingredients is the historical imagination of the researcher.

Spreadsheets

Spreadsheet software gives more ways of looking at numerical data such as that for the Russian elections. A computer spreadsheet, like an accountant's, is composed of a large number of *cells*, arranged in horizontal *rows* and vertical *columns*. A spreadsheet program links these cells together electronically; the data in the cells is usually numerical, and the program allows a wide range of calculations. Powerful spreadsheet programs available for desktop computers are another product of the microcomputer revolution; among the first examples were VisiCalc (1979) and Lotus 1-2-3 (1982). Given the wide commercial market of this kind of software (especially in small businesses) there are now available a number of powerful and well-documented products.

A simple commercial spreadsheet is shown in Figure 9.3. It is set up in general in the same way a database is set up; the user

A Sample Spreadsheet

	A	B	C	D	E	F	G
1		Cost	Margin	Profit	Price	Sales	Total Profit
2	Widgit	5.00	0.2	1.00	6.00	600	600.00
3	Mini Widgit	4.00	0.2	0.80	4.80	1000	800.00
4	...	...	...	...	...	...	...
5	Total		...	...	...	...	...

Figure 9.3   A sample spreadsheet

creates a file, is confronted with a blank grid, and decides what
will go in the rows and columns. He or she has control over the
format of the cells, e.g. how wide they are or what kinds of data
they contain. The data is entered from the keyboard (often from
the numeric pad) and the user moves around the screen using a
mouse or the arrow keys. Rows are numbered 1, 2, 3, etc., and
columns are labelled A, B, C, etc. Cells are identified (like grid
squares on a map) by the appropriate column label and row
number (A1, A2, A3, etc., B1, B2, B3, etc.). Each cell contains
one piece of information (usually numeric but sometimes alphanumeric), like a field in a database record.

Product names are in column A, production cost in column B,
and percentage of expected profit in column C. Column D can
be set to equal the resultant unit profit for the specific product in
column A by entering in cell D2 a *formula*: '= B2*C2'. This
means that the value in cell D2 will equal cell B2 times cell C2.

What appears in D2 is not the formula, but the result of the
formula, in this case 1.00 (5.00 × .20 = 1.00). What the formula
'B2*C2' in cell D2 really means is that D2 will equal 'the value
contained in the cell two cells to the left plus the value contained
in the cell immediately to the left'. In other words the *cell addresses*
contained in this formula are *relative* rather than *absolute*. This
being the case, when the formula is be copied to the cells below
D2 (D3, D4, D5, etc.) – a simple operation – the results calculated
are those required in the appropriate rows (B3 + C3, B4 + C4,
etc.).

Column E, the selling price, could also be based on a formula
(= B2 + D2) in cell E2, and column G on another (= D2*F2). A
further adding up of all rows in column G could be in G5 (= G2
+ G3, etc.) and would give the firm's potential profit for all
products. The special usefulness of the tool for the business

community is that the software can instantly calculate the overall implications of any change – a 'what-if analysis'. For example it could find out what the total profit would be if the percentage of profit for all products was lowered from 20% to 15%. 'What-if analysis' is less useful for historians, although there is such a thing as 'counter-factual' history.

The spreadsheet, then, is a kind of supercalculator. One of the best ways to learn to use a spreadsheet is to enter data from a table of historical material that is of direct interest; the examples below come from Spirin's tables and the British census, but any similar data could be used.

Something very like Spirin's original tables of Constituent Assembly election results (Figure 9.1) could easily be transferred to a spreadsheet. It would not be necessary to key in all of Spirin's columns; the percentages column for each party and the Total column could be calculated by the software. Assuming the Bolshevik vote was in cell B2, and the Kadet vote was in B4, etc., the total could be in cell B16, based on a formula (= B2 + B4 + B6 + B8 + B10 + B12 + B14), and each percentage could come from another formula. The Bolshevik percentage would be in B3 (= B2/B16*100). The same formula could be copied into the rows below for all the other election districts.

So far Spirin's original columns would simply have been reproduced; the spreadsheet can, however, also be used to enrich the data. Some of Spirin's original columns could be temporarily combined (for example getting the *socialist* vote – and percentage – for all districts by combining the Bolsheviks, the Mensheviks, the SRs, and the left nationalists). The spreadsheet software could also be used to get the total for all parties in particular regions (adding together the Total column for all the North Russia rows). Assuming that the data was entered into the spreadsheet in roughly the same form as in Spirin's original three tables, operations could be carried out involving *two* tables. For example, in one operation the garrison vote in Table 3 could be subtracted from the total city vote in Table 2 to get a *civilian* city vote in a new Table 4.

Spreadsheet programs now have an array of useful features. There are various special financial and scientific functions, facilities for including dates, *macros* for avoiding repetition of commands, and database-like tools. Modern spreadsheets normally have good

Sample Historical Spreadsheet: North Region Election Districts

AREA	BOL	KD	SR	MEN	LNAT	RNAT	OTHER
ARKHANGELSK	36,522	12,086	106,570	7,335			6,192
OLONETS		20,278	127,120				2,813
VOLOGDA	84,358	25,357	348,239				11,946

Figure 9.4 An example of part of an historical spreadsheet: the vote for the three election districts in the Northern region (Russca database)

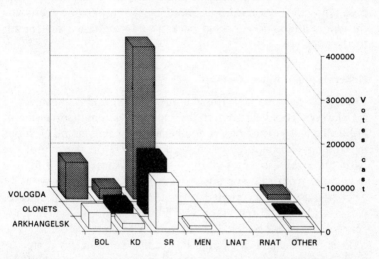

NORTH REGION VOTE

Figure 9.5 A three-dimensional bar chart created from the data in Figure 9.4

graphics, producing bar charts, pie charts, etc., which can also be extremely useful.[3] (If the spreadsheet does not have graphics software the enriched data could be exported into a graphics program.) Rows and columns can be selected from the spreadsheet and shown graphically. Figures 9.3 and 9.4 show how the votes for the three provinces in the Northern region can be isolated in part of a spreadsheet and then translated into a striking three-dimensional bar graph. (It is worth taking a moment to see how each element in the spreadsheet is illustrated in the graph.) These graphics can be incorporated into a written presentation in a number of ways. The scissors-paste-photocopy method is a practical possibility, but good modern software charts can be *pasted* electronically into a word-processor document file.

One drawback of the spreadsheet is that while it is usually possible to retrieve – for example – every row where the Bolshevik percentage of the vote was over 25%, the process can be more cumbersome than in a database (which is why the latter was used for the teaching application in the first part of this chapter). Spreadsheets are also less convenient when a lot of text is to be found in some of the columns. Finally, the complex operations performed with a relational database would be awkward or impossible with a spreadsheet. There is no reason, however, why the data cannot be exported back into a database manager for further analysis.

Generalisation: other elections

There was only the one Russian election. Normally, however, a spreadsheet could also chart the changing strength of different political parties over time. A good example would be the elections in Weimar Germany between 1920 and 1932 on the eve of the Nazi takeover, as entered in a spreadsheet (Figure 9.6) and developed from that spreadsheet into a line graph (Figure 9.7). The spreadsheet was created very quickly from printed tables of electoral data, and the graph was created within seconds.[4] Only certain rows were selected for the graph to preserve clarity. The SPD is the Social Democratic Party, the Zentrum/BVP are the Catholic parties, the KPD are the Communists, and the NSDAP are the Nazis. The interesting question that might be asked is where the millions of Nazi voters came from between 1928 and 1932. The answer in part is that Hitler was taking votes from parties not shown on the graph; the voters of the SPD, Zentrum/ BVP, and KPD stayed loyal.

Spreadsheet with Data on German Elections

	A	B	C	D	E	F	G	H
10		Jun-20	May-24	Dec-24	May-28	Sep-30	Jul-32	Nov-32
11	SPD	6104	6009	7884	9153	8576	7960	7251
12	ZENTRUM/	5084	4861	5256	4658	5186	5792	5327
13	KPD	589	3963	2712	3285	4590	5370	5980
14	NSDAP		1918	903	810	6407	13779	11737

Figure 9.6   Spreadsheet with data on German elections in the 1920s and 1930s

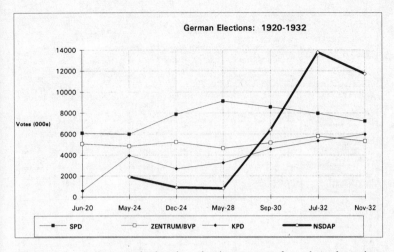

Figure 9.7 A line graph showing election returns for selected parties, created from data in Figure 9.6

Similar graphs could be used for any 'series' of election returns for any country. Electoral data much fuller than that used in this chapter is readily available in printed tabular form. Much electoral information in machine-readable form can be obtained from the Data Archives of the Economic and Social Research Council (in Britain) or the Inter-university Consortium for Political and Social Research (America) – see the Bibliography.

Spreadsheets and the British census

Spreadsheets can be used with any numerical information in tabular form. Figure 9.9 is an example of using a spreadsheet with some aggregate census data from the printed census, which is printed in Figure 9.8. This *aggregate* data, the printed results of the census, is about a group of people; it should be contrasted with the *nominal* data like the enumerator's books, which is about individuals. The spreadsheet is a good way of handling the aggregate tables, carrying out basic mathematical operations (e.g. getting percentages), combining and manipulating rows and columns (categories), and putting the information in graphical form.

BIRTH-PLACE	PRESENT IN															
	* Galashiels (Municipal or Police Burgh)				Glasgow (Parliamentary Burgh)				* Glasgow (Municipal Burgh)				* Govan (Police Burgh)			
	MALES		FEMALES		MALES		FEMALES		MALES		FEMALES		MALES		FEMALES	
	Under 20 Yrs.	Above 20 Yrs.	Under 20 Yrs.	Above 20 Yrs.	Under 20 Yrs.	Above 20 Yrs.	Under 20 Yrs.	Above 20 Yrs.	Under 20 Yrs.	Above 20 Yrs.	Under 20 Yrs.	Above 20 Yrs.	Under 20 Yrs.	Above 20 Yrs.	Under 20 Yrs.	Above 20 Yrs.
SCOTLAND	3,564	3,235	3,487	4,149	100,763	93,409	101,870	110,201	105,739	97,145	106,791	113,923	10,954	9,143	10,688	9,465
Portions.																
NORTHERN	129	354	154	400	5,348	24,313	5,520	26,234	5,686	25,681	5,861	27,401	899	3,632	833	3,364
SOUTHERN	3,435	2,879	3,312	3,744	95,238	68,927	96,147	53,886	99,873	71,291	100,720	86,232	10,041	5,497	9,848	6,082
Not Stated	-	2	1	5	177	169	203	281	180	173	210	290	14	14	7	19
Divisions.																
I. NORTHERN	-	12	-	28	145	1,081	156	1,138	152	1,109	161	1,168	32	161	27	161
II. NORTH-WESTERN	6	14	7	30	370	2,474	396	2,633	392	2,664	425	2,759	89	589	81	483
III. NORTH-EASTERN	22	57	29	56	624	3,028	632	2,474	654	3,185	665	2,578	118	456	106	350
IV. EAST-MIDLAND	65	214	68	225	1,597	7,761	1,394	6,633	1,725	3,249	1,494	6,991	287	1,110	224	771
V. WEST-MIDLAND	36	57	50	61	2,612	9,969	2,942	13,356	2,763	10,474	3,116	13,905	373	1,336	395	1,599
VI. SOUTH-WESTERN	79	133	63	181	92,698	60,849	93,612	75,214	97,168	62,787	98,045	77,384	9,787	4,806	9,624	5,348
VII. SOUTH-EASTERN	2,752	1,880	2,735	2,345	1,858	5,017	1,955	5,406	1,990	5,326	2,073	5,678	176	384	156	409
VIII. SOUTHERN	604	866	514	1,218	682	3,061	580	3,066	715	3,178	602	3,170	78	307	68	325
Not Stated	-	2	1	5	177	169	203	281	180	173	210	290	14	14	7	19
Counties.																
1 SHETLAND	-	-	-	-	18	86	11	122	19	88	11	127	6	20	5	24
2 ORKNEY	-	1	-	4	29	192	26	213	31	194	27	216	2	28	5	29
3 CAITHNESS	-	6	-	14	77	502	102	542	80	516	106	556	21	87	16	80
4 SUTHERLAND	-	5	-	9	21	301	17	261	22	311	17	269	3	26	1	28
5 ROSS & CROMARTY	3	6	1	8	124	876	120	932	127	923	122	966	40	234	26	190
6 INVERNESS	3	8	6	22	246	1,598	276	1,701	285	1,736	303	1,793	49	335	55	293
7 NAIRN	-	2	-	2	21	107	18	109	22	111	19	113	3	16	3	12
8 ELGIN	2	8	5	7	96	507	96	435	98	536	98	460	24	117	19	90
9 BANFF	4	12	5	5	79	446	59	330	85	465	70	342	10	52	15	38
10 ABERDEEN	16	29	15	35	396	1,615	426	1,400	414	1,705	443	1,445	75	242	65	187
11 KINCARDINE	-	8	4	7	33	353	33	200	35	388	35	218	6	29	4	23
12 FORFAR	7	22	9	11	600	1,843	461	1,334	627	1,934	489	1,387	107	319	74	155
13 PERTH	4	47	3	56	462	3,138	496	2,879	499	3,292	520	3,010	57	298	59	276
14 FIFE	15	57	24	64	368	2,062	320	1,902	423	2,257	360	1,940	106	401	81	273
15 KINROSS	3	12	3	14	37	245	18	173	38	256	19	179	3	18	1	13
16 CLACKMANNAN	36	76	29	80	130	473	99	445	138	510	106	475	14	74	9	54
17 STIRLING	33	51	49	53	856	3,557	1,141	4,578	925	3,783	1,227	4,307	76	284	94	343
18 DUMBARTON	-	2	1	2	896	2,159	907	2,828	959	2,300	992	2,963	150	264	157	298
19 ARGYLL	3	4	-	5	681	3,717	681	5,242	679	3,843	711	5,418	121	684	108	851
20 BUTE	-	-	-	1	199	536	213	708	200	548	216	717	26	104	36	107
21 RENFREW	10	20	7	31	3,083	7,063	3,087	3,925	3,123	7,275	3,183	9,145	1,028	965	950	1,019
22 AYR	14	22	3	31	2,157	7,947	2,057	8,958	2,213	8,134	2,114	9,170	331	920	274	951
23 LANARK	55	91	48	119	87,508	45,839	88,468	57,331	91,832	47,378	92,748	59,069	8,428	2,921	8,400	3,278
24 LINLITHGOW	13	19	10	29	241	572	279	841	255	629	294	885	28	60	27	68
25 EDINBURGH	187	354	212	445	1,478	3,613	1,545	3,790	1,590	3,809	1,642	3,986	133	349	112	270
26 HADDINGTON	17	46	25	61	62	362	54	388	63	392	55	403	5	38	11	38
27 BERWICK	147	389	144	479	29	258	33	238	33	271	37	245	4	22	4	17
28 PEEBLES	46	116	59	144	31	145	24	98	32	155	25	108	3	10	1	10
29 SELKIRK	2,342	976	2,285	1,187	17	67	20	51	17	70	20	51	3	4	1	6
30 ROXBURGH	546	751	489	1,080	71	362	63	270	74	372	65	275	6	27	10	28
31 DUMFRIES	49	99	41	110	300	1,315	255	1,207	315	1,373	268	1,283	15	82	11	87
32 KIRKCUDBRIGHT	7	11	3	22	77	411	67	378	80	430	72	389	10	26	4	28
33 WIGTOWN	2	5	1	6	234	973	195	1,211	246	1,003	197	1,243	47	172	43	182
Not Stated	-	2	1	5	177	169	203	281	180	173	210	290	14	14	7	19
ENGLAND	72	132	89	159	2,628	5,048	2,616	4,609	2,784	5,299	2,777	4,817	402	540	387	486
WALES	-	1	2	-	47	137	49	85	54	146	54	93	8	10	7	14
IRELAND	21	178	25	164	4,304	27,610	4,300	26,341	4,786	29,702	4,897	25,924	774	3,382	591	2,211
MAN, GUERNSEY, JERSEY	-	1	-	-	30	55	22	62	34	61	22	68	5	9	5	4
BRITISH COLONIES	8	15	5	11	403	433	389	481	421	447	400	493	68	124	34	33
BRITISH Subj's { By Birth	1	11	1	2	259	162	264	194	268	168	271	203	31	29	28	12
Born in Foreign { Natural-ized Parts	-	-	-	-	14	90	6	62	14	90	7	62	1	19	1	6
FOREIGNERS { European	2	9	-	3	129	868	63	263	129	873	64	263	3	42	-	8
{ Others	-	-	-	-	28	139	11	46	28	139	11	46	1	27	1	4
BORN AT SEA (British)	-	-	-	2	11	26	15	46	15	46	16	46	1	4	-	-
TOTAL INHABITANTS	3,668	3,582	3,591	4,489	108,616	127,977	109,605	142,390	114,270	134,096	115,110	147,939	12,246	13,329	11,742	12,243
Of the above, there were Born in																
ABERDEEN TOWN	-	9	12	17	251	713	284	778	261	754	294	796	43	100	29	78
DUNDEE TOWN	4	7	6	3	385	750	501	583	407	789	328	610	92	143	49	61
EDINBURGH TOWN	72	118	85	146	1,123	2,558	1,171	2,662	1,196	2,670	1,233	2,787	97	163	64	181
GLASGOW TOWN	37	41	27	60	83,175	38,196	83,576	47,179	87,016	39,820	87,395	48,475	3,589	1,740	3,582	2,060
GREENOCK TOWN	2	2	3	8	616	910	700	1,469	635	943	725	1,510	191	204	156	237
LEITH TOWN	12	15	3	26	158	392	174	412	174	427	192	431	25	40	33	39
PAISLEY TOWN	4	13	2	15	669	2,442	634	3,052	694	2,505	650	3,109	138	281	133	316
PERTH TOWN	2	8	1	1	121	665	105	590	138	707	178	622	21	63	14	67

* See note at p. 73.

Figure 9.8　　1881 Census Table

A typical task might be to explore the nature of internal migration in Scotland. There is nothing new or confidential about the information which relates to this; the printed census has been available since 1882. As with any table, it is worth taking a few moments to look at the information in Figure 9.8. The 'Total inhabitants' row, towards the bottom, breaks the population of 'Glasgow (Municipal Burgh)' into four sub-groups (columns) by sex and age; the total of all four is 511,415. There is information about adults and non-adults, about males and females, and from this table the number in each sub-group born in a particular county can be seen. Of the 511,415 people, only 19 were males under 20 years of age who were born in '1 Shetland'. Although this is not immediately clear, the table already aggregates Scottish 'Counties' rows into eight groups ('Divisions') (e.g. I. Northern = 1/Shetland + 2/Orkney + 3/Caithness + 4/Sutherland). Once this data has been transcribed into a spreadsheet, percentages can easily be calculated for any of the categories, and bar charts, pie charts, etc., could be drawn to illustrate the data.[5]

Figure 9.9 should make clearer the complex relationship between three variables concerning the inhabitants of Glasgow: age, sex, and region of birth. For example, the difference in age distribution between those born around Glasgow and those born in other parts of Scotland is clearly brought out. The South-Western 'Division' (VI) comprises the counties of Renfrew, Ayr, and Lanark; the Glasgow metropolitan area was within Lanark, and Renfrew and Ayr are nearby; it is older people who migrate in from areas beyond this south-western 'core'. The spreadsheet allows a range of questions to be asked of tabular data like this, and at the very least suggests questions for more detailed research, perhaps using the nominal data.

In this chapter we have looked mainly at the potential of the computer for analysing numerical data. Elections were chosen on purpose to be the centrepiece of the chapter because they were 'political'; it not just the economic or social historian who benefits from an ability to manipulate numbers. Interesting conclusions can be drawn without vast amounts of data.

The same data can be analysed using different computer tools: a database manager, a spreadsheet program, or even a statistics package. The spreadsheet program is an invaluable tool for the

GLASGOW (Munic. Burgh), 1881: Birth-Place

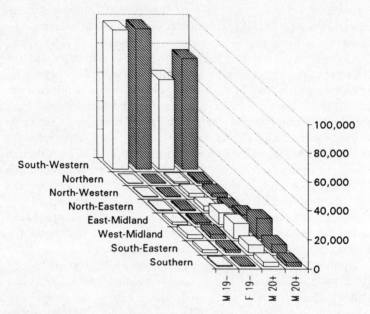

Figure 9.9 Bar chart showing aspects of the Glasgow population, created from Figure 9.8

relatively simple calculations involved in aggregating and splitting any sort of data. In this area it is more flexible than a straightforward database manager. The graphics capabilities of modern spreadsheets, in addition, add not just 'pretty pictures' but provide a means of making a mass of complex historical data – political, economic, or social – understandable and accessible.

Notes

1 Oliver H. Radkey, *Russia Goes to the Polls: The Election to the Russian Constituent Assembly of 1917*, Ithaca, 1990; L. M. Spirin, *Klassy i partii v grazhdanskoi voine v Rossii (1917–1920 gg.)* [Classes and Parties in the Russian Civil War: 1917–1920], Moscow, 1968. For an analysis of Russian politics in late 1917, based loosely on the Constituent Assembly elections, see Evan Mawdsley, *The Russian Civil War*, Boston, 1987, pp. 5–15.

2 For a useful introduction to the whole question of using maps, see H. Southall and E. Oliver, 'Drawing maps with a computer . . . or without?', in *History and Computing*, II, 1990, pp. 146–54.
3 The graphics in this chapter were partly prepared used the Microsoft Excel spreadsheet program.
4 Georges Castellan, *L'Allemagne de Weimar: 1918–1933*, Paris, 1969, pp. 86–106.
5 There are similar tables for the 1851 census, which would have related more directly to the nominal data discussed in previous chapters, but these did not contain information about gender or give the clear regional layout seen here. See *Census of Great Britain, 1851. Populational Tables II. Ages, Civil condition, Occupations and Birth-Place of the People . . .* , II, London, 1854, p. 1041.

Chapter 10

Using existing databases: economic perspectives

Computers are useful not just for research starting from raw primary material. In Chapter 9 we used printed aggregate data from the Russian elections of 1917; in this chapter we shall tackle some very different types of data, relating to trade and to taxation. Clearly each type of source material and each kind of research topic will tend to favour certain methodological approaches over others.[1] The present chapter is intended to illustrate some basic techniques for historians using data with specific economic orientation. Some of the examples will be based on aggregates from recent research; but the potential in using existing machine-readable datasets will also be explored.

Setting up one's own database is an exciting but in many ways difficult task: the research project itself has to be thought out in some detail first, and the data carefully scrutinised to reveal both its implicit structure and its inherent weaknesses. It is therefore worth remembering that it may in some cases be possible to skip the data-entry stage altogether: now that historians have applied computing techniques to their typically bulky sources for over a generation, there are large sets of machine-readable data already in existence.[2]

It has to be recognised that there may well be problems associated with the use of such imported datasets, and that these problems may prove serious if the data has been heavily edited. Nevertheless, datasets which respect the original source to a reasonable degree – ideally if they are designed as a machine-readable source edition – may prove highly versatile. As an example, we shall start by looking at a dataset of enormous potential for economic historians of the eighteenth century: the toll books which record the trade through the Sound into and out of the Baltic. Some preparatory calculations will be made on the material, using a few of the techniques discussed in Chapter 7. We shall then explore ways of presenting results both from this and from other types of quantitative historical data.

The Sound Toll data

One of the most valuable long-term sources of income for the Danish crown since the late Middle Ages were the tolls levied on all maritime traffic through Danish territorial waters to and from the Baltic. The best route was via the straits between Elsinore and what until 1660 were the Danish provinces east of the Sound, now part of southern Sweden. There were other access routes to the Baltic, but those by sea were less convenient (and also subject to Danish tolls), and transport overland through northern Germany (for example via Lübeck) was far more costly. So most bulky western trade with Poland, the Baltic provinces, Russia, Finland, northern Germany east of Schleswig, and much of Sweden, came through the Sound. Because of the growing importance of this trade, the Danish kings, who traditionally had completely unrestricted use of the toll revenue, took pains over the collection procedure and the bureaucracy that went with it. Protocols were kept, recording in consistent format information about every shipment passing Elsinore (except local Danish coastal traffic).

By the 1780s, around 10,000 ships were recorded annually. Each ship might carry any range of commodities being taken from/to one or more ports; or, if going east, it might be just in ballast. When passing Elsinore, each commodity in the cargo would be quantified and valued, and the resulting toll calculated. These details, together with information on the ports of origin and destination of the cargo, information on the captain, and sometimes on the ship itself, were recorded quite systematically (see Figure 10.1). A great deal of information is thus available, with considerable research potential. It is possible to observe which ports were the most important participants, and how each was affected by economic and climatic fluctuations over time. The direct commercial disruption caused by political factors before and after the outbreak of the French Revolutionary Wars is clearly visible. The roles of the main trading partners in northern

Europe can be quantified. The routes taken by individual captains can to a considerable extent be mapped. Even the significance of individual products can be assessed: although actual tolls were fixed by a series of bilateral international treaties, some a century old, so that the data does not always reflect current price-structures, fluctuations in supply and demand are nevertheless indicated in the actual quantitative information given for the hundreds of common goods going through the Sound.

Because of ice and bad weather, there were generally very few sailings before late March or early April each year. Then the number increased rapidly, and from May to August there were often 1,500 transits per month, or on average 50 every day. Depending on the weather, a marked decrease was usually clear by later September or October, but some captains managed to fit in four or five journeys every season (each one being recorded separately). Others worked over very long distances, for example to the Caribbean or the Far East, therefore reaching the Baltic much less frequently.

Judging from information on the port of origin for the ships and captains, it is clear that four nationalities between them accounted for around four-fifths of the entire Baltic trade: Britain, Sweden, Denmark and the Netherlands (usually in that order). War, however, substantially upset the balance at times – notably for Sweden, during its conflict with Russia from 1788 to 1790, and indeed for all the participants after the start of the revolutionary wars of 1792/93.

There are relatively few problems with the source material as such. Minor errors and inconsistencies in the original have of course been found, for example regarding the information on the home port of the captain, or the ports of embarkation and destination. Some (unquantifiable) smuggling also occurred, revealed through checks against other sources. For example, a heavily taxed product like coffee was at times falsely declared as prunes, which carried only one-tenth of the duty. There are also difficulties with a few specific goods, such as coal, for which no tolls were levied. But overall, and by the standards of the age, the Sound Toll records are regarded as reliable, carefully kept, and above all consistent over time.[3]

The Sound Toll archive, created over several centuries by the customs officers employed at Elsinore, is extremely voluminous.

The historian wanting to use the information in its original form is likely to find the bulk almost overwhelming. Accordingly, an attempt was made earlier this century to summarise some three centuries' worth of aggregate information (up to 1783) in published tables. Although this printed edition could be used for certain types of study, its organisation is unwieldy and the editorial procedures adopted impose severe limitations.[4]

The obvious answer is a computerisation of the data. The files now available in electronic form, for the period 1784–95, were prepared by a team under Professor Hans Chr. Johansen of Odense University. There is one file for every year covered. Each file is essentially a transcription of the original protocols, with only a minimum of interpretative structure. The data is therefore ideal for a variety of historical purposes.[5]

In a straight translation from Danish, a single entry in the original manuscript Sound Toll records reads as shown in Figure 10.1. It shows an unnamed vessel under a British captain, sailing west from Riga to Liverpool, clearing the toll office on 27 June 1784 with a typical cargo of shipbuilding supplies (mostly timber).[6]

This is, with minor variations, the type of information given in each of the 10,000 or so annual entries in the Sound Toll protocols. When loaded into a computer, the actual layout will be determined

27 June
No.1256
Benjamin Huntley of and to Liverpool from Riga with

60 shippounds hemp	9	rdl	47	sk
124 ....flax	30	-	46	-
869 pieces of balks	27	-	8	-
100 ....masts	2	-	24	-
87 ....deals			4	-
4 1/5 threescores of caskwood			5	-
1 2/5 .... planks	1	-	21	-
2 1/2 .... ships planks	1	-	12	-
	73	rdl	23	sk
- discount	2	-	41	-
	70	rdl	30	sk
+ light duty	4	-		
	74	**rdl**	**30**	**sk**

Figure 10.1 An entry in the Sound Toll records for 1784

by the particular software application and version of the data being used, but the original structure will be readily recognisable.[7]

Money and units of measurement

A glance at the record given above reminds us that not all the information can conveniently be used in the form that it takes in the source. Both monetary and measuring units need to be converted to something simpler before any statistical operations can be carried out, with or without a computer. Provided tables of equivalents are available, this is not a difficult operation.

Monetary units are generally easy to deal with, especially if (as here) they were used consistently in a given source. Assuming there are no uncertainties over the commonly used moneys of account (accounting units just like the *écu* of today's Common Market – as opposed to money in circulation, that is, the actual coins in your pocket), decimalisation of money composites into one standard unit is easily accomplished using the arithmetic functions of the database manager. The coinage system used in the United Kingdom until decimalisation two decades ago is typical of what may be found in historical sources. With one pound (L) made up of 20 shillings (S), each made up of 12 pence (P), the instruction to convert a sum in pounds, shillings and pence to decimalised pounds (LD) is:

> multiply the value in S by 12, add it to the value in P, and divide the result by 240; then add that result to the value in L to make a value in a new column LD

In the algebraic form required by most database managers, using brackets to denote the correct sequence of operations, this would be:

$$LD = L + (((S \times 12) + P)/240)$$

Such a computation is done quickly by a good database manager, and once the correct result is achieved the original three monetary columns in the database can be deleted. In the case of the Sound Toll data, conversion of the sums levied is even simpler since there are only two units, the *rigsdaler* and the *skilling*. In Figure 10.1, the first toll payment of 9 *rdl* 47 *sk*. could be decimalised to 9.98 *rdl*.

Units of measurement for actual commodities present a different level of complexity. Depending on the commodity, the customs officers at Elsinore generally reckoned either by piece, by weight or by volume. Around 65 different units of measurement were used regularly. Some of these units varied depending on the commodity: a barrel of beer (or other liquids) had a volume of 150.7 litres, but a barrel of grain 146 litres, and one of salt rather more. As a measure of solids like butter, the barrel became a unit of weight (usually around 110 kg). Similarly, a *last* could either be a unit of weight – equivalent to 893 kg for hemp, tallow and related products, but double for potash – or it could be a unit of volume measuring up to 2,921 litres (the Dutch rye last). Units cited in the same format in the accounts may in fact vary depending on the port of origin of the commodity.[8]

In the processed datasets, the quantity of each commodity is given in the form in which it appears in the source. For the major commodities (notably grain and liquids) reliable quantitative equivalents make conversion relatively straightforward. A database manager will be able to identify the commodity by its code, if necessary take regional variations into account, look up the appropriate equivalent for that commodity in a conversion table (by means of a relational join), and do the arithmetical conversion accordingly. Not all items in the Sound Toll records, however, lend themselves to this type of conversion. Timber is often, as in Figure 10.1, quoted by piece, the dimensions of which were subject to infinite variation. We also find some strange commodities where reliable conversion is out of the question: pigeons' dung, window glass, reindeer hoofs, and spermacet candles, to pick just a few. For such commodities – and perhaps to check other conversions that appear suspect – an alternative is to use the sum paid in toll. The official register of toll rates[9] will provide the standard rate per unit of measurement, and this information can then be used to work back to the actual quantity of the commodity concerned. Alternatively, the toll can in itself be regarded as an approximate comparative quantitative indicator for a single commodity.[10]

In the Sound Toll datafiles, there is another category of information codified during data-entry: the home port of the captain, together with the ports of origin and destination of the cargo. The coding scheme adopted for the Sound Tolls project is slightly

more complex than that suggested above, p. 72: it consists of
three digits and three letters. Liverpool, the port of the captain in
the above example, is 652LIP – the 600s being used for the
United Kingdom, the 52 being a particular part of the coast, and
LIP being unique to Liverpool.[11] A straight tabulation of this
coding scheme, against the original geographic terms, allows
the user to 'decode' the three items of geographic information
efficiently during retrievals by means of a simple table join.

Using the Sound Toll data

It is well known that in the early modern period the price of
grain, the staple food, fluctuated dramatically. Although state
intervention might help to cushion the worst extremes, these
fluctuations were the result largely of unreliable supply (usually
harvest failures) or of speculation in the anticipated supply. Since
in effect the west depended on Baltic grain to supplement domestic
production, the repercussions of these fluctuations on international
transactions in northern Europe are clearly reflected in the Sound
Toll records. The quantity of each main cereal, and the routes
taken from east to west, reveal a dramatic instability in the years
before and after the outbreak of the French Revolution.

  This instability is summarised in Figure 10.2. It shows a tabulation of the major Baltic grain-exporting ports for the years
1784, 1787, 1789 and 1793. The table is in fact the result of a
succession of database operations. First, all wheat shipments were
selected from the original files for each of the years concerned
(each year being in a separate file). These shipments were then
merged into a single file, similar in structure to the original yearly
files but containing no commodities other than wheat. All tolls
paid on these wheat shipments were then added together by port
of origin and by year (so that, for example, the tolls paid on all
the 59 wheat shipments that left Riga in 1784 were summed to
produce the figure 3848.0 *rigsdaler* in the 1784 column). Any port
whose wheat exports never rose to 250 *rigsdalers* in any one of
these four years was eliminated. The result was then cross tabulated
as shown, and the percentages on that crosstabulation added
using a statistical function in the database manager.

  The left-hand column thus includes all ports which shipped a
total quantity of wheat sufficient to attract a cumulative toll of at

PORT	1784	%	1787	%	1789	%	1793	%
COPENHAGEN	198.6	0.53	0.0	0.0	0.0	0.0	1580.9	3.77
ST.PETERSB.	1171.0	3.1	0.0	0.0	2.8	.01	951.0	2.27
ARENSBURG	269.3	.71	0.0	0.0	0.0	0.0	0.0	0.0
RIGA	3848.0	10.19	1.4	.02	895.0	3.17	3491.	8.32
LIBAU	645.5	1.71	5.5	.06	137.9	.49	744.5	1.77
KOENIGSBERG	5600.6	14.82	1376.0	14.47	4631.6	16.4	4737.1	11.28
MEMEL	2045.4	5.41	.5	.01	157.0	.56	964.0	2.3
PILLAU	8733.5	23.1	4786.5	50.32	11785.5	41.72	12152.6	28.95
DANZIG(A)	14885.4	39.4	3222.4	33.88	7364.2	26.07	13668.9	32.56
STETTIN	0.0	0.0	0.0	0.0	258.7	.92	884.7	2.11
SWINEMUNDE	0.0	0.0	4.0	.04	471.3	1.67	1258.2	3.0
GREIFSWALD	34.2	.09	53.8	.57	308.1	1.09	55.8	.13
WOLGAST	34.6	.09	49.2	.52	496.4	1.76	160.7	.38
ROSTOCK	89.3	.24	1.0	.01	1198.1	4.24	538.9	1.28
WISMAR	224.0	.59	12.0	.13	541.5	1.92	789.0	1.88
TOTAL	37779.4	100%	9512.2	100%	28248.1	100%	41977.4	100%

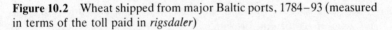

KEY TO ANNOTATIONS:

A = port of origin of the grain (the reference or index field for the retrieval)

B = sum (in rigsdaler) of tolls paid on all grain from Danzig

C = Danzig's grain represented as a percentage of all grain shipped that year (that is, 3222.4 / 9512.2 x 100)

D = total toll paid on wheat shipped from all 15 ports in 1793

Figure 10.2 Wheat shipped from major Baltic ports, 1784–93 (measured in terms of the toll paid in *rigsdaler*)

least 250 *rigsdaler* during any one of these years. The actual toll (in *rigsdaler*) accruing on the wheat shipped from each port is shown for each year, alongside the port's percentage share of the total wheat shipped that year.

Although over a period of years the toll is not an exact reflection of real quantities, some impression of the scale of the fluctuations in total Baltic wheat exports to the west is seen from the summation line at the bottom of the table: as one would expect from the overall economic environment, the figure for 1793 is very high, even though a major customer, France, was by then under nearly total British naval blockade. No less striking, however, is the variation (both in relative and in real terms) for some individual ports, notably St Petersburg and Copenhagen. By contrast, the biggest centres, like Danzig (now Gdansk), retained a more constant share of total exports from one year to the next.

Comparative statistics are readily prepared by means of the functions available on good database managers. In Figure 10.2 the percentages and totals were done on vertical columns, that is, by year. It would have been just as simple to produce *horizontal* percentages and totals – that is, relating to a particular port over time (say, how the exports from Memel from one year compared to its total exports over the four years). A good database manager (or indeed a spreadsheet application or a statistical analysis package) will equally readily produce horizontal or vertical averages (mean, median, mode and standard deviation). In the case of the ports included in Figure 10.2, for example, we would discover that the mean level of tolls collected in 1784 from these ports was 2518.63 *rigsdaler* (with, given the huge range, a predictably high standard deviation of 4123.22); the median (middle value) was 224.01, and the mode (most common value) 0. These measures of central tendency are, each in their own way, illustrative of the characteristics of this restricted group of ports. It is also easy to see that they would have been very useful measures if we had included *all* wheat-exporting ports – or indeed if we wanted to compare over time the relative significance of *different* commodities from a particular port or region.

In other words, datasets as substantial as the Sound Tolls can be used to plot import and export patterns (by region or by commodity) over time, to quantify changing relative strengths of particular nations in the northern European trade before and after the outbreak of the French Revolution, and even to illustrate typical sailing patterns against changing weather conditions. Datasets which are in effect source editions will permit as wide a range of analysis techniques as the original historical material can support – subject only to the restrictions of the hardware and software available. Conversion tables readily allow standardisation of units of measurement; similarly, data which was codified during data-entry can be decoded during retrievals, if desired. If standard statistics functions are brought to bear, the results can readily be converted to a form (such as percentages) suitable for comparative purposes. Equally, as we shall see in the next section, graphics could be used to highlight some of the key trends.

Using existing aggregate economic data

The Sound Toll datafiles are the result of a major research and transcription project. It is worth bearing in mind, however, that large datafiles are not indispensable for interesting quantitative results. Meaningful results are also attainable from smaller properly designed samples (see p. 93). Equally, aggregate data (by its nature likely to be much less bulky) may lend itself just as well to computer-aided analysis. The aggregate data on the 1917 elections in Russia used for Chapter 9 is a good example of how much can be done with a relatively limited but well-chosen set of information in a political context. Here we shall examine something quite different, namely a small set of data summarising the conclusions of a recent research project on the financial fortunes of *ancien-régime* France.

Early modernists will be familiar with the significance of various fiscal 'abuses', in an age before national debts and parliamentary auditing procedures forced the finance officers of the state to become more accountable to their taxpayers. The French monarchy before the Revolution is a classic example of tax-farming (tax-collection privatised in the hands of bankers and financial agents through competitive bidding), financial irresponsibility and consequent fiscal instability.

In 1978 the historian Alain Guéry published a study of what the summary 'budgets' of the French crown might have looked like if the information had been accessible at the time.[12] The figures, once adjustments have been made for major problems in the source material, allow us to trace the gross and net incomes of the French crown, as well as its total expenditure, on a year-by-year basis. Tabulated, the results for the first years of Louis XIV's reign, in thousands of *livres tournois*, look as follows:

	Gross income	Nett income	Expenditure
1662	87,603	44,451	65,169
1663	88,906	51,122	46,546
1664	89,243	53,718	63,068
1665	88,454	58,648	50,744
......	...	...	
1714	118,396	32,190	213,530

Even for the 54 years of Louis XIV's reign, the total information given in Guéry's tables is too dense for a quick visual analysis. With a pocket calculator it would be easy (if rather boring) to work out the difference between gross and net incomes (produced in part by the cut taken by the tax-farmers), or the size of the deficit when such occurs. Equally, it would be possible to work

F

out the size of the 'overheads', or of the deficit, in relation either
to each year's total turnover or, say, to the 'normal' turnover in
some suitably chosen base-year. However, such calculations would
be laborious and inflexible.

The obvious approach is to enter the three columns of figures,
alongside the year, into the columns of a spreadsheet (see above,
p. 126). The data will retain its layout and appearance unchanged.
But any of the calculations can now be done painlessly, the
parameters of, say, an index-year can be changed at will, and the
results graphed for maximum clarity. Even a simple line chart of
the three columns of information given in the table, distributed in
a time series as shown in Figure 10.3, will allow the historian of
the reign to see the financial background to some key foreign
policy decisions of Louis XIV: not only the obvious impact of the
war of the League of Augsburg (1688–97), but also the virtual
collapse of fiscal credibility in the last years of the reign, when
the overheads of tax-collection (the difference between gross and
net income) took on alarming proportions.

A spreadsheet gives easy access to a variety of graphical rep-
resentations of the results, complete with layout editing facilities.
It also allows many other arithmetical operations to be carried
out on data such as this. For example, the relationship between
the real deficit and the cost of fiscal overheads can be explored –
on the hypothesis that, even if the crown's bankers did not have
exact information on the true state of wartime expenditure, they
had enough information not only to increase the charges for
anticipatory borrowing on expected income, but also to take a
larger share of actual tax receipts in the hope of covering the
mounting costs and risks they faced as tax-farmers. Even with
gaps in the information (reflected in the graph lines), it is apparent
that Colbert's moderating influence, waning as it probably was
even before his death in 1683, gave way to a period of growing
financial irresponsibility. Illustrated in this way, the misery of
French taxpayers in the last years of Louis XIV's reign becomes
almost tangible.

This chapter has attempted to show that both small and large
quantitative datasets can yield highly significant results when subjected even to simple forms of analysis. Many historians, especially
those who are not orientated towards economics and econometrics,

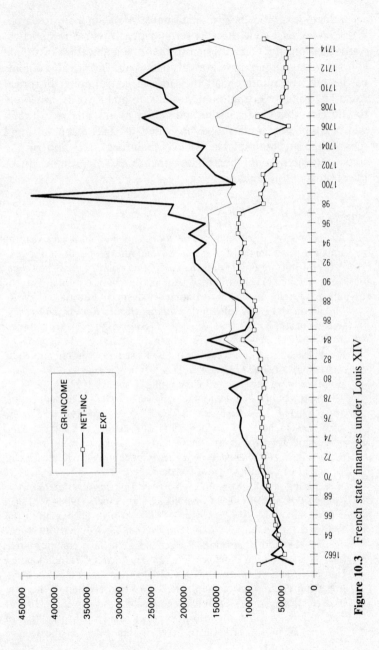

Figure 10.3 French state finances under Louis XIV

are reluctant to use 'heavy' quantitative data in their research. The techniques used in this chapter, however, involve no statistical sophistication: they are little more than the application of simple computing techniques to historical sources and historical problems of the kind encountered all the time in conventional historical research. Some basic quantitative skills, in other words, are likely to add considerable precision and clarity to any analysis of data which is not purely narrative. Provided the user keeps in mind the limitations both of the source materials used and of the statistical operations themselves, the scope for simple quantification is considerable.

Notes

1 An exhaustive discussion of the tools and methodologies current amongst economic historians is beyond the scope of this book. A useful starting point from the computing point of view, however, is the detailed and informative 'Annual review of information technology developments for economic and social historians', by R. Middleton and P. Wardley, in *Economic History Review*, 2nd series, starting in vol. XLIV, 1991, pp. 343–72 (spreadsheets) and continued in XLV, 1992, pp. 378–412 (database managers).
2 For a list of readily accessible datasets, see K. Schürer and S. J. Anderson, *A Guide to Historical Datafiles in Machine-readable Form*, Association for History and Computing, London, 1992.
3 The best detailed guide to the material is Hans Chr. Johansen, *Shipping and Trade between the Baltic Area and western Europe 1784–95*, Odense, 1983, which contains a summary of the checking procedures used to identify error and smuggling (*passim*, but esp. p. 7f and 98–101), as well as a survey of the main overall conclusions that can be drawn from the data.
4 N. E. Bang and K. Korst, *Tabeller over Skibsfart og Varetransport gennem Öresund*, 7 vols., Copenhagen and Leipzig, 1906–53. For a general survey see W. S. Unger, 'Trade through the Sound in the 17th and 18th centuries', *Economic History Review*, XII, 1959–60, pp. 206–21; and P. Jeannin, 'Les comptes du Sund comme source pour la construction d'indices généraux de l'activité économique en Europe', *Revue historique*, CCXXXI, 1964, pp. 55–102, 307–40.
5 For a full description of the procedure of transcription of the data into electronic form, see Johansen, *passim*, and esp. pp. 115–23. The data is available in two forms: either as a straight rendition of the original punch-cards on to magnetic tape, held in the Danish

Data Archive in Odense and available in the UK through the ESRC data archive at the University of Essex; or in a reorganised hierarchical format on floppy diskettes (suitable for analysis for example under SPSS), in the series *Databases as Editions*, available also from the Danish Data Archive (in collaboration with the Max-Planck-Institut für Geschichte, Göttingen). Since two readily accessed and well documented versions of the data are available, downloading procedures will not be discussed here. See Chapter 11 for a more complex example of how to handle raw ASCII data from tape.

6 The example in Figure 10.1 is from Johansen, p. 120.

7 The Sound Toll records are not unlike portbooks of the kind found all over Europe. See for example P. Wakelin, 'Comprehensive computerisation of a very large documentary source: the portbook project at Wolverhampton Polytechnic', in *History and Computing*, ed. P. Denley and D. Hopkin, Manchester, 1987, pp. 109–15.

8 For details of the main units of measurement, see Johansen, pp. 125–9. These equivalents do not always correspond to the standard set of measurements used domestically in Denmark after the 1683 reform of weights and measures.

9 The last such register, the *Öresunds og Strömtoldrulle*, Copenhagen, 1842, not only includes the regulations governing the actual collection, but also forty-five pages detailing commodities and their ratings.

10 As noted, the listed toll rates, being fixed, do not correspond to actual market values: however, for piece-rate commodities, and for some relatively uncommon goods, levies were nominally around 1 per cent of the market value. Provided absolute accuracy is not required, the tolls can, therefore, be used as a guide. See Hans Chr. Johansen, 'Baltic timber exports in the late 18th century', in *The Baltic as a Trade Road*, Proceedings of the Seventh Baltic Seminar, 1989: publication no. 16 in the series of the Provincial Museum of Kymenlaakso, pp. 17–35.

11 See Johansen, *Shipping and Trade*, pp. 133–9, for a full listing of the geographic coding adopted for this project. For a broader methodological discussion of how to deal with complex datastructures such as this, see C. Harvey and J. Press, 'Relational data analysis: value, concepts and methods', *History and Computing*, IV, 1992, pp. 98–109; and L. Burnard, 'Principles of database design', in *Information Technology in the Humanities*, ed. S. Rahtz, Chichester, 1987, pp. 54–68.

12 A. Guéry, 'Les finances de la monarchie française sous l'ancien régime', *Annales*, XXXIII, 1978, pp. 216–39. It is well known that the first contemporary budgetary summary in France was Necker's highly controversial *Compte Rendu* of 1781. Its credibility has been

the object of controversy ever since its appearance, just as the overall finances of pre-revolutionary France have been the object of detailed study, even a summary of which cannot be attempted here.

Chapter 11

Linking sources: comprehensive analysis of a community

Earlier in this volume, in Chapters 4–6, we looked at a single, clearly structured descriptive source, the census, which might serve as an obvious starting point for a certain kind of social history. We observed how the computer might help simply as an efficient index to the original source. But we also looked briefly at ways of enhancing our dataset, partly by adding fields and coding, partly through the creation of an hierarchical framework. In a relational database manager, that in turn would give us the means of bringing in other historical sources to help clarify difficulties (like the definition of the household unit).

This chapter will discuss three common aspects of working with large linked datasets: (1) how to adapt (download) existing bigger research datasets; (2) how to go about relating different historical sources through record linkage; and (3) what approaches might be adopted to make the most of loosely structured source material. To illustrate these, we shall use a large existing set of data covering a wide range of typical primary source material. Since centrally-controlled local administration in early modern Britain was minimal by continental European standards, and some types of records therefore rudimentary, we shall turn instead to a more bureaucratised continental example: the Danish town of Odense during the second half of the eighteenth century. Many of its more structured administrative sources have, through the work of another research team led by Professor Hans Chr. Johansen of the University of Odense, been assembled into a quite remarkable database.[1]

It has to be admitted that not all databases created in connection with big research projects will be of much use to other historians.

Data entered in the days of mainframe computing – with space at a premium and heavy numeric coding inescapable – was often subjected to so many irreversible compression and editing processes that it no longer reflected the original historical source satisfactorily.

However, fortunately there are exceptions. In Chapter 10 we explored the potential of a very large dataset designed as a source-edition, that is, transcribing the original as faithfully as was practical in the 1970s. Such an editorial policy creates excellent conditions for secondary analysis (that is, analysis by historians other than the originator). Inevitably, most datasets depart somewhat from the ideal of faithfulness to the source: constraints of space and resources, as well as inconsistencies in the primary material itself, will often have led to some intrusive editorial policies during the data-transcription process. Yet compromises of this kind do not invariably invalidate use of the data by others. After all, the primary sources were themselves often written up as standardised summaries of a more complex reality. Since in any case no electronic dataset can at present be an exact replica of the original source, all database work will in fact involve some degree of compromise. Provided those compromises are fully justifiable and documented, an imported dataset which is not explicitly a source-edition can still be of great value.

The Odense data

The Odense datafile is a typical example of a research dataset where compromises have been made, but in a clearly visible way. In accordance with standard practice for large-scale mainframe computing in the 1970s and early 1980s, each source chosen for inclusion had to be adapted to fit the constraints of the 80-character line (derived from the 80 columns of the now antiquated standard punched card). In many cases this created no great problems; but certain items of information (like occupational labels, or annotations in the original) were too varied to escape compression or editing. Moreover, certain types of potentially relevant freer textual sources, notably judicial records, were omitted altogether. Much of the material that was keyed in, however, was more or less as it appeared in the original sources.

By the later eighteenth century, Odense (on the island of

Funen in Denmark) was a town of around 5,000 people, on the main road from Copenhagen to Jutland (and north-western Germany). Typically for the period, it was not particularly thriving. It was accessible by sea through shallow waters, but was not a major port; it was the administrative, judicial and ecclesiastical centre for Funen, but did not grow much on that basis. Traditional small crafts predominated: most numerous were the shoemakers and cobblers, glove-makers, tailors, bakers, cabinetmakers and weavers. There was a small sugar refinery and a soap manufactory, but neither was a substantial contributor to the economy. An attempt was made in 1754 to bring to Odense a large cotton-weaving enterprise run by an entrepreneur in Wiesbaden (Germany), but it was not in the end a success: the arrival of nearly 400 people (the workers and their families) imposed a noticeable strain on the community.

Of the nearly 1,070 households in Odense in the 1787 census, 351 were headed by master craftsmen, another 89 by journeymen, whilst 105 were headed by administrative office-holders or members of the liberal professions, 43 by innkeepers, and only 35 by merchants or shopkeepers. Because of its garrison status, Odense also had 114 households headed by a soldier. It is probably safe to say that Odense was, not unlike many other communities before the advent of industrialisation, static (even if many of its inhabitants displayed mobility during their life-cycle) and not very prosperous (seasonal underemployment remaining a recurrent problem).

The datafiles for Odense proper cover various types of demographic, social and administative sources from around 1740 to 1790: (1) the actual censuses of 1769 and 1787; (2) birth, marriage and burial registers; (3) tax registers; (4) fire insurance building valuations, rate and probate registers; (5) guild and citizenship rolls; (6) hospital and workhouse admission protocols, and one poor relief register. Except for the last mentioned, there is no sampling: all cases given in the historical source are included.

Unlike the Sound Toll data discussed in the last chapter, however, the Odense data did not during compilation retain an overall form visibly close to the historical original. The most important change was in the sequential structure of the information itself: in the machine-readable datafile each line is located in sequence first by house, then by date and type of source (see

```
90    5
 1  402    TORVET            13          13    585       5      4
 4         1743      5      SKRAEDER  HANS      MOELLER              1    1  20
 3         1761      5      SKRAEDER-LAUGET                             62    80
 3         1731    585      SKRAEDER-LAUGSHUUS                          72   600
 5         1851    585                          SKRAEDER-LAUG
 6         1803    585      SKRAEDERNES-LAUGSHUS                     3 1 16  9 304 304
 3         1811    585      SKRAEDER-LAUG                            3    2K 1  72 1260
95
43    5 20  5152106432HANS      MOELLER  ANNA      MOELLERS  SKRAEDDER 11        10
2200400          743    5 11HANS                    MOELLER-SKRAEDERS-ENKE        3
2200400          743    5 13                                                   A F
95
2200400          743    5 21GIERTRUD                NIELSDATTER-ENKE             3
2200400          743    5 23                                                   A F
95
2300400  1749    5      CAPITAIN          FRISCHES-ENKE            PENSION
43    5 24  343090558    FRISCH                                                -13
12  4 4          758    3221                         FRICHE                      3
12  4 4          758    32231605    2                                  5
95
80                       PEDER     LUNDE      FRA 132    1751
13  4 4          754    1311PEDER              LUNDE-SKRAEDER                    2
13  4 4          754    1322KIRSTINE           HANSDATTER                        3
13  4 4          754    13 30612130255
2400400  1759    5      SKRAEDER  PEDER    LUNDE              312N
2500400  1762    5      SKRAEDER  PEDER    LUNDE      2            1 2
43    5 25  3640312662PEDER     LUNDE    KIRSTEN  HANSDATTERSKRAEDDER  1 KA   -3
12  4 4          766    7611PEDER              LUNDE-SKRAEDER                    3
12  4 4          766    76130812                                   2
2100400          769    5 21PEDER              LUNDE-SKRAEDERS-ENKE              3
2100400          769    5 23         1                                          3
30                       PEDER     LUNDES-ENK   TIL  834      1769-75
95
3000400SKRAEDD  1801HANS            HUNDERUP                                     3
3000400SKRAEDD  1803            260871
80                       METTE-CATHLIEBEN     FRA  663    1772
13  4 5          772    811HANS                HUNDERUP-SKRAEDDER                2
13  4 5          772    822METTE-CATHRINE      LIEBEN                            3
13  4 5          772    823    2210                             1               5
13  4 5          772    825PETER               LIEBEN-SKRAEDDER
11  4 4          773    5521ANNA-MARIA                             0612          4
11  4 4          773    5524HANS               HUNDEROP-SKRAEDER-TORVET
11  4 4          775    1311JOCHUM-PETER                          0804          4
11  4 4          775    1314HANS               HUNDEROP-SKRAEDERMESTER
2600400  1775    5      SKRAEDER  HANS    HUNDERUP
45    5 27  399020276  HANS      HUNDERUP  JOHAN-JOCKHUNDERUP  FAR      399   -43
3100400SKRAEDE  312 HANS            HUNDERUP                    210276
12  4 4          777    1911JOCHUM-PETER                                        3
12  4 4          777    19131502                               1                5
12  4 4          777    1915HANS               HUNDEROP-SKRAEDER-TORVET
30                       HANS      HUNDERUP   TIL    9      1777
95
80                       ANNE-SOPHIBRANDT     FRA  11    1775-31
2500400  1781    4      JOMFRUE        BRANDT      1 1 1 L
200040020010047870040012 1ANNE-SOPHIE           BRANDT                          3
20004002001004787004001231061          0210
23004002001004787004002 21MARGRETHE            PHILIPSDATTER                    3
20004002001004787004002231074          0260
2700400  1789    4      JOMFRU  ANNE-SOPHIBRANDT    S  4
```

Figure 11.1 Sample of raw Odense data (house no. 5) straight from tape

Figure 11.1), rather than the reverse. To achieve this, the addresses of all buildings had to be standardised: in many of the original sources there is, in addition to personal information, some indication either of household structure or of the physical building, but these indications naturally vary from one source to the next. During data-entry, therefore, a consistent house-identification system was constructed, such that each line of data (from whatever source) could be slotted into a standard map of the whole town.

This did not pre-empt decisions about, for example, the demarcation of the household unit in the census listings (cf. above p. 76), but, as we shall see, it does mean that one important stage in the process of *linking* records across different sources has already been completed. Such an approach is in fact typical of what social historians regularly have to try to do in order to make use of descriptive sources.

From ASCII data to relational database

The data covering the whole population within municipal jurisdiction, in the form just described, takes up just over 90,000 lines of 80 characters each. If each line had been fully used, the amount of data would be $80 \times 90,000 = 7,200,000$ bytes (7 megabytes), but in practice it is around 4 megabytes. It is only very recently that the storage capacity and quality of software have become available to make database work on such a scale possible on a desktop machine. Given that large datasets often come in a format broadly like the one just described, it may be helpful to summarise how such raw machine-readable data can be mounted in a new computing environment for secondary analysis.

The Odense data was stored in ASCII form, that is, according to the American Standard Code for Information Interchange commonly used for data transfer. Since data stored in this way is independent of any specific software requirements, a transfer should present no immediate problem. As with any computer tape, all that was initially required was to identify the tape standard used.[2]

Editing a datafile of this size, however, requires large amounts of memory and file store, and software to match. Therefore the first step was to mount it on one of the mainframe computers at Glasgow University, as a transitional stage before downloading to a relational database manager.

As is apparent from Figure 11.1, each line in the raw datafile starts with a two-digit code. This denotes the source from which each line is derived ('11' for baptismal registers, '12' for burial ones, and so on). It made historical sense, therefore, to begin by breaking the 90,000-line datafile up into separate files, one for each type of historical source. Since, in the Odense datafile, all entries were ordered by house (house no. 5 is identified in the first two lines of Figure 11.1), each line was first tagged with the house number under which it appeared, and was then copied into its appropriate source-file. This is a relatively straightforward job on a mainframe computer, but anyone not acquainted with programming and mainframe editing will be well advised to seek technical assistance for this stage.

The sorting just described not only made historical sense, but was also essential given that the allocation of information (the field structure) across each 80-character line in the original raw datafile varied from one source to another. During the sorting, single entries of information that in the original datafile had had to be spread over a sequence of more than one 80-character line – such as the 1769 census recorded in Figure 11.1 on lines starting with '21' – could (given modern database technology) be 'unfolded' and joined end-to-end, so that each row in the resulting files always represented one entry (record) from the original source. So, instead of a single flat file of some 90,000 lines, there were now around 30 smaller files, each of which represented the data taken from a particular primary source, and none of which contained more than 6,000 records. This initial sorting was the only stage where outside technical assistance was required. The source-files were now small enough to be downloaded to a desktop computer with a large hard disk and a good DBMS.[3] Each source was placed in its own table (file) within the relational database.

The core of the resulting data structure is summarised in Figure 11.2. At its centre is naturally the thorough and generally reliable 1787 census (similar in contents and design to the British 1851 census). Around it are groups of related material, each giving certain types of information: the tax records often add useful detail on occupations and household structure, the church records are more specific on family links, whilst the guild, citizenship and poor relief records give economic clues which can usefully supplement the fiscal returns. Consistently with the original primary material, the rows of one table are not linked by unique identifiers to those of any other table; however, the house-number added to each record provides the nearest alternative that the data allows at this stage.

In practice this means that the relational link between tables is ambiguous. A head of household in a tax file will be listed under the number of the house where he lived, but if we try to relate

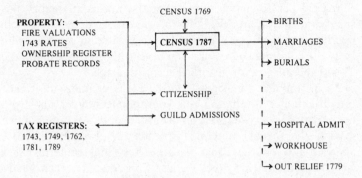

Figure 11.2 Odense data organised into tables by source

him by means of that house number to, say, the information in a contemporary census, we may find that the particular building was occupied by several heads of household at the time. As we shall see in the next section, we have to use other information in the sources (names, occupations, ages, or whatever) to supplement the house number before we can be sure we are dealing with the same person. From a computing point of view, such ambiguity is clearly less than ideal; from a historical point of view, however, this reflects the true nature of the sources. What we have done, in effect, is to create a relational database where each table represents one primary archival source complete with many of its original inconsistencies: the first task of the historian (just as if working without a computer) is to establish reliable links between these sources.

Record linkage

Historians have to make judgements about inconsistent data all the time, and these files are no exception. In order, for example, to get an impression of the overall social and economic characteristics of the town, the historian might wish to sort all the households in the 1787 census according to occupational groups, and then link that information not only to the information on the co-residential household unit in the census itself, but also to the quite specific information on earnings and wealth contained in the 1789 tax register. Given the two-year interval between these sources, a perfect match would of course not be attainable; but a significant overlap might reasonably be expected. To identify this overlap, however, the historian has to be able to establish which individuals in one source are identical to those listed in another. This is the purpose of historical record-linkage.

As mentioned, the Danish 1787 census contains information broadly similar to that in the later nineteenth-century British ones.[4] The 1789 tax-register, on the other hand, was rather unusual in that the taxable potential of each breadwinner was to be assessed not on the usual flat-rate basis but in terms of his (or, more rarely, her) real means. Consequently, each head of household had to submit a simple tax-return. The amounts payable were then itemised under two headings: partly as a 0.5% levy on any wealth over a certain minimum, partly as a 5% levy on earnings of various kinds, including (1) office-holding salary, (2) unearned income, or (3) earnings from trade, crafts and other ordinary occupations.

There clearly are problems in using any tax return as an historical source. Each head of household was responsible for declaring his own wealth and earnings, and whilst those of public employees would be fairly easy to verify (and hence are presumably reasonably reliable), the returns of ordinary craftsmen and traders would be more difficult for the authorities to check.[5] Nevertheless, the source clearly has far greater historical interest than the usual register of flat-rate taxes.

Some rows (records) from each of the two tables are juxtaposed in Figure 11.3. For the census table, only the lines for heads of households have been included, complete with an editorial code (HHCODE) representing the composition of the household (described above, p. 76). For the tax table, the information under each potential category of levy, originally in a composite monetary form not unlike the system used in Britain before decimalisation, has been converted into the lowest monetary unit (the *skilling*) by using the database facility of multiplication and addition.[6]

So, first of all, how far can the historian link individuals in the two different sources? It is unsatisfactory to go by surname alone, since some names are very common (like Hansen in house 143), and others have widely variant spellings (like Moegs/Mychs in house 148). In any case patronymics were customary in Denmark at the time: Ane-Margrethe Andersdatter in house 146 here

1787 CENSUS TABLE:

HHCODE	HOUSE	FORENAME	SURNAME	SEX	MC	AGE	OCCUPTR
AACJJXXSLLLLL	143	JOACHIM	HANSEN	M	M1	34	TAILOR MST
ACGL	143	SOPHIE-CHRISTIANA	JACOBSEN	F	W1	57	SEAMSTRESS
AACRXL	145	PEDER	WARNICHE	M	M1	44	TAILOR
AACCCXS	146	LUCAS	FRANDSEN	M	M1	63	SHOEMAKER
AC	146	ANE-MARGRETHE	ANDERSDATTER	F	W1	64	MIDWIFE
AA	147	PEDER	RANDERS	M	M1	56	GLOVER
AAC	147	SCHACH	GROENVALD	M	M1	23	SERVANT
AAC	147	DITLEF	HILLEBRAND	M	M1	35	DRAGOON
AAC	147	JOHAN	JISMAN	M	M1	30	BONE-TURNER
AA	147	OVE	THOMASEN	M	M1	68	DAY-LABOURER
LLL	147	SIDSEL	OLSDATTER	F	U	35	SPINNER-BINDER
ALCCCC	147	KNUD	THOMASEN	M	M1	36	COBBLER/SOLDIER
AC	148	JOHANNE	MOEGS	F	U	30	SALESWOMAN
AAC	148	PEDER	PHILIPSEN	M	M1	60	BEGGAR
AACXSL	150	HANS	THOMASEN	M	M1	70	COOPER
AACC	152	POUL	CHRISTENSEN	M	M1	67	GLOVER-J.
LLL	152	MAREN	LAUSDATTER	F	W1	74	BEGGAR

1789 TAX REGISTER TABLE:

HOUSE	OCCUPTR	FORENAME	SURNAME	XWEALTH	XOFFICE	XINCOME	XEARN
143	DYER/W	SOPHIE-CHR	KOELSNERS	0	0	0	0
143	TAILOR	JOCHUM	HANSEN	0	0	0	384
144	PROFESSOR/W	METTE-ELIS	NANNESTAD	0	0	0	114
145	-/W	RASMUS	NIELSENS	0	0	0	120
145	RET.SERVANT	JOHAN	SIM	24	0	0	0
145	TAILOR	PETER	WARNICHE	0	0	0	96
146	SHOEMAKER	LUCAS	FRANDSEN	0	0	0	0
147	GLOVER	PEDER	RANDERS	48	0	0	240
148	PEDDLAR WOMAN	JOHANNE	MYCHS	0	0	0	96
150	COOPER/W	HANS	THOMSENS	0	0	0	96
150	SPINSTER		HOLSTEIN	0	0	672	0
152	POOR			0	0	0	0

Figure 11.3 Heads of household in the 1787 census (houses 143–52) and taxpayers in the 1789 tax register (same houses)

carries a patronymic (the daughter of Anders, equivalent to Anders's son), but since she is a widow (marital condition = W1) she might equally well have carried her dead husband's surname. Indeed the widow in house 145 in the tax table, recorded in the source as Rasmus Nielsens *enke* (widow), is being referred to by nothing but her husband's forename *and* surname.

What if we add in the forenames? That would not help for the last case just mentioned, but might for others. Our tailor in house 143 is still not without problems, as his forename is written in two different ways (Joachim and Jochum). These two spellings, however, are close enough to be matched through the 'sounds-like' facility which many sophisticated database programs have. Since in this dataset we can also rely on the house-numbering link already in place, such a procedure would almost certainly deal satisfactorily with a large part of the acceptable linkages. Some new problems might be created, however. Those women widowed in the two-year interval, but retaining their husband's name might, given the absence of reliable information on marital condition in the tax register, be identified with their husbands, even though in reality they were in a very different fiscal position (the '/w' for widows, under occupation, is not consistent).

Would the information on occupation help, as an additional criterion for linkage? It might help the historian, but not always the computer. Sophie-Christiana Jacobsen, widowed seamstress in house 143 in the census, is probably the same person as Sophie-Chr. Koelsner, the dyer's widow, in the tax register – but the computer would have little chance of spotting her unless it had been given categories of related occupations. Even if it had, the two occupations here are not obviously connected, the way the 'tailor' and 'tailor master' (house 143) clearly are.[7]

The normal procedure for record linkage is in fact to go through several such stages in a systematic and logical way. First of all links are established using the most reliable part of the data (if the records are individual people, as here, this will often mean starting with surnames). Successive additional criteria for matching can then be added, progressing from the most reliable information (often forenames or initials, or the name of a spouse if available) outwards to less reliable parts of the data (age, place of origin, and so on). At each stage, especially if the 'sounds like' facility is used, it is essential to examine manually all the linkages proposed by the computer. If the matching criteria are too slack, then errors may become evident either through common-sense judge-ment (checks against birth and death records might suggest an improbably long life-span) or on the basis of detailed critical assessment of the reliability of the source itself. In the end, the difficult cases will need to be re-examined manually on their merits. Those not matched might either not have any link at all, or may (like Rasmus Nielsen's widow in house 145 in the tax register) need to be sought by cross-reference to entirely different source material.

Perfect accuracy will of course never be possible, but a sequential procedure like the one outlined here, with at least three independent co-ordinates (items of information to help linkage)[8] will give as reasonable a set of results as the data can support. Those records that cannot be matched will more often be from the lower end of the social spectrum – in the present dataset some of the poor were exempt from taxation altogether, whilst others of course positively evaded it – so due allowance must be made if, using this particular data, conclusions about the social stratification of the whole population are to be drawn.

Demographers have for many years used techniques such as these, especially on birth, marriage and burial registers, in order to clarify the cyclical patterns in household composition typical of any society. Identification of such cyclical fluctuations, by means of systematic family reconstitution, is indeed an essential corrective to the apparently static 'snapshot' of the census. Record linkage, however, is also necessary for other types of sources, including some where the individual case (record) being observed, the row of the database, is not a person: for example building- or ship-registers, auction sale catalogues, and other sources.

Using conversion tables with linkages

Having established acceptable linkages between the 1789 tax list and the 1787 census, it is worth using the information thus gained on some of the other sources. First of all, in order to deal more consistently with variants of spelling, we might compile 'conversion tables' (double column equivalents) of all successfully matched pairs of names, one for forenames and one for surnames. Basically, we would convert all acceptable equivalents of a variable into one standard form: in the surname column, for example, 'Smith', 'Smythe' and 'Smit' might all be treated as equivalent to 'Smith'.

Any database software will produce an alphabetically ordered list of unique occurrences of each variable (in effect a 'keyword count'). If all surname variants from both lists are consolidated into a single sorted list, a 'standard' spelling can be entered in a new column against each variant, in keeping with the distinctions pinpointed in the original set of matched pairs. The resulting double-column table is then in effect a 'translation table' or conversion table which (by means of a relational join) can convert all surnames into the chosen standard form.

For less reliable parts of the data, such as the occupational information, a deliberately simplifying coding scheme might be used in a similar way. All occupations in the dataset would have to be reduced to simple broad categories. For example, all tailors, cloth-merchants, weavers, dyers, seamstresses and related could be converted to a single general category such as 'cloth' – or even more comprehensively, 'trades'. If the categories are carefully designed, such a conversion table may well help with difficult linkages.

The three conversion tables suggested here (surname, forename, occupational categories) need of course not be used to *replace* the original information, but will give the computer a set of standard conversions to help linking further tables with less manual checking. The standardisation of values achieved in this way will help to ensure that all potential pair-combinations will be identified consistently – not just those deemed equivalent by the often arbitrarily fixed criteria of the 'sounds like' linkage-system on a given database manager.

Conversion tables are also a simple and quick way of translating archaic terms – or (as in the Odense case) actually translating from a foreign language. In order to translate the occupational labels in the Danish census and tax registers, for example, a procedure was used similar to that for the surnames: instead of judgements on standard spellings for names, judgements were made about historically appropriate translations for variant descriptions of similar occupations.[9]

Creating a framework for socio-economic classification

Given the information in the 1789 tax table regarding apparent earnings and wealth, distributed by occupations, and the linkage potentials just discussed, analysis of the socio-economic hierarchy in Odense can now be undertaken. The historian might well go about such a task by establishing, first of all, how best to group all the taxpayers in a meaningful classificatory scheme. A good database manager will allow a grouping by occupation all those individuals paying each specific category of tax; it will give the mean tax (and preferably also a maximum and minimum) for each occupational group. It may also be possible to add the wealth tax information to such an analysis. This will help provide the historian with the information needed to work out where social dividing-lines can reasonably be placed, checking the occupational categories, where necessary, against the 1787 census and other tables in the dataset. This is not the place to discuss the actual results in detail,[10] but it will be apparent that techniques such as the ones described here will be of use on a wide range of historical source material. Typically for the early modern period, the Odense data reveals a community with quite sharp horizontal dividing lines in terms of wealth and occupational groupings. The elite was small and largely confined to titled families, office-holders, military and church staff, with only the rare manufacturer. At the bottom of the social scale were older journeymen who had never secured economic independence, as well as unskilled and semi-skilled workers, servants and transient single people.

Thanks to the availability on computer of this wide range of sources, eighteenth-century Odense can be studied in surprising depth. Of course not all problems are solved: some of the Odense sources are evidently too widely spaced for linked analysis, so that for example the 1769 census is of little use in connection with the 1743 rates register. Equally, not all the information in the complete range of tables can be taken at face value – after all, even the 1789 tax ratings were based on self-assessment of a kind not tried on any scale before. Nevertheless, it will be readily apparent that a combination of computerised record-linkage techniques, statistical functions and coding schemes can, without locking the historian into an inflexible framework, achieve some very interesting results without an impossibly large investment of time and effort.

Incorporation of loosely structured information

The Odense database can usefully illustrate another quite different but equally important technique for historians: how to fit inconsistently structured (or 'free-form') text into a more formal database. A case in point is the admission protocol of the workhouse in Odense.

Like all early modern towns with less than thriving economies,

Odense had many unemployed or underemployed, some of whom had come from the surrounding countryside. In an effort to deal with begging and vagrancy, the town established a workhouse (bridewell) in 1752, which characteristically admitted people from the hinterland (all of the island of Funen) as well as from the town itself. Like workhouses elsewhere in Europe, it was intended as a disciplined environment, extracting penal labour from basically fit vagrants, beggars, disobedient servants and youngsters, quarrelsome individuals and those guilty of moral offences. It was also, however, meant to look after those 'deserving poor' and orphans who could neither gain admission to the city hospital nor cope by themselves just with support from the seriously underfunded municipal out-relief system.

A typical entry in the original admission protocol reads in translation as follows:

23 November 1752 No. 57 Joen Biörn from Kerteminde, born in the same place, upwards of 70 years old, who according to submitted examination and witnessed report has for many years lived restless and dissipated with drink, irreconcilable in his marriage, quarrelsome and brawling to all his neighbours, so that he latterly has behaved as if deranged, with everyone afraid of him, in case he in drunkenness should inflict a misfortune on someone; which indeed he finally did, when he attacked the town official in the middle of the street, trying to stab him with a knife; for which he will, according to the district governor's decision, be judged by the *byfoged* (town authority), pending which he is placed here in the Workhouse. [With a marginal note:] Released

To incorporate this in a conventional structured database might require (for efficiency both in storage and retrieval) a simplification of the information. A summary version might include admission number, date, names, sex, place of origin, age, offence and outcome as separate fields, thus:

57, 521123, JOEN BIOERN, M, KERTEMINDE, 70, DRINK/VIOLENCE/ATT.STABBING, RELEASED

But to such a summary one might want to add details regarding the not entirely clear committal procedure, the pending judgement, or the sources of information cited. Equally, one crucial item of information – the reasons for arrest – might well deserve fuller rendition than just the three keywords given here: drink, violence, attempted stabbing. Indeed the order in which these keywords are listed here (underlying cause, general problem and immediate trigger) imposes an editorial view inconsistent with the source as a whole, and not readily applicable to some of the more complex cases in the protocol. In other words, such editorial 'tidying' takes us away from the actual source, disguising some of its characteristics.

With 900 individuals admitted over the 40-year period covered by this set of data, however, some structure is necessary to enable efficient linkage with any of the other more structured sources in the Odense database. A summarised data-entry such as the one suggested here may serve as an index to a fuller version of the text. Such a fuller version, perhaps a verbatim rendering of the protocol with mark-up code, would allow the kind of detailed analysis which judicial records, for example, often require. This will be discussed in the next chapter.

This chapter has illustrated how the historian might go about structuring and processing a set of related but characteristically uneven primary sources (whether from an imported dataset or compiled afresh). The starting point was, once more, a census, but a representative range of other administrative and parish records were added to try to create a fuller and more reliable foundation for a detailed analysis of the community. As in all historical research, each type of source raised new problems, and some of these problems have a bearing on how the historian might incorporate the data into a database.

There are no simple answers to many of the problems encountered, and decisions will depend partly on manpower and resources, partly on the purposes for which such a database might be created. A detailed examination of the circumstances surrounding the creation of each source, its purpose, and its level of accuracy is often a precondition of its effective use. This, however, is as true for historians who do not use computers as for those who do; indeed, it could be argued that the process of editing data into a database structure is likely to make the historian more conscious of the strengths and weaknesses of his/her source material. With some ingenuity, and a flexible adaptation of relational database technology, the historian will be in possession of materials and tools sufficient for a level of analysis effectively unattainable by non-computerised methods.

Notes

1　The datasets are stored in the Danish Data Archive, and are available in ASCII format through the normal data exchange channels. Hans Chr. Johansen himself used the data for parts of his history of eighteenth-century Odense, *Næring og Bystyre: Odense 1700–1789*, Odense, 1983, on which some of the background comment given here is based. See also his brief article on 'Growing old in an urban environment', *Continuity and Change*, II, 1987, pp. 297–305. Professor Johansen also very kindly made available to us a considerable amount of additional background information, for which we are very grateful.

2　Computer tape behaves much like a high-quality cassette tape. Unlike a floppy disk, tape is not very fast to access, since spooling will slow down searches. On a 9-track mainframe tape each of the 8 bits of one byte (or character) is assigned to its own track across the tape, and the last track is used to check parity. Lengthways, a density of at least 800 or 1,600 bits per inch (bpi) is common. A sequence of bytes (often 4,000 or 8,000) constitutes a block of information on the tape, separated from the next by a small gap. It is essential to have a note of such technical information before a tape can be read.

3　For practical reasons, an intermediate stage may be necessary, as it was here. The raw Odense data did not have field markers (field delimiters) so it was essential to load it first into a database where it would be easy to specify that, say, columns 10–24 belong to the field SURNAME, and so forth. To define which columns of the original lines belong to which fields, the Odense data was processed first by means of SQL in Ingres (running on a VAX cluster), before being downloaded to a desktop computer. Some good DBMS (like Borland's Paradox) can perform this operation on a desktop computer, but might be slow in dealing with some of the largest files.

4　There are a few differences: for example the Danish census indicates, for married or widowed individuals, how many times they had been married, and which marriage any resident child came from. There is a considerable literature in Danish on the census material: as with the British material, there are doubts for example about the consistency of definition of the co-residential unit, and the placing of marginal individuals like lodgers, but generally speaking the censuses from 1787 onwards have stood up well to scrutiny.

5　For an instructive British parallel, see E. Baigent, 'Assessed taxes as sources for the study of urban wealth: Bristol in the later 18th century', *Urban History Yearbook*, 1988, pp. 31–48.

6　One might simplify further, and lump together the taxes payable on office, unearned income, and ordinary earnings from crafts and trade (no one paid more than one of these). That, however, could destroy important historical information: even at a glance it is clear that assessments in the columns for office-holders and unearned income are generally much higher than for the ordinary earnings. This clearly has relevance for social stratification. If one were to combine these different tax-ratings into a single column, therefore, it would be essential first of all to add a column with a code indicating which of the taxes each individual was rated for.

7   Using occupational information for primary linkages is often not to be recommended either for the early modern period or for industrial society: the degree of variation in nomenclature at all times is very high, and individuals are far too likely either (a) to change their occupation, or (b) to give the same general occupations significantly different specific labels. This is a problem for all European and North American data. Occupational information, as a rule, is better used as subsidiary corroboration for linkages proposed by other means.

8   For further discussion of historical record linkage, see M. Thaller, 'Methods and techniques of historical computation', in *History and Computing*, ed. P. Denley and D. Hopkin, Manchester, 1987, p. 150f; and K. Schurer, J. Oeppen and R. Schofield, 'Theory and methodology: an example from historical methodology', in *History and Computing II*, ed. P. Denley *et al.*, Manchester, 1989, pp. 130–42. S. W. Baskerville, 'Preferred linkage and the analysis of voter behaviour in 18th-century England', in *History and Computing*, I, 1989, pp. 112–20. See also the special issue of *History and Computing*, IV, part 1 (1992), devoted to Record Linkage. For a detailed practical illustration, relating to very complex Portuguese sources, see A. Kitts, D. Doulton and E. Reis, *The Reconstruction of Viana do Castelo* (Research Studies in History and Computing, I, Association for History and Computing), 1990, *passim*, but esp. pp. 18–22.

9   To do this, a list of all unique occurrences of the terms to be translated is saved as a single-column table. A new (blank) column is added to that table, into which appropriate translations are added against each of the original terms. These translations are then re-inserted into the original table by means of a standard relational join.

10   See T. Munck, 'Social identity and community in 18th-century urban Denmark', in *The Cultural and Political Formation of Social Identities in European Communities*, ed. C. Bjørn, A. Grant and K. Stringer, Copenhagen, forthcoming.

Chapter 12

Beyond the database: text analysis, hypertext and Computer-Assisted Learning

So far in this book the emphasis has been on the types of historical source material which have fairly obvious and consistent structural features: for example administrative records designed to convey specific information in a standard and repetitive form, tabulated censuses and election results with a sequence of similar entries, or biographical dictionaries where each entry to some extent follows a standard pattern. However, historians just as often work with sources where the structural features are not so obvious: say, in the prose of longer memoranda, the complex and formulaic language of judicial records, the popular jargon of newspapers – and even the idiosyncratic style of the private writings of individuals, or the diverse contents of fictional writings, cartoons and other material.

Many of the written sources that historians habitually employ – not to mention visual ones – do not lend themselves well to conventional database manipulation. This does not, however, mean that historians should necessarily abandon the computer when they reach something which will not fit into their relational database or spreadsheet. On the contrary, it could be argued, massive textual sources require computer-assisted analysis at least as much as, say, the census. It may even be that 'textbase'[1] applications, being capable of representing any kind of historical text in something much more akin to its original form, will in fact supersede the database as the 'normal' tool for computer-using historians.

Text analysis

The written language, given its very complex evolutionary history, does not lend itself readily to programmable (i.e. fully logical)

analysis of a kind that will produce convincing historical conclusions. Quite apart from the complexities of non-standard spelling, non-standard abbreviations and units of measurement,
regional dialects, shifts in meaning over time, and subtler nuances
that may initially escape even the trained researcher (let alone a
computer program), every language has a vast range of associ-
ations, contextual undercurrents and implicit values which can be
lost through attempted systemisation. A historian specialising in a
given period gradually acquires a subjective 'feel' for the language
of the period. Some of this expertise could conceivably be system-
atised, but the potential pitfalls are endless, and the scope for
informed disagreement no less so. Not without reason, therefore,
have historians had considerable difficulty in applying computing
techniques to any but the most basic levels of text analysis.

Getting a text into a machine-readable form is the least of
these problems. With the services of a keen copy-typist, text may
be entered (like any other data) at the keyboard. Alternatively, a
moderately priced *scanner* and some suitable Optical Character
Recognition (OCR) software should work efficiently on a clearly
printed text. Standard modern typefaces can be scanned in on,
say, a basic Apple Scanner at the rate of about a page a minute.
If the font is clear and consistent, correction of misreadings will
then not be a prolonged editorial job on a word processor.
However, although some scanners can 'learn' to recognise difficult
and non-standard fonts, even the most sophisticated machines
(such as the Kurzweil scanners) have difficulty with books set in
hand-cast type (because of the irregularities of appearance) or set
in a way that produces slightly wavy lines. Books more than
about 150 years old, therefore, are not easily scanned straight
into text – though they can of course be image-scanned to produce
a visual facsimile.[2]

The next stage, choosing a suitable tool to analyse the text that
has been entered, is more difficult. Chapter 3 briefly discussed
some features of word-processing systems, notably searching,
which have obvious potential in the study of new text. Equally,
such search facilities can be applied to the historian's primary
textual sources to locate some previously identified characteristics,
or to add textual mark-up for later use. But, apart from a complex
academic text processor like Nota Bene, with its facilities for
multilingual word processing and concordances (listing words in

their context), few applications satisfactorily cover both text preparation and simple text analysis.

For certain types of work, more composite systems may prove helpful. IdeaList, for example, is an unusual type of database manager allowing extremely flexible field structures. This makes it suitable for the handling of variable and unstructured texts such as those one might assemble from heterogenous archival material. It can be run alongside other programs within a single environment like Microsoft Windows, and this facilitates easy exchange between word processor, database manager and other analysis software. Using a common windows-type environment is of course not the same as having a single application with enough flexibility for effective processing of all types of written historical data, whether structured or free text; but it can be very useful just the same.

For serious text analysis, however, the historian is likely to need more specialist and versatile software. Some sophisticated textual analytic software for micros, even if concentrating on specific and relatively limited tasks, is so large and unwieldy that, as in the case of BRS/Search, it still behaves much like its mainframe ancestor. As far as freely-structured text is concerned, historians are in some ways still facing the kinds of software problems which they had to contend with when working on structured historical databases in the mid-1980s.

Good full-text retrieval applications, like the Oxford Concordance Program (OCP), WordCruncher or Tact, are designed primarily for literary analysis: they will be of great help to the historian wanting an initial overview of word usage in a historic text, but will probably not (at least without sophisticated mark-up) be able to help with some of the more complex issues of syntax, rhetorical style or meaning that arise.

In contrast to the earlier chapters on database design and analysis, therefore, this chapter will not convey even a semblance of consensus. Rather, it will explore some very diverse approaches which may not so far have proved definitive, but which are certainly fruitful.

Analysis techniques for free-form texts

Computers have been used for textual and literary analysis for over forty years, and some of the techniques developed can be of relevance to historians. The study of vocabulary, syntax, style and dialect, for example, will be useful for certain very specific tasks: say, to identify a large body of text of uncertain origin, or perhaps to identify characteristic patterns of usage and ideas in a particular community. Equally, word counts and stylistic analysis might be of importance in clarifying disputed or unknown authorship. Similar kinds of analysis might also, for early corrupted texts which exist in uncertain or incompatible versions, help establish a 'tree' of the mutual relationship between variant readings, and thus help reconstruct a plausible text through collation.[3]

Most historians, however, are likely to be primarily interested in thematic content analysis: how concepts evolve within one work or over a period of time, what meanings are attached to words used to express these concepts, what logical framework is used to support a particular argument, and so on. For this, they may well start with a check through the visible literary features of their source. To get such an overall impression of a text it may be helpful to use some standard techniques taken from literary analysis:

- Comprehensive *word-counts*, listing all the words in a text, together with a count of the number of times each occurs. This might be done either for the entire vocabulary in the text, or perhaps excluding very common functional service-words like 'the', 'and', 'is', etc. Most text analysis applications will allow the word-count to be qualified in various ways, and will display the resulting list in alphabetic order or order of frequency.
- *Indexing* of selected words, giving information on where each occurs in the text, and, at request, perhaps giving a minimal context.
- *Keywords in context* (often abbreviated KWIC), a kind of concordance where chosen words are displayed within a fuller context, the extent of which (in number of words or lines) can be specified.
- *Collocations*, which consist of formal analysis of the extent to which certain pairs of words or phrases tend to occur in proximity to one another, as measured in their 'z-score'.[4]

All of these techniques are well known to those literary researchers who use computers, but can be of great value to historians, too. Collocation analysis, in particular, has obvious

value in determining shifts in the contextual and historical usage
of key words over periods of time. Collocations, in conjunction
with controlled selections and KWIC, may also help offer some
initial clues regarding the significance of phrases or particular
pairings of words.[5]

Practical results from text analysis

For historians, the text analysis techniques just described are
likely to be particularly fruitful when comparing two or more
separate texts (from different authors or over a certain period of
time). In texts written in the last years before the French Revolution, for example, the historian may wish to look for changing
views about fiscal and judicial reform, press censorship, notions
of 'social contract', or suggestions regarding political representation. For the present purposes, however, a single text will
suffice: Abbé Sieyes's controversial polemic *What is the Third
Estate?*, published a few months before the meeting of the French
Estates General in 1789. It is not a long work: it runs to around
35,000 words in the slightly extended second edition, and an
English translation[6] takes up 170 Kb (not counting the original
footnotes).

What is the Third Estate? is a book designed to influence the
debate then occurring in France regarding the system of representation and voting to be adopted in the forthcoming meeting of
the Estates General (May 1789) – itself the first general parliament
in France since the Estates General of 1614. During the previous
years there had in fact been significant experimentation with
provincial assemblies, some of which (notably in the Dauphiné)
had already opted for a doubling of representation of the third
Estate (the Estate which, by the historic conventions of the time,
included all those who were neither nobles nor clergy). More
importantly, the Dauphiné provincial assembly had also decided
that voting within it would be by head rather than by Estate,
thereby creating the potential for a defeat of the privileged first
and second Estates (clergy and nobles) by the third. For the
forthcoming Estates General of 1789, however, the Crown, while
allowing a doubling of the third Estate, had not indicated any
willingness to consider voting by head. This was the central issue
which Sieyes now addressed.

Sieyes made his point clear in the very opening sentences of his book, well-known to historians of revolutionary France:

The plan of this book is quite straightforward. We have three questions to ask ourselves.
1. What is the Third Estate? EVERYTHING.
2. What has it so far been in the political order? NOTHING.
3. What does it ask for? TO BE SOMETHING.
It will become clear whether these answers are right. Until then, it would be wrong to dismiss as exaggerations those truths for which the actual arguments have not yet been studied. We shall then examine those steps that have been tried, and those that need to be taken, in order for the Third Estate to become, in effect, *something*.

The rest of the text is a detailed and readable discussion partly of the iniquities of the political system of the old order, partly of the inadequacies of crown policy in a variety of areas. Not surprisingly, the book became a major influence on the debates of early 1789.[7]

Running this text under the text-analysis program Tact,[8] one can rapidly gain a rough impression of the language and orientation of the book to supplement an actual reading. A frequency count of all words in the text, in alphabetical order, may not on its own say very much, since there are naturally a large number of very common function words (definite and indefinite articles, conjunctions, auxiliary verbs, and similar). However, a quick scan of the entire list of nearly 4,000 different words in the English text immediately reveals some that are worth studying more closely.

As noted, *What is the Third Estate?* was written with the express intention of influencing political opinion in the run-up to the Estates-General. Not surprisingly, therefore, certain words are used by the author in a rather loaded way. Take as example an adjective like 'unjust'. It is used only five times in the text; but even the basic index listing in Tact of these five occurrences, with a short context added, gives some indication of the slant:

(296)   common rights and it was totally >**unjust** to deprive the people
(828)   anything unconstitutional in this >**unjust** advantage. They feel
(2098) And how violent and profoundly >**unjust** the second! In vain

(2626) every privilege is by its nature >**unjust**, hateful and
     against
(2844) by purging themselves of their >**unjust** privileges, and

The number in brackets gives the line reference; the 'target'
word itself is marked with a pointer. However, a short context
citation like this may (as in the third occurrence, in line 2098) be
too truncated to give a sense of the tone. Instead, a fuller KWIC
(keywords-in-context listing) of the same passage can be called
up to provide a wider context:

the petitions of the municipalities and of some of the pays d'état. Compare
these to the equally authentic step taken by the princes against the
people, although the people had carefully refrained from attacking the
princes. How modest and measured the first are! And how violent and
profoundly **unjust** the second!
   In vain will the Third Estate await restitution of its political rights and
the fullness of its civil rights from . . .
   [line 2098]

A text analysis program like Tact will allow the user to increase
or reduce the amount of text included in such a KWIC retrieval
at will, to suit the language and circumstances of analysis.
   In such a study of a chosen list of particular words, the historian
is in effect using the computer simply as a quick and reliable
index- and counting tool. However, a *collocation analysis* using a
span of three words on either side of the target word produces
more complex results, as shown in Figure 12.1.
   What has happened is that each occurrence of the target word
'unjust' has been located, all words occurring within three words
of the target have been turned into a *mini-context*, and all these
words listed individually. The table tells us that although for
example 'hateful' occurred only once close to 'unjust', it only
appeared twice in the text altogether. Had these two occurrences
of 'hateful' been distributed at random throughout the text, the
chances of one of them occurring so close to 'unjust' would have
been very small; the fact that it happens at all gives the 'hateful –
unjust' collocation a high *z-score*, meaning that it is highly unlikely
that these two words were used close together purely by accident.
Further down the list in Figure 12.1 are simpler function words
('was', 'and') with lower z-scores, which are not likely to be
relevant for historical purposes.

	COL. FREQ	TYPE FREQ	Z-SCORE
predominance	1	1	30.288
profoundly	1	1	30.288
violent	1	1	30.288
deprive	1	2	21.394
hateful	1	2	21.394
totally	1	2	21.394
unconstitutional	1	2	21.394
feel	1	5	13.487
opposed	1	7	11.374
nature	1	16	7.450
second	1	16	7.450
therefore	1	33	5.092
themselves	1	36	4.859
privileges	1	37	4.787
was	1	48	4.152
and	3	568	3.062
their	1	125	2.349

Figure 12.1   Collocations of 'unjust' (span: three words either side)

Pursuit of such clustering of words can reveal a great deal about the author. Given that Sieyes was trying to argue for a break with the privileged inequality of the past, he uses techniques of association which are clearly less than impartial. A collocation analysis on the word 'feudal' is given in Figure 12.2. This time, the analysis takes note of the fact that the target word is an adjective (the word it qualifies is likely to *follow* it): the span has been reduced to nil preceding, but increased to 4 after the target. Again, the lower z-scores include a number of ordinary function words of no great historical significance; but there can be little doubt that the very high z-scores at the top suggest that Sieyes tended to use the word 'feudal' very much as a generally pejorative descriptor – as a word useful for denouncing the 'barbarisms' and 'superstitions' of the past.

It will be apparent that, as with database applications, Tact has not done anything which the assiduous historian of language could not do with pencil and paper. However, even basic indexing

	COL. FREQ	TYPE FREQ	Z-SCORE
barbarism	2	3	32.354
debases	1	1	28.036
disappeared	1	1	28.036
oppress	1	1	28.036
tribunals	1	1	28.036
superstition	1	2	19.800
rural	1	3	16.146
add	1	6	11.374
servitude	1	6	11.374
philosopher	1	7	10.517
me	1	8	9.825
further	1	10	8.766
chamber	1	13	7.659
possible	1	14	7.371
free	1	22	5.820
like	1	24	5.558
still	1	26	5.326
let	1	32	4.764
just	1	36	4.468
power	1	36	4.468
was	1	48	3.808
when	1	50	3.721
has	1	96	2.520

Figure 12.2 Collocations of 'feudal' (span: four subsequent words only)

is extremely time-consuming if done by hand; and collocation analysis of a fairly short work like Sieyes's little book could well take years if done by hand. So while text-analysis software may not produce conclusive results on its own, it undoubtedly gives a great deal of help in the early stages of establishing what is important. Any one result is likely to produce new questions, which can be answered within seconds. Insignificant leads can be abandoned, but promising ones can be pursued, in preparation for more detailed work on context and undercurrents of meaning.

Text encoding and mark-up

All historical source-material has implicit and explicit structural features at several levels. In the case of Sieyes's *What is the Third Estate?*, as in most other books, there is an explicit structure in the form of chapters, sections, paragraphs (and of course sentences). There is also an implicit structure marked out by recurrent questions, which serve to bring out new developments in the argument. In some paragraphs particular words are picked out in italics, ensuring that the reader takes notice; whilst other parts of the argument are relegated to the author's own footnotes. A historian will use these more or less obvious markers – just like a literary or music analyst would do with their equivalents – as a guide to the overall structure of the argument itself. Equally, these markers, and the more implicit structures of the text, give an indication of how the author deliberately or instinctively intended his/her ideas to come through.

Much government-produced historical source material has a rather more obvious structure than that of a published book. Take for instance the entry in the Odense Workhouse admission protocol quoted at the end of the previous chapter (p. 164). The short heavily structured summary which was adopted there for database use clearly did less than justice to the source. Ideally, the historian would want to keep all the significant parts of the text in a form as flexible as if marking up a paper copy of the source with, say, coloured markers to distinguish the different separate bits of information in each entry (the date, the name of the person admitted, his/her age, the reasons for admission, and so on).

One way of doing this for a machine-readable version of the protocol would be to write the structural mark-up into the text in such a way that the markers are readily distinguished from the text itself. One could simply put the mark-up in a different font. But as noted in connection with word processing (above, p. 28), such a distinction would be lost during as ASCII transfer. It would therefore be more reliable to flag the mark-up codes by means of particular signs or strings reserved for that purpose. For maximum clarity, both the beginning and the end of a structural element could be indicated – just like the fields in a database copied into ASCII format will, whether the user sees it or not, in fact be marked off by field delimiters such as commas.

Suppose, for example, that we decide to indicate the beginning of each of the units of information (the structural features) by enclosing its label (in effect its field name) in pointed brackets; and similarly to mark the end of each item by means of the same label preceded by a forward slash, again within pointed brackets. Identifying the most obvious items of information, the unabbreviated entry (record) from the workhouse protocol might then look as follows (its subdivisions suitably laid out just for clarity):

<entry>
<date> 23 November 1752 </date>
<num> No.57 </num>
<name> Joen Biörn </name>
from <town> Kerteminde </town>,
<birthplace> born in the same place </birthplace>,
<age> upwards of 70 years old </age>,
   who <div1 = case> according to submitted examination and
    witnessed report
   <div2 = reason> has for many years lived restless and
    dissipated with drink, irreconcilable in his marriage,
    quarrelsome and brawling to all his neighbours, so that he
    latterly has behaved as if deranged, with everyone afraid
    of him, in case he in drunkenness should inflict a mis-
    fortune on someone; which indeed he finally did, when he
    attacked the town official in the middle of the street . . . </
    div2>
   </div1>
</entry>

<entry> [followed by a similarly marked-up transcription of
   the next record in the protocol, and so on]

If such mark-up was applied consistently throughout the source, it could be used as a kind of field structure for retrieval purposes – without changing the text of the original, and hence without any loss of semantic material. Each entry in the protocol could be made the object of analysis as if it were a record in a database: one could retrieve the age, sex and reasons for admission for each of the individuals recorded, just as we did in Chapter 11. In addition, however, because the original text of the protocol is now preserved complete and intact, it would also be possible to analyse the details of explanation given under 'reason for admission', and to study the actual kind of language used by the authorities in describing the people they admitted. In other words, the historian would be liberated from the rather brutal editorial decisions of the person compiling the database for Chapter 11.

If, at the beginning of the datafile, a header or Document Type Definition (DTD) were inserted, describing how the mark-up was designed, the file might become conformant with the international Standard Generalized Markup Language (SGML). That would allow analysis by different programs, and ASCII transfer would become fully reliable. If one were to revise the mark-up in accordance with the highly detailed guidelines of the Text Encoding Initiative (TEI), the datafile would meet an internationally recognised standard.[9] The editorial decisions of the original researcher would be clearly identifiable, and if necessary reversible; and the original text of the source could be reconstituted verbatim at will, say for publication.

Not all of this can readily be done at the moment. It will be obvious that a comprehensive mark-up of just one source (let alone different types of sources) is not only time-consuming (even with a dedicated application running pre-programmed routines); it is also historically very demanding. Agreement on standards across several disciplines (including linguists and historians from different cultures) is naturally not achieved overnight. There are also currently problems with suitable retrieval software. But when these difficulties are overcome, it will be possible to use sources like the Odense workhouse admission protocol far more effectively. A vast range of loosely structured source material – typical of the kind which historians use all the time, including judicial records, newspapers and manorial ledgers, to name a few – will become much more accessible to systematic analysis.[10]

The initial effort in adopting such a system may at present seem very considerable; but in the long run such costs could well be outweighed by the advantages of having machine-readable sources which are both faithful to the original and, being software-independent, accessible to whatever computer analysis the historian selects.

Computer-Assisted Learning and hypertext

Until software becomes available that can make full use of text-encoding schemes like those just discussed, historians are unlikely to have a fully satisfactory tool for computer analysis of text. Existing textual analysis packages fall short of this, in that (as we noted earlier) they may help establish some of the basic characteristics of word usage in a given source, but are not able to go very far either in helping to compare structural features or in analysing underlying meanings.

Traditional literary and historical methodologies, however, have given rise to some very different computer applications working at simpler levels. They often use selections of traditional historial source material, selected and prepared by an expert, and placed in a framework intended more for instruction than for original research.

Computer-Assisted Learning (*CAL*) programs, for example, come in a great variety of forms. All are intended to give the user wider scope for independent enquiry and wide-ranging searches than conventional printed material usually can give. CAL programs might take the form of historical simulations, where the user is encouraged to make decisions in a particular historical context using a variety of freely structured sources. A well regarded recent example is Carolyn Lougee's 'The Would-Be Gentleman', in which the user has to learn about wealth and status criteria in the age of Louis XIV, taking decisions on property deals, offices and marriage alliances in order to try to 'succeed' by the standards of the age.

There are many other ways in which historical material can be made easily accessible, involving varying degrees of factual and interpretative skills on the part of the user. Some – like the Great American History Machine, mapping US election and census data from 1840 onwards – are really highly edited information-banks which exploit current computing techniques very fully to present massive quantities of information in a graphic or spatial context.[11]

CAL systems are often designed to allow considerable flexibility in use. The integrated teaching packages developed by the HiDES Project at the University of Southampton, for example, are intended to prepare students for tutorials and seminars by giving them access to a wider range of sources than they would otherwise usually have. The backbone of each HiDES package is a varied set of textual and visual historical materials. The student is drawn constructively into a major debate by means of a set of questions. These are tackled using various software tools, and the resulting answers are processed partly by means of an expert query system (where the user has his/her historical analysis constructively compared against expert knowledge). A notepad application facilitates *pre-tutorial dialogue* with the tutor, to clarify basic points, and also allows the transfer of quotations to written reports and essays. The tutor, in turn, may design his/her own sets of material through the HiDES authoring facilities.[12] CAL packages require a substantial amount of preparation in order to work well, but they derive naturally from the kind of methods used in undergraduate history teaching, and are likely to become more widely used.

Hypertext applications, in contrast to CAL, have so far largely been used in literature and non-historical courses. In many ways, however, hypertext offers great potential for history students, and has a somewhat closer resemblance than CAL to the text analysis techniques discussed earlier in this chapter. Basically, a hypertext system (for example Guide, or one of the applications developed using Hypercard on the Mac) holds texts on *cards* such that patterned cross-references can be mapped out by the compiler with as much flexibility as resources allow (and in ways impossible in conventional print). The user follows these cross-references in any order by means of *buttons* on the screen – areas (for example a word or phrase of particular interest or complexity) to which the user can point and click in order to obtain a second level of information, a quotation from elsewhere, a set of notes, or whatever. Hypertext is like a complex set of interrelated footnotes, more flexible than anything which can be printed on paper.

Sieyes's *What is the Third Estate?*, in a hypertext version, would as its top 'layer' have the actual text. Certain words in that text ('estate', 'feudal', 'representation') would be encoded in such a way that the reader, by clicking the mouse on each word, would see a subsidiary window with a brief explanation of its meaning and usage. Further historical background material, illustrations, collocation tables, and other instructional aids might be offered in additional subsidiary layers, accessed on request by an appropriate selection. Although hypertext requires considerable amounts of memory, hardware developments over the last few years have greatly increased the viability of fairly complex developments in this direction.

Extended into non-textual information, such as images, sounds or video recordings, hypertext becomes hypermedia. Whilst very expensive to develop, and quite demanding in terms of current hardware and storage facilities, hypertext and hypermedia have obvious potential in bringing together different types of historical material at different levels of instruction and research.[13]

It is too early to predict what effect Hypermedia will have on historical work at different levels. At the very least it will make a wider range of source materials more readily available, and thereby enhance both teaching and research. The flexibility of hypermedia will also, once powerful computers become more widely available, pose a real challenge to authors and publishers, who might exploit the potential of what is already called the 'electronic book'.[14]

This chapter has looked at some areas where the historian is seeing, and will continue to see, important technical developments. Historians have always relied heavily on textual source materials of various kinds, but – in so far as they have tried at all – have had difficulty using standard software to analyse such sources for at least two major reasons. First of all, historical source material, typically, is inconsistent, incomplete, ambiguous and heavily conditioned by a great variety of contextual factors which are not easily recorded unambiguously for computer analysis. Secondly, historical interpretation often relies on detailed knowledge of implicit meanings, non-standard turns of phrase, shifts in the meaning of words, and other subjective factors which require more than formal logic and consistency for analysis. These problems, as we noted earlier in this volume, affect both relatively structured sources and free text – but have in practice caused more difficulties with the latter. There is no denying that there is a long way to go before computers will help the historian as much with loosely structured texts as with more structured datasets; but while recognising current limitations, the historian already has a good range of tools at his or her disposal.

Notes

1 Just as the word 'database' can be defined in several ways, no uncontroversial definition of 'textbase' exists. However, one might say that a textbase is the machine-readable free-form version of a text, rendered in such a way that it is not abbreviated or forced into the tabular limitations of a database manager.

2 Image scanning is fundamentally different from text scanning: during text scanning, the computer will recognise the letters on the page as standard alphanumeric characters (and translate them into ASCII or other code suitable for a word processor or other application), whilst in image scanning it will store what it scans as dots (which it can reconstitute much like photographs in newspapers – as a large number of small blobs of varying shape and size). Image scanning consumes far more memory than text scanning.

3 For a good survey of such literary and linguistic applications, see S. Hockey, *A Guide to Computer Applications in the Humanities*, London, 1980, esp. Chs. 3–4 and 6–7. For a recent specialised application, see S. Nenadic, 'Identifying social networks with a computer-aided analysis of personal diaries', in *History and Computing III*, ed. E. Mawdsley *et al.*, Manchester, 1990, pp. 188–94.

4 The z-score can be defined as a measurement of the frequency with which a word occurs as a collocate (that is, within a specified distance – or span – from the reference word) compared to the expected frequency of occurrence within such a span if its distribution throughout the text was totally random.

5 For a clearly presented case-study, see M. Olsen and L.-G. Harvey, 'Computers in intellectual history: lexical statistics and the analysis of political discourse', *Journal of Interdisciplinary History*, XVIII, 1988, pp. 449–64.

6 It is naturally best to analyse a text in its original language; but in order to make the most of the illustrative potential a translation is used here.

7 There is no space here to give full references for this central aspect of the early Revolution. For a general introduction, see W. Doyle, *The Oxford History of the French Revolution*, Oxford, 1989, pp. 86–122; and M. Forsyth, *Reason and Revolution: the Political Thought of the Abbé Sieyes*, Leicester, 1987.

8 Tact is a text-analysis package prepared at the University of Toronto and available to the academic community free of charge, provided it is used unaltered.

9 SGML was first developed in the early 1980s, and was formalised as a standard in 1986 (ISO 8879). Since then, it has become increasingly

widely used as a norm under which specific schemes for textual mark-up such as TEI are being worked out. See L. Burnard, 'What is SGML and how does it help?', in *Modelling Historical Data*, ed. D. Greenstein, Göttingen, 1991, pp. 65–79; and his 'An introduction to the Text Encoding Initiative', *ibid.*, pp. 81–91.

10 A number of examples are given in *Modelling Historical Data*, ed. D. Greenstein, Göttingen, 1991, pp. 111–223.

11 For a brief description of a wide range of major CAL programs of various kinds, see D. A. Spaeth, *A Guide to Software for Historians*, CTI Centre for History, Glasgow, 1991, pp. 7–48. See also D. W. Miller and J. Modell, 'Teaching United States history with the Great American History Machine', *Historical Methods*, XXI, 1988, pp. 121–34.

12 For a further development of the HiDES initiative with a wider range of historical material, see W. Hall and F. Colson, 'Multimedia teaching with Microcosm-HiDES: Viceroy Mountbatten and the partition of India', *History and Computing*, III, 1991, pp. 89–98.

13 For a useful discussion of hypertext and the Macintosh Hypercard application, see G. Russell, 'Hypertext', and D. Gilbert, 'Hypercard: new ways of writing, new ways of reading', *History and Computing*, III, 1991, pp. 183–5; *ibid.*, pp. 186–94.

14 For a short survey of this topic, see *Byte*, XVII, June 1992, pp. 263–8. A fuller discussion is found in F. Mastroddi, ed., *Electronic Publishing: the New Way to Communicate*, Brussels, 1987.

Conclusion

The computer has become a tool from which every historian can benefit. The 'micro' is cheap enough to be affordable, it is small enough to use in a study or library, and – most important – it is easy to use. It can carry out some tasks that otherwise would be impossible, but more important it can do everyday tasks more easily and efficiently. We have tried to show that, unlike many other tools used by historians, from card files to microfilm readers, the computer is designed not for a single task: it is a truly multi-purpose machine able to carry out a wide variety of complex operations quickly and accurately. Many historians are likely to start by using the computer for one such everyday task – as a word processor; it is our hope that this book will have been of help to those who want to go further and exploit the wider potential offered by modern computers and their software.

The technology is no longer a challenge to the non-technical historian. Since the mid-1980s there has been an extraordinary parallel development in which desktop computers and their software have become both much more powerful and much more easy to use. Admittedly the initial set-up of a computer system has pitfalls, and manuals often leave something to be desired. But once the system is running, additional software is usually easy to load and use; on-line help and tutorial systems will then often solve remaining difficulties.

Leaving aside the presentation of findings through word processing, it is the storage and analysis of sources which is central to 'historical computing'. Historians apply a very wide variety of techniques to their bulky and varied raw material. Whether as local historians, genealogists, industrial archaeologists, students or teachers, they are likely to encounter both primary and secondary sources which present challenges of analysis and interpretation. The computer will seldom be able to help make fundamental decisions about the strengths and deficiencies of actual source material; but given sound instructions, it will make it much easier to handle the data to best effect, test alternative interpretations, and carry out checks and analytic procedures with far greater speed and accuracy than would be possible by hand.

A central theme in this book has been the delicate relationship between the 'raw' source and the way the historian converts it into something that a computer can use. Any kind of transcription, into notes, file cards, or a computer database, is bound to involve some editorial intrusion, some decisions about what is significant and what is not. Formerly, historians did not as a matter of course make their own notes available for scrutiny by others. Unlike handwritten notes, however, computerised data can in theory be of use to others either for secondary analysis or simply as a source edition for a different project.

We would not wish to labour the case for more data exchange: such exchange can work, but using another researcher's data is not always satisfactory in a discipline where the problems of interpretation of the raw source material are so complex. Nevertheless, some fundamental points can be made.

First of all, anyone creating a machine-readable data source should document carefully each step taken: what sources are used for particular items of information, what decisions have been taken regarding alternative readings and interpretations, what categories of information have been summarised or coded rather than transcribed *verbatim*, and what information has been left out. This will not only be indispensable for anyone else trying to assess the data and the conclusions drawn from it, but may well also become crucial for the originator him/herself. Modern computing technology being what it is, substantial transformations and sorting of data are so easy that even the originator may well loose track, especially if the project runs for any length of time. The great value of the computer is that it gives the opportunity for factual accuracy and quantitative or qualitative underpinning of conclusions: but such gains can easily be lost in scores of variant codified datafiles and selective retrievals.

Secondly, although software is now versatile and powerful the historian should think carefully in advance about how the data will be processed. It is vitally important to test the analysis on a small 'pilot' set of data before undertaking full-scale data entry. And it is essential, whatever combination of hardware and software is used, that the data be portable, i.e. that it can be moved to other software. If a project was started on an older machine, and the limitations either of the hardware or the software become clear, all data can usually be moved to a better environment. It is worth making sure, before starting any project, that the data will not be locked into a format from which it is not easily extricated.

Recent developments, especially in computer software, mean that the historian now has a genuine and convincing choice. Not all of the historian's needs are fully or inexpensively met. This was discussed in connection with text analysis, and the same could be said about mapping software; but it is likely that even this will change in the next few years.

This book has outlined some of the basic types of software that are most likely to be of relevance to historians; but we have also been at pains to stress that it is often possible, with a little ingenuity, to get more out of a particular application than may at first be obvious. Carefully designed coding schemes can do more than just classify the information into categories: they can actually be used to extract information which (like the household structure code in Chapter 6) is not explicit in the source. Similarly, while some historians may feel less than fully confident about how to handle quantitative data, both statistical routines (Chapter 7) and simple tabulations and graphics (Chapters 9–10) can add a clarity and precision not otherwise attainable. Even text, as we noted at the end of Chapter 11 and in Chapter 12, may lend itself to computer analysis to a greater degree than would have seemed possible a few years ago. The computer should never be regarded as more than a very pliant tool: but it will remove much of the drudgery from the analysis of historical sources.

In the end, however, the attraction of using the computer as an historical tool is not just one of convenience. Most historians who have used a computer for some time will admit that it adds a distinctive dimension to their work. This distinctiveness can perhaps best be summed up by saying that, because of the accuracy and rigorous logic of the machine itself, historians using a computer are often forced to become more aware of the nature and implications of their source material. Whilst at times this can be frustrating, at other times it can be little short of exhilarating. The computer is no guarantee of constant historical exhilaration, but its versatility and speed allow historians at all levels and in all branches of the discipline much easier and more reliable access to the past than was practicable even just a few years ago.

Appendix I

The Gorbals census dataset

This appendix contains the census records for 1851 for 100 people from the Gorbals district of Glasgow.

Although these records can simply be inspected as a small example of a source suitable for computer analysis, it is recommended in Chapter 4 that at least a 'paper' database structure be created for them. If possible some or all of the records should be keyed into a computer; the data is used with examples in Chapters 5, 6, and 7.

In 1851 the Gorbals was a poor district on the south side of the River Clyde; the district would gain notoriety 75 years later as one of the worst slums in Europe. The 100 inhabitants listed beyond were recorded as having been present on the night of 30 March 1851, living in houses on the north side of Malta Street, from Portugal Street to Main Street. No claim is made that this group of 100 people is typical of the Victorian working class or the city of Glasgow. They may well not even be typical of the 59,408 inhabitants of Gorbals Parish or of the rest of Malta Street; this is not a 'sample' in a statistical sense. It may, however, be valuable in giving a sense of the texture of life in 1851.

The data is a reproduction of the first five pages of an Enumeration Book for Enumeration District No. 22, Parish of Gorbals, Parliamentary Burgh of Glasgow, County of Lanarkshire, Scotland (CEN.RET. 644/2). The original Enumeration Book is held by the Registrar General for Scotland, New Register House, Edinburgh, EH1 3YT; microfilm copies are available elsewhere. The data is reproduced with various anomalies that might be found in any manuscript original. A facsimile of the first 20 records is also reproduced in Figure 4.1, with the permission of the Controller of HMSO.

In assembling this data the authors benefited greatly from the work carried by Alison Gray at Strathclyde Regional Archives. The current appendix is based on computerised data provided by one of her projects; it has been altered back to nearer its original state and elements of coding removed.

Fuller general details are given in Chapter 4; for background information see especially Edward Higgs, *Making Sense of the Census* (1989).

Enumeration Book / Page 1

No	Street, No. of House	Name and Surname		Relation to Head	Condition
1	Malta Street, No 35	Grace Young	Piggie	Head	Widow
		Robert	Piggie	Son	U
		William	Piggie	Son	U
		Janet	Piggie	Daur	U
		Jean	Piggie	Daur	U
		Alex[r]	Piggie	Son	
2	Malta Street, No 35	William	Ross	Head	Mar
		Janet	Ross	Wife	Mar
3	Malta Street, No 33	Andrew	Wallace	Head	Mar
		Margaret	Do	Wife	Mar
		Andrew	Do	Son	U
		Marion	Do	Daur	
		John	Do	Son	
		James	Do	Son	
		William	Do	Son	
		Mary	Do	Daur	
4	Malta Street, No 33	Robert	Graham	Head	Mar
		Susanna	Do	Wife	Mar
		Henrietta	Do	Daur	U
		Jean	Do	Daur	U

Enumeration Book / Page 2

No	Street, No. of House	Name and Surname		Relation to Head	Condition
	Malta Street, No 33	Susanna	Graham	Daur	U
		James	Graham	Son	
5	Malta Street, No 29	John	Hussey	Head	Wid[r]
		John	Do	Son	Mar
		Janet	Do	Son's Wife	Mar
		John	Do	Grand Son	
		Mary	Do	Grand Daur	
		James	Do	Grand Son	
		Robert	Do	Nephew	U
6		Margaret	Speirs	Head	U
		Ann	Do	Sister	U
		Robert	Do	Brother	U
		Finlay	McQueston	Lodger	U
7		John	Wright	Head	Mar
		Janet	Do	Wife	Mar
		Mary	Do	Daur	
		Margaret	Do	Daur	
8		James	Wilson	Head	Mar
		Catherine	Do	Wife	Mar
		Elizabeth	Do	Daur	U

Male	Female	Rank, Profession or Occupation	Where Born	
	36	Housekeeper	Fifeshire. Dunfermline	
20		Light Porter, Muslin Warehouse	Kinrossshire. Kinross	
17		Carriers Porter	Do	Do
	15	House Servant	Do	Do
	10	Scholar at Home	Do	Do
5			Do	Do
60		Gardener	Edinburgh. Westchurch	
	50	Wife of Do	Stirlingshire. Larbert	
40		Rope Spinner	Lanark. Glasgow	
	39	Wife of Do	Do	Do
13		Errand Boy	Ayrshire. Kilmarnock	
	11	Scholar at Home	Do	Do
9		Wheel Boy to Rope Spinner	Do	Do
6			Do	Do
3			Do	Do
	4 mos		Lanark. Glasgow	
47		Confectioner	Renfrew. Greenock	
	47	Wife of Do	Lanark. Glasgow	
	16	Flower Maker	Do	Do
	16	Do Do	Do	Do
	13	Flower Maker	Lanark. Glasgow	
7		Scholar	Lanark. Glasgow	
67		Tailor	Middlesex. Edmanton	
32		Tailor	Lanark. Glasgow	
	32	Wife of Do	Do	Do
5			Do	Do
	3		Do	Do
10 mos			Do	Do
16		Glazier	Do	Do
	34	House Keeper	Do	Do
	29	Steam Loom Weaver	Do	Do
22		Blacksmith	Do	Do
18		Confectioner	Renfrew. Greenock	
30		Dyer	Lanark. Glasgow	
	29	Wife of Do	Do	Do
	5	Scholar	Do	Do
	2		Do	Do
40		Lamplighter	Do	Do
	40	Wife of Do	Do	Do
	15	Power Loom Weaver	Do	Do

Enumeration Book / Page 3

Malta Street, No 29	Alexander	Wilson	Son	U
	James	Do	Son	
	Archibald	Do	Son	
	David	Do	Son	
	Donald	Do	Son	
9	John	Scott	Head	Mar
	Margaret	Do	Wife	Mar
10	John	Crosbie	Head	Mar
	Euphemia	Do	Wife	Mar
	Elizabeth	Do	Daur	
	Mary	Do	Daur	
	Agnes	Do	Daur	
11	John	McGhie	Head	Mar
	Ann	Do	Wife	Mar
	Ann Jane	Do	Daur	
	James	Do	Son	
	Matthew	Do	Son	
	Ellen	Do	Daur	
	Edward	Kinlock	Lodger	Mar
	Catherine	Do	Lodger	Mar

Enumeration Book / Page 4

12	Malta Street, No 27½	Ann Fimester	Head	Widow
	Alex^r Do	Son	Mar	
	Maria Do	Daur		
	Ann Do	Daur	Widow	
	John Duncan	Son in Law	Mar	
	Amelia Do	Daur	Mar	
	Adam Do	Grandson		
	James Do	Do		
	John Ross	Lodger	Mar	
	Janet Do	Lodger Wife	Mar	
	Alexander	Do	Lodger Son	
13	Malta Street, No 27	James Summers	Head	Mar
	Margaret	Summers	Wife	Mar
	Elizabeth	Taylor	Servant	U
14	Malta Street, No 25	Henry Murray	Head	Mar
	Jane Do	Wife	Mar	
	Jane Do	Daur		
	Catherine	Do	Daur	
15	Joseph Gibb	Head	Mar	
	Mary	Do	Wife	Mar

		Occupation	Birthplace	
13		Errand Boy	Lanark. Glasgow	
8		Scholar	Do	Do
5		Scholar	Do	Do
3			Do	Do
5 Mos			Do	Do
29		Silversmith	Perthshire. Redgorton	
	30	Wife of Do	Lanark. Glasgow	
39		Blacksmith	Do	Do
	39	Wife of Do	Do	Do
	9	Scholar	Do	Do
	3		Do	Do
	7 Mos		Do	Do
42		Gardener	Ireland	
	34	Wife of Do	Ireland	
	8	Scholar	Lanark. Glasgow	
6		Scholar	Do	Do
4			Do	Do
	2		Do	Do
39		Gravedigger	Renfrew. Strabungo	
	26	Wife of Do	Ireland	
	67	Eating House Keeper	England	
27		Glazier	Ireland	
	25	Cotton Mill Worker	Ireland	
	30	Hawker of Hardware	England	
27		Boiler Maker	Forfarshire. Dundee	
	24	Wife of Do	Lanark. Glasgow	
2			Do	Do
1			Do	Do
22		Boiler Maker	Forfarshire. Dundee	
	27	Wife To Boiler Maker	Edinburgh. Leith	
2			Edinburgh. Leith	
34		Spirit Dealer	Stirlingshire. Stirling	
	38	Wife of Do	Lanark. Glasgow	
	18	House Servant	Linlithgow. Linlithgow	
39		Hatter	Midlothian. Edinburgh	
	37	Wife of Do	Renfrewshire. Greenock	
	9	Scholar	Lanark. Glasgow	
	1		Do	Do
24		Shoemaker	Lanark	Glasgow
	22	Wife of Do	Ayrshire. Girvan	

Enumeration Book / Page 5

Malta Street, No 25	Isabella	Gibb	Daur	
	John	Gibb	Brother	U
16	Isabella	Melville	Head	Widow
	John	Do	Son	U
	Janet	Do	Daur	
	Agnes	Do	Daur	
	Thomas	Do	Son	
	William	Do	Son	
17	Thomas	Fergus	Head	Mar
	Mary	Do	Wife	Mar
	Janet	Do	Daur	
	Neil M	Do	Son	
	Alexander S P	Do	Son	
	John	Mathieson	Nephew	
18	Peter	Heron	Head	Mar
	Bridget	Do	Wife	Mar
	Mary	Do	Daur	
	Peter	Do	Son	
19	William	Prentice	Head	Mar
	Elizabeth	Do	Wife	Mar

		Occupation	Birthplace	
	5 Mos		Lanark. Glasgow	
28		Shoemaker	Do	Do
	37	Lodging House Keeper	Ayrshire. Dalrymple	
11		Errand Boy	Stirling. Campsie	
	9	Scholar at Home	Lanark. Glasgow	
	7	Do	Do	Do
4			Do	Do
2			Do	Do
31		Blacksmith	Clackmannan. Alloa	
	30	Blacksmith's Wife	Lanark. Glasgow	
	6	Scholar	Stirlingshire. Stirling	
3			Lanark. Glasgow	
11 Mos			Do	Do
11		Scholar	Do	Do
55		Night Watchman	Ireland	
	50	Wife of Do	Ireland	
	24	Cloth Weaver	Ireland	
25		Baker	Guernsey (British Subject)	
30		Labourer in a Coal Yard	Lanark. Hamilton	
	26	Lace Worker	Do	Hamilton

Appendix II

CD-ROM and on-line historical bibliographies

This book has been about how historians can best make use of computers today. The stress in the main text has been on historical databases; since word processing is the aspect which actually involves most historians it also has been given some attention. There is a third area of relevance to historians which has not been directly treated in the main text but which, as a tool of growing importance, certainly deserves mention: the computerised bibliography. This is also an intcresting area because it involves technologies that will become increasingly important to historians in the near future.

Libraries have over the past decade been installing computer-based catalogues, in effect databases of books. Aside from allowing the user to check whether the library has a particular volume, such catalogues make it possible to conduct searches by general subject area. The procedures used are similar to those mentioned in Chapter 12 for searching textbases. It is possible to produce paper copies of the results of searches and, with permission and the right software, to 'capture' citations electronically on to a PC, where they could, for example, be edited electronically and incorporated into a bibliography. It is increasingly easy to obtain remote access to the electronic catalogues of other libraries. This can speed interlibrary loan requests, or indicate whether a trip to a nearby library is worthwhile.

Other valuable bibliographical information is available through *CD-ROM* (Compact Disc Read Only Memory) or *on-line* via a remote Mainframe computer (a *remote host*); many important bibliographies are available on both. Usually this material is also available in – paper – book form, but the electronic versions will in the long term be easier to use and probably more up to date. Searches by subject area are extremely useful, and abstracts of books and articles are frequently provided.

Most large libraries will now have available to readers desktop computers with an attached CD-ROM drive. These computers, or similar machines functioning as terminals, will allow access to on-line sources. Reference CD-ROMs, which are regularly updated, are still quite expensive and only the largest libraries can keep more than the most important items. Use of a commercial service like Dialog on a remote host will allow access to almost any material, but involves expensive telephone time, often expensive *international* telephone time. The assistance of a specialist librarian may well be required for the use of on-line services; it is essential to think through the questions (searches) in advance. A useful British service available to subscribing institutions and making available the key *Social Science Citation Index* and *Arts and Humanities Citation Index* is the ISI Data Service at Bath (BIDS).

Because new information and sources are appearing all the time it will be valuable to consult a reference librarian. In the meantime, two useful lists of available resources are:

The CD-ROM Directory, London, 1991.
The Online Database Directory, London, 1991.

Recent books

Books in Print Plus. (CD-ROM/On-line) (Bowker Electronic Publishing). Books in print in the United States.
Whitaker's Bookbank (British Books in Print). (CD-ROM/On-line) (Whitaker's). Books in print in the United Kingdom.

Recent articles in history

America: History and Life. (CD-ROM/On-line) (ABC-CLIO). Articles on American History.
Arts and Humanities Citation Index (Arts and Humanities Search). (On-line) (Institute for Scientific Information). General humanities periodical articles, including history.
Historical Abstracts. (CD-ROM/On-line) (ABC-CLIO). Periodical articles on post-1450 history other than American history.

Humanities Index. (CD-ROM/On-line) (H. W. Wilson). General arts and humanities periodical articles.

Serials Directory. (CD-ROM) (EBSCO). Lists of current serials world-wide.

Social Science Citation Index (Social Science Search). (CD-ROM/On-line) (Institute for Scientific Information). Articles in social science periodicals.

Social Sciences Index. (CD-ROM/On-line) (H. W. Wilson). Articles in social science periodicals.

Recent articles from related disciplines

Philosophers Index. (On-line) (Bowling Green State University). Articles on philosophy, with much of interest to historians.

Religion Index. (On-line) (American Theological Library). Articles on religion and the history of religion.

MLA International Bibliography. (CD-ROM/On-line) (H. W. Wilson/Modern Language Association). Articles relating to foreign language and literature; many are historical.

Recent theses

ASLIB Index to Theses. (CD-ROM) (Association for Information Management). British higher-degree theses.

Dissertation Abstracts. (CD-ROM/On-line) (University Microfilms). American and Canadian theses.

Glossary

One notable feature of historical computing is the extent of the technical vocabulary – some might say 'jargon'. The field combines the language of computers with that of the social sciences, statistics and even printing. Much of this is necessary, some is not. The most well-intentioned historian eventually falls into the trap of referring to programs as 'products' and teaching materials as 'courseware'. Leaving aside all aesthetic judgements, however, it is at least useful to know what the jargon is supposed to mean when reading technical articles and books; this glossary is intended to help do that. No claims are made for completeness or for total technical correctness; the computing side – focused on microcomputer terminology – will certainly date quickly. The glossary is, however, based on hard-earned experience and designed specifically to meet the needs of those involved in historical computing.

Terms italicised in the explanatory text are cross-references to other entries.

adaptor   Video adaptor. A circuit in a computer, usually an *expansion card*, which connects it to the *monitor*. There are various levels, e.g. CGA, EGA, VGA, SVGA.

aggregate data   Information about a group, e.g. of individuals.

AHC   The Association for History and Computing. The major interest group in the UK and mainland Europe.

algorithm   A series of instructions to a computer used to solve a specific problem. Similar to a *program*.

alphanumeric   Data which takes the form of letters and numbers.

append   To add *records* to a *database*, usually with the same structure (see *join*). Also, to put two similarly-structured *files* together.

application, applications package   The purpose to which a computer tool is supposed to be put. This now normally means the particular *program* to be used. 'Various applications can be run on this machine at the same time'; 'data can be transferred from one application to another'. However, history in general may be seen as an application.

application language See *language*.

archive Something historians should be working in rather than messing around with computers. Also, as a verb, to make a safe copy of data.

artificial intelligence AI. An advanced form of *software* which can learn how to solve problems.

ASCII American Standard Code for Information Interchange. A standard character set used by most computers; useful in transferring data from one *program* to another.

attribute In a database, same as *field*.

back up To create copies of data and programs on other *floppy disks*, *hard disks* or on tape.

bar chart A common kind of graphic used with nominal-scale data, for example to show how many records there are in each category. See also *histogram*.

BASIC A relatively simple programming *language*.

batch file A *file* giving a set of instructions to the computer.

batch mode An overall method in which a group of commands are given together to a computer, which then executes them and produces a result in its own time. This is the way that computers operated in the past, and it is still used for large jobs on mainframe computers. Batch mode is the opposite of *interactive mode*.

baud rate Used as a measure of speed in communications; usually the number of *bits* per second that can be transferred. Named after French inventor J. M. E. Baudot (1845–1903).

bit *Bi*nary digi*t*, 1 or 0. A modern 16-bit *CPU* can transfer 16 bits of information to or from *memory* at one time. The first generation of *microcomputers* had 8-bit *chips*, but 32-bit chips are now common.

bit mapping In *graphics*, making each *pixel* on the screen correspond to one or more *bits* of information.

bitnet A major American academic network for *electronic mail*.

board See *card*.

boolean searching At its simplest, the use in a *database* or a library *on-line* catalogue, of terms 'and', 'or', 'not', etc. (select/from TABLE/ where NAME = 'SMITH' *or* 'JONES'). A combination of algebra and logic. Named after mathematician George Boole (1815–64). A common use would be in library on-line searches, where Boolean algebra is used to narrow the results of searches to find just the titles/topics required.

boot To load *operating system* into memory, i.e. one of the first steps in a computing session.

bubble jet printer See *ink jet printer*.

buffer A temporary storage area for electronic data. A typical use is where data is transferred faster than the *printer* can print; the data has to be held in the buffer until the printer is ready for it.

bug An error in a *program*.

bulletin board *Electronic mail* clearing house. Bulletin boards exist for many special interests.

bus A channel of electronic communications, e.g. within a computer.

button An area of the screen which can be selected with a *mouse* to cause an action. Also, the buttons on the mouse which execute commands.

byte A unit of memory or storage capacity, normally the equivalent of one *character*.

cad Computer-Aided Design.

cal Computer-Assisted Learning. *Software* for teaching, often using question and answer techniques. Comparable to a short-answer quiz, and expensive to set up.

card A printed circuit *board*, typically one that fits into slots within the computer.

case The basic unit of analysis in a *database*. Something about which data is collected. Same as *record*.

case-sensitive A program is said to be case-sensitive if it does not regard upper- and lower-case letters as indistinguishable.

categorical variables Another name for *nominal-scale data variables*, or for *variables* that relate to either *nominal-scale data* or *ordinal-scale data*.

CD-ROM *Compact Disk Read Only Memory*. Storage device of large capacity from which data, images, etc can be *read*; similar to hi-fi compact disc.

cell One box on a *spreadsheet*, the intersection between a *row* and a *column*.

cell address In a *spreadsheet*, the location of a particular block of information: thus the information on the third line of the second column is said to be at cell address B3.

CGA See *adaptor*, *monitor*.

character A single number, letter, punctuation mark or other symbol.

chartjunk Over-complex flashy *graphics* created for their own sake and generally meaningless.

CHEST Combined Higher Education Software Team. An organisation devoted to negotiating and publicising discount *software* prices for higher education.

chi-squared test χ^2, χ being the Greek letter *chi*, pronounced 'kye'. A statistical test used with a *contingency table* to test whether two *variables* are independent of one another. It provides a way of checking whether the difference between the observed and expected numbers (in a contingency table) is greater than could reasonably be due to chance alone.

chip See *CPU*.

clean To correct (edit) mistakes in a *database*, etc. Cleaning a database includes checking for possible errors, inconsistencies and missing data, and making corrections and deletions.

cliometrics An approach to history which uses quantitative methods and a model-building approach from the social sciences (sociology, politics, economics). Major applications are in economic history, demography, urban history, parliamentary and electoral history. From Clio, the muse of history.

clock speed The speed of the *CPU* measured in *MHz*.

clone A copy, usually of *hardware*.

cluster 'Friendly' name for a group of computers, in a computing lab, e.g. the 'arts faculty cluster'. Often a cluster will be linked together via a *local area network* (*LAN*).

code To assign a number or abbreviation to a particular piece of information in a standardised way. Words are often coded as numbers ('male' = '1', 'female' = '2'), and coding sometimes involves *aggregating* the data at the *data entry* stage (e.g. 15 variants of related jobs might be coded as '316').

Coding was more important when many programs could only handle numbers, data was limited by the 80 character IBM *punched card*, and file storage space was at a premium; *codebooks* and data sheets were then a standard part of the researcher's tools. Coding can mean loss of information, and many historians now prefer *post-coding*.

codebook A systematic list of variables and coding instructions. See *code*.

collapse Like 'to *aggregate*'; an example would be if there were 65 different professions in a *dataset* and they were collapsed into 18 categories.

collocation In *text analysis*, the location of one word in proximity to a another chosen *keyword*.

column Vertical division of data; sometimes the same as *field* or *variable*.

command driven Software which the user operates by typing in a command. The opposite of *menu driven*.

compatibility Ability of two computers to run the same *software*.

concordance List of all or selected words in a text, with their location and context; useful for the analysis of the text. Also, the *program* that creates such a list.

confidence level In sampling, the percentage of instances where a given *sampling error* applies. A confidence level of .99 means that 99 samples out of 100 will meet this level of sampling error.

configuration The structure and composition of a computer system, affecting its power and speed.

content analysis The systematic analysis of the form and substance of texts.

context sensitive See *help*.

contingency table A *crosstabulation*.

continuous-scale variable A term for *interval-scale data* or *ratio-scale data*; this might be thought of simply as numerical data.

coprocessor A *processor* run with the main processor (*CPU*) to accelerate specific functions. A maths coprocessor does this with certain mathematical calculations.

co-residential unit (CRU) A term used by social historians for a group of people living together; sometimes used as a synonym for 'household', but to be distinguished from 'family'.

correlation coefficient A number (index) showing how closely related two *interval-scale* values (e.g. age and income) are. Designated as 'r', it ranges from +1 to −1, with results close to +1 and −1 indicating a high correlation (direct or inverse, depending on the sign). Also called *Pearson's r* – after British statistician Karl Pearson (1857–1936). A high correlation coefficient should correspond to a *scattergram* where all points are grouped close to a line.

courseware Nasty jargon word for *software* designed specifically for teaching.

CPS Characters per second, a measure of the speed of a *printer*. A typical *dot matrix printer* might have a speed of 120 cps.

CPU Central Processing Unit. The silicon *chip* at the heart of a microcomputer. See *processor*.

crash Unexpected stop of computing operations owing to an unforeseen fault.

crosstabulation, crosstab A table showing the relationship between two *fields* (*variables*); widely used with two *nominal-scale* variables. See *contingency table*.

CTICH Computers in Teaching Initiative Centre for History. A nationally-funded centre based at Glasgow University and intended to promote the use of computers in history teaching. The Computers in Teaching Initiative (*CTI*) provides general support for such teaching in various disciplines across higher education.

cursor Symbol (often flashing) on *monitor* screen which tells where the next operation will take place. In a *word-processing program* the cursor will indicate where the next character will appear.

daisy-wheel printer Essentially a keyless electric typewriter. Capable of producing better quality print than a *dot matrix printer* but less flexible, and generally being replaced by it and the *laser printer*.

data   Narrowly defined information that is being processed by a *program* in a computer.

data bank   Generally the same as a *database*.

database   The common meaning is a collection of (historical) information held in *machine-readable* form. Strictly speaking, a database is a name for a collection of *files*, but it may now mean only one file. A database is composed of *records*, each record has the same *fields (variables)*, and the fields (variables) have particular *values*.

    The term 'database' is also a common name for a database management system (*DBMS*), i.e. the *software* to manipulate a database.

database management system   DBMS. A *program* designed to organise and give access to a *database*. Sometimes the *program* itself is simply called a 'database'.

data capture   Jargon for getting information from (usually) paper sources and storing it in a computer. See *transcribe*.

data entry   Putting historical information into a computer, usually from a *keyboard*.

data file   Can be the same as a database, or part of a database. Like a *file*, a data file is a unit of storage.

dataset   Similar to *database*.

dbms   *Database management system*.

dedicated   Designed for a specific task, e.g. a computer might be a 'dedicated *word processor*'.

default   What the computer thinks unless it is told to think something different. The default *drive* is the one to which the computer will send data unless another drive is specified. A default can normally be selected by just pressing the *enter* key, i.e. by making no special selection; this is often a means of saving time.

demography   The study of population change over time.

density   See *floppy*.

dependent variable   DV. A *variable* whose value is influenced by a change in another variable (the *independent variable*). See *regression*.

descriptive statistics   Statistics devoted to decribing or displaying data. Compare with *inductive statistics*.

desktop publishing   *DTP*. Producing publishable text and graphics using a computer. DTP *software* goes beyond *word-processing* software in that it includes more powerful tools for page layout, etc.

digital   Information represented in numbers; in the binary system used in computers, these numbers are 1 or 0.

directory   Group of *files*, usually defined by the user. The object is clear organisation; all files relating to project RUSSIA might be put in a directory called 'RUSSIA'. Directories can contain sub-directories ('RUSSIA1', 'RUSSIA2' containing different aspects of RUSSIA), indeed, there may be a whole structure of sub-directories and 'sub-sub-directories' like the branches of a tree.

disk Magnetic disk used to store information; same as *floppy disk*. Also, more loosely, other media used to store *files*. See *hard disk*.

disk drive Slot in the computer which holds *floppy disk*.

diskette Same as *floppy disk*.

documentation Manuals for *software* and *hardware*, explanatory text for *databases*, etc. Generally opaque and poorly indexed.

DOS Disk Operating System. A standard *operating system* used with IBM-type personal computers; the most common type is MS-DOS, from the American *software* firm Microsoft.

dot matrix printer Common type of *printer*, which prints words and *graphics* as a group of dots; two standard types are 9 pin and 24 pin.

download To transfer data from a large computer (e.g. a *mainframe*) to a smaller one (e.g. a *microcomputer*).

draft mode A *dot matrix printer* printing in its fastest mode; the minimum number of dots are used to make up the letters; the dots are more obvious than if the printer were working in the slower *NLQ* mode.

drive See *disk drive*.

DTP See *desktop publishing*.

EARN European Academic Research Network. Major (continental) European academic network for *electronic mail* and *file transfer*.

ecological data Attributes of geographical units (e.g. number of farmers in a county); not the same as data about individuals.

ecological fallacy In statistics the drawing of misleading conclusions about individuals from data about their community. A high correlation between the percentage of Catholics and the percentage of Democratic voters in the voting districts of a US county does not necessarily mean that Catholics voted Democratic.

econometrics The use of mathematical and statistical methods in the study of economics (and economic history), which has wide application to advanced computing methods. Creation and testing of economic models is a standard part of econometrics. The term was coined by the Norwegian economist Ragnar Frisch (1895–1973).

edit Changing (usually correcting) the content or structure of information stored in a computer. In word processing it means, specifically, to enter or change text.

editor Program for editing text in *files* (including programs). A word-processing *program* is a special kind of editor.

editorial field A *field* added to the records of a database in the process of editing it; i.e. data that was not present in the original paper data.

EGA See *adaptor*, *monitor*.

electronic mail A system for sending messages from one computer to another.

e-mail See *electronic mail*.

emulator A *program* which lets programs intended for one computer system be run on another. One use would be to allow *microcomputers* to act like *mainframe terminals*.

entry-level Elementary or introductory.

environment What we should all take more care of. One computing meaning is the general system within which a computer is being operated, e.g. a *Windows* environment.

eprom (Erasable Programmable *Read Only Memory*) *ROM* which can be written to (and changed) by the user. Used in some portable computers.

ESRC Economic and Social Research Council, whose Data Archive, based at Essex University, is a major source of *machine-readable* historical data.

ethernet Set of standards for *LAN* communications, defined by *ISO* 8802/3.

expanded memory *Memory* above the normal 640K limit of a *PC* or *clone*. Technically different from *extended memory*.

expansion card A *card* fitted inside a computer, to increase *memory* and add functions.

expert system Advanced *software* that uses *artificial intelligence* to solve specialised problems. It stores rules and formulates new rules from data.

extended memory *Memory* above and normal 640K limit of a *PC* or *clone*. Technically different from *expanded memory*.

family reconstitution Systematic study of parish and census records to identify and link all members of a set of families over a period of time.

field Pieces of information which are the same for each and every *record* in the *data file* or *table*. In a census *database*, for example, each person in the census district might count as a record; each person's record might have fields for 'name', 'age', and 'place of birth'. The same as *variable*.

fieldname Name given to a *field*.

file A unit of storage. Some files contain data, others text. *Programs* are also stored as files.

filename The name of a particular computer *file*, often assigned by the user. Many systems limit filename length to eight characters. Different kinds of files may automatically have a particular suffix (ending). A text file from a word processor might be called 'ESSAY1', to which the *program* might assign the suffix.DOC, to make the filename 'ESSAY1.DOC'.

file transfer The copying of data from one computer to another using agreed standards of exchange.

firmware *Programs*, usually connected with the general operation of the computer, which are held in its *ROM*.

flat file A relatively simple *data file* consisting of only one type of *record*, each with the same set of *fields*; a synonym might be *table* in which the *rows* are the records and *columns* are the fields; also called a rectangular file. A *relational database* might be thought of as several flat files (rectangular tables) which have a common field and can be *joined* by that common field.

floppy, floppy disk A flexible *disk*, stored in a (hard) protective packet. The main sizes are 3.5 in. and 5.25 in. See *format*.

Floppies come in various densities, and those with the most capacity may not be readable by older computers. The 5.25 in. disks are able to store 360*KB*, 720*KB*, or 1.2*MB* of data. For 3.5 in. disks. 'double density' is 720*KB* and 'high density' is 1.4*MB*.

font A particular size and style of typeface, e.g. 12*pt* (size) Times (typeface) Roman (style). *Font* is sometimes loosely used as a synonym for typeface.

format As a verb, to arrange the tracks and sectors of a *floppy disk* so that it can be used with a particular kind of computer. Newly-purchased floppy disks usually need to be formatted, which is done by placing them in the *disk drive* and typing in the required command. Hard disks also need to be formatted. If serious faults occur, both floppy and hard disks can be re-formatted, but all data stored on them will be lost in the process.

fortran See *language*.

4GL *Fourth generation language*.

fourth generation language *4GL*. A programming *language* facilitating the design of *applications* by non-programmers.

free text, free-form text *Machine-readable* information that is not structured in tabular (*database*) form. Text is usually held as documents (*records*) which may be further divided into paragraphs (*fields*). Indexes provide a fast means of finding information. See also *textbase*.

frequency count Same as *frequency distribution*.

frequency distribution Ordered count of the number of instances each *value* occurs.

front end *Software* addition to an *application* to make it look and behave in a particular way; the front end is what the user sees and is generally designed to be simple to use.

GB *Gigabyte*.

gigabyte *GB*. About one billion (10^9) *bytes*, i.e. a thousand *megabytes*.

graphical user interface See *GUI*.

graphics Diagrams, graphs, maps, etc., created by the computer.

GUI Graphical user interface, pronounced 'gooey'. A system or *environment* for relating to the computer using images. The first widely-available GUI was that used in the Apple Mac; Microsoft *Windows* is currently a common GUI. See also *WIMP*.

hacking Anti-social and often illegal use of computer systems, trying to gain access to confidential *files* without permission, etc.

hard copy A paper copy produced by a printer, i.e. output which is not just on the *monitor* screen.

hard disk A permanently mounted stack of magnetic disks for storing large files; unlike a *silicon disk*, data on the hard disk is not lost when the computer is turned off. Most modern microcomputers now come with a hard disk. Same as *Winchester*.

hardware Computer equipment (as opposed to programs, which are *software*).

help One of the most important features of a computer *program*. The help system gives background information about how a *program* works; it takes the form of a series of screens and usually has an index. In modern *software* help can be related to the particular task being carried out when it is called up (i.e. it is 'context sensitive').

hertz See *MHz*.

hierarchical data structure A structure where some *records* are subordinate to (nested within) others, e.g. in a census database each person might be subordinate to (nested within) a household.

highlight (verb) In word processing and certain other applications, a way of making more than one character active (see *cursor*), usually by drawing the pointer of the *mouse* across the screen while holding down one of the buttons on the mouse.

high resolution graphics Graphics created with a relatively high density of *pixels*, giving a sharper image.

histogram A *graphic*, generally similar to a *bar chart*, which breaks *interval-scale* data into a number of ranges and draws bars whose length corresponds to the number of *records* in each *range*.

host A computer, usually a large one, providing a service which other computers or terminals can gain access to via a network. On-line databases are often stored on a *remote host* and accessed from distant sites.

hypermedia *Hypertext* incorporating graphics, sound, etc., perhaps using *CD-ROM*.

hypertext Linked full-text *records* (documents), allowing easy cross-reference. Typically a word in one document could lead to another document or to an explanation. Guide is an example of hypertext *software*.

IBM compatible A *microcomputer* (*clone*) similar to the IBM Personal Computer, the *industry-standard* microcomputer of the 1980s and early 1990s. IBM compatibles use similar *software* and *operating systems*. The other type commonly encountered in education, and not IBM compatible, is the Apple Mac.

IC *Integrated circuit.*

icon A graphical symbol for a particular *program* or action. It is selected from the screen with the mouse. Icons are a vital part of a *graphical user interface.*

ICPSR Inter-university Consortium for Political and Social Research, based at the University of Michigan, whose Data Archive is a major source of *machine-readable* historical data.

independent variable IV. A variable whose change in value influences another variable (the *dependent variable*). See *regression.*

inductive statistics Statistics which makes generalisations about a whole *population* from a *sample*. Compare with *descriptive statistics.*

industry standard Jargon adjective attached to a piece of *hardware* or *software* that is widely used, especially in the 'real world'.

ink jet printer A *printer* which produces high quality print by squirting tiny quantities of ink on to the paper. Less expensive than a *laser printer.*

input device A device for entering data into the computer, e.g. a *keyboard.*

integer A whole number. Sometimes used as a type of value in a database field, as distinct from a word or other *alphanumeric* data.

integrated circuit IC. Another name for a silicon *chip*, which contains a large number of electrical circuits. It was the development of the integrated circuit that made possible the miniaturisation of the computer.

integrated package A group of *programs* – e.g. a *word processor*, a *spreadsheet*, and a *database* – which work in much the same way. Often bundled for sale with a computer system; these are relatively simple programs.

interactive mode An overall method in which the user conducts a dialogue with the computer. The user puts in commands using the keyboard, etc., and the computer responds via the monitor. Most microcomputer programs work interactively; the opposite is the older *batch mode*, which is used on mainframe computers for large jobs.

interface In general, a link between two systems. An interface can also be the link between the user and the machine, allowing them to interact easily (Microsoft *Windows* is a *graphical user interface*). Also, *software* which links applications together or adapts *applications* to a particular use.

internet A major American network system for *E-MAIL* and communication, similar to the British *JANET.*

interval-scale data Normally taken to mean data on a continuous-scale that has equal intervals. In crude terms this is data on which mathematical operations can be performed; examples would be age in years, or income in monetary units. Sometimes called *continuous variables.* Strictly speaking, however, interval-scale variables are those that do

H

not have an absolute zero point. See *nominal-scale data*, *ordinal-scale data*, *ratio-scale data*.

ISO　International Standards Organization, which establishes standards for various industries, including computers.

JANET　Joint Academic Network. A system for electronic mail and file exchange within UK academic institutions.

join　To merge data, not by adding new (identically structured) *records* to the end of an existing *data file* or *table*, but by adding fields from one data file to another. Also to perform an operation in a *relational database* which joins together two tables based on their common *fields*. See *append*.

justify　In *word processing*, to make the right hand edge of the text a straight line, as in a book. Justification may or may not involve *proportional spacing*.

K, KB　See *kilobyte*.

kermit　A *file transfer program*, especially for transfers between *microcomputers* and *mainframes*.

keyboard　A *peripheral* device used for entering text and other data into the computer; an expanded version of the keyboard on a typewriter.

key table　In a *relational database*, a table which holds the 'key' to the other tables, in the form of unique numerical identifiers or similar information by which each row (record) can always be identified.

keyword　One or more words specified in a search within a *textbase*. See *KWIC*.

kilobyte　KB. About 1000 *bytes* (1024 bytes).

KWIC　*Keywords*-in-context. In a *text analysis program* the retrieval of selected words (*keywords*) and the words around them.

LAN　*Local area network* (of computers).

language　Usually a *programming language*, a means of writing instructions (a *program*) for the computer. There are different languages for different purposes, e.g. *BASIC*, *PASCAL*, *FORTRAN*, *C*, etc. With the development of modern *software* (pre-written instructions) it was quite possible to get good historical results from a computer without knowing anything about languages.

　　Some large modern commercial programs contain their own limited application language as an option for those who want to customise a *program* for a particular use; these are called *fourth generation languages* or 4GL. As an example, the Borland Paradox *DBMS* contains a programming language called PAL.

laptop　Portable computer, often battery powered and with an LCD screen. Typically weighing 3–7 kg.; smaller than a *transportable* but bigger than a *notebook*.

laser printer   High quality fast *printer* using laser technology.

lcd   Liquid Crystal Display. A kind of screen used in small portable computers.

level of confidence   For example, a confidence level of 95 per cent means there are 5 chances in 100 of being mistaken. For example, the level of confidence with which the *population mean* can be estimated from the *sample mean*.

level of significance   In statistics, a 95 per cent level of significance (given as 0.05) means 5 chances in 100 of being mistaken. The expression 'p < .05' means 'the result is significant at the .05 level', or literally that the probability (p) is less than .05 (less than 5 chances in 100) that the *null hypothesis* can be accepted, and that the alternative hypothesis can safely be accepted. The expression '$p < .01$' would mean that the probability that the null hypothesis can be accepted is less than 1 chance in 100 and that the result is significant at the .01 level.

linear relationship   A relationship between two *variables* that can be graphed as a straight line; not all relationships are linear – some would be graphed as a curve or some other shape.

line of best fit   See *regression line*.

linking   See *record linkage*.

load   To bring information into the computer's memory from a permanent storage device like a *floppy disk*. A *program* or *file* is loaded into the computer. Similar to *read*; the opposite of *save*.

log off   Leave a computer network in the proper way (opposite of *log on*).

log on   Gain access to a computer network by giving user identification and password.

longitudinal   Social-science jargon for long term, i.e. change over time.

M, MB   See *megabyte*.

Mac   Abbreviation for the Apple Macintosh, one of the standard microcomputers in education; it is noted for its innovative *graphical user interface*.

machine-readable data   Information that is stored on a disk or tape, etc., and can be interrogated using a computer.

macro   A means of running several commands together to reduce the number of keystrokes required. Complex operations in commercial *programs* (e.g. for *word processing* or *spreadsheets*) can be recorded and then replayed as a macro with one or two key presses.

mainframe   A large central computer, usually accessed simultaneously by a number of remote *terminals*.

mark-up   Encoding of structural or descriptive features in textual data. See *SGML*.

MB   See *megabyte*.

mean   Average; the value of all *records* added together and divided by number of records.

median   The value of the middle *record* when the records are listed from lowest to highest value.

megabyte   MB. About one million *bytes*.

megahertz   See *MHz*.

memory   The electronic storage facilities of a computer, especially those where *programs* and *data* are held when they are being executed or processed. Memory takes various forms: see *RAM* and *ROM*. Sometimes taken to mean the size of those storage facilities, measured in *bytes*.

menu   A list of options which a user can choose from. A menu serves as a reminder of choices available. Menus are important parts of *graphical user interfaces*.

menu driven   Software which the user operates by making choices from a *menu*, often with the aid of a *mouse*. The opposite of *command driven*.

MHz   Megahertz. A measure of how fast a computer's *CPU* operates. A hertz – named after the German physicist Heinrich Hertz (1857–94) – is a measure of frequency, i.e. one cycle per second. A megahertz is a million hertz. A relatively fast modern microcomputer would operate at 25 MHz.

micro   See *microcomputer*.

microcomputer   General name used in the 1980s for a small desktop computer, as distinct from the larger *workstation*, *mini* or *mainframe*.

microprocessor   Another name for the *processor* in a microcomputer.

microspacing   Same as *proportional spacing*.

minicomputer, mini   A medium-sized computer, smaller than a *mainframe* but larger than a desktop *micro*. Often accessed by remote terminals.

mips   Million instructions per second. A measure of how fast a computer processes.

mode   In statistics, the most frequently occurring *value*.

modem   Modulator/demodulator. A device to allow information in a computer to be transmitted via a telephone line.

monitor   Television-type display attached to the computer. There are several standards for IBM PCs and compatibles. *CGA* (Colour Graphics *Adaptor*) is a relatively old, low definition, display. *EGA* (Enhanced Graphics *Adaptor*), *VGA* (Video Graphics Array) and *SVGA* (Super VGA) have a higher quality display.

monochrome   Video with only one colour, black and white, black and green, etc.

motherboard   The printed circuit board on which the *CPU* and other major elements of a *microcomputer* are mounted. The motherboard may contain expansion slots into which plug-in *expansion cards* can be fitted.

mouse A small box attached to the computer which can be rolled across the desktop. The movement of the mouse moves a pointer on the computer's *monitor*. Typically used to select operations by pointing at *icons* on the screen, then executing by pressing the *mouse* buttons.

MS-DOS Microsoft Disk Operating System, pronounced 'em-ess-doss'. See *DOS*.

multitasking The ability to perform several functions at the same time, i.e. a user might be running a *database manager* and a *word processor* simultaneously.

multivariate analysis, multivariate statistics Statistical analysis involving several *variables* simultaneously.

network Several (micro-) computers wired together in one system.

NLQ Near letter quality. Print from a *dot matrix printer* where the density of dots is increased; the effect is to make the letters look nearly like normal print from an electric typewriter. The printer works more slowly in NLQ mode than in *draft mode*.

nominal-scale data Data which is in non-ordered categories; an example would be if people were divided up by their county of birth. See *ordinal-scale data*, *interval-scale data*.

non-trivial Computer jargon for complicated or serious; 'I'm afraid we have a non-trivial problem here.'

normal distribution A basic concept of statistics by which most *observations* are concentrated near the middle of the distribution of values. Many statistical techniques assume normal distribution of the data.

notebook A portable computer about the size of a piece of A4 paper and in the 2–4 kg. range, i.e. smaller than a *laptop*.

null hypothesis A temporary hypothesis (H_0) designed to be disproved so that an alternative hypothesis (H_1) can be accepted.

observation Sociological jargon for a *record*.

OCR Optical character recognition. A process by which a computer can read and later manipulate letters and numbers. See *scanner*.

on-line To have a terminal connected to a computer, e.g. a *remote host*. In another sense the immediate availability of some facility, e.g. 'on-line help' is on tap throughout a session.

operating system A control *program* through which the user manages *files* and performs other tasks such as running *programs*. *MS-DOS* is the operating system for IBM PCs and *compatibles*. Other operating systems are *UNIX* and *OS/2*. In some cases operating systems functions are carried out using a *graphical user interface* like Microsoft WINDOWS.

operationalise Sociological jargon for a measurable concrete test for a particular hypothesis.

operator   In database queries an element such as 'and', 'or', 'greater than', 'equals', 'minus', 'plus', etc.

optical disks   Large scale storage device with great potential for future use; the most common form available now is the *CD-ROM*.

ordinal-scale data   Data which has an order in a series (i.e. is ranked), but which is not divided by equal intervals. An example would be if people were divided up into social groups; there would be an obvious order from highest to lowest, but mathematical operations could not be carried out on this data. See *nominal-scale data*, *interval-scale data*.

OS/2   An IBM-backed *operating system* designed to replace *DOS*. Whether it will do so, given competition from Microsoft *Windows*, is still open to question.

output device   A device showing the results of a computer's work, e.g. a *monitor*, *printer*, or *plotter*.

p   Probability that the observed data would occur if the *null hypothesis* were true.

package   Essentially, a synonym for a *program* or a piece of *software*.

pad   Packet Assembler/Disassembler. A translating computer providing access to a packet switching network, e.g. to a mainframe computer.

palmtop   A very small pocket-sized portable computer currently suitable for taking notes and storing basic information.

parallel interface   A means of transferring data between *memory* and a *peripheral* (e.g. a *printer*) by which *characters* are communicated simultaneously along several lines. The physical connection on the PC is the *parallel port* (Centronics port). See *serial interface*.

parallel port   See *parallel interface*.

parameter   Characteristic of a *population*, as opposed to that of a *sample*.

pascal   See *language*.

password   A word, known only to a particular user (and the *network* manager), which allows that users to *log on* to a computer network and access to their own files and programs. Often used together with a more widely known user identity or user name.

PC   *Personal computer*. Also, the IBM PC or a computer compatible with it.

Pearson's r   Pearson product-moment correlation coefficient. See *correlation coefficient*.

peripheral   Devices outside the computer used to send data to it, receive data from it, or store data from it (e.g. *printer*, *disk drives*).

personal computer   Used in general for a desktop computer or microcomputer; also the IBM PC or a computer compatible with it.

pixel   Picture element. A unit of screen display. The more pixels the computer can put on the screen the higher the resolution. For example, the EGA standard allows a resolution of up to 640×350 pixels.

platform Nasty jargon for a computer or computer system, ranging from *microcomputers* to *mainframes*, e.g. 'Rank the importance of the following *hardware* platforms with respect to your department's current overall computing needs.'

plotter Output device which uses a pen or pens to draw *graphics* on paper, often in colour.

pocket computer A very small computer, smaller than a *notebook*.

point Unit (1/72 in., 0.35 mm.) for measuring the height of a *font*.

population In statistics, all the *cases* being studied in a particular survey. Same as 'universe'. *Samples* are selected from a population.

positive relationship Relationship between two *variables* where a change in one leads to a change (in the same direction) in the other, e.g. where older people are richer.

post-coding To assign a code to data *after* it has been entered into the computer rather than at the data entry stage; *database management systems* often have a *recode* function to help do this. The user then has two items, e.g. 'woollen merchant' *and* '60319'; it is always possible to refer to the original data. This is a form of having your cake and eating it.

printer A *peripheral* device used to produce *hard copy* of computer output; in effect a keyless electric typewriter.

printer driver A piece of *software* required to transfer output from a computer to a particular *printer*.

printout A paper copy (*hard copy*) of the work done on the computer, usually produced by a *printer*.

processor A central part of the computer, which executes *programs* and processes data. See *CPU*.

product Generic jargon term for *software*; Microsoft Word or Borland Paradox are products. A term to be avoided.

program A set of instructions for a computer, i.e. *software*.

programming Writing a *program* to instruct a computer to carry out a task. It is not usually necessary to know how to program to use modern *microcomputers*, as they have pre-prepared programs.

programming language See *language*.

prompt A symbol on the screen that shows the computer is ready to accept a command, e.g. '>'.

proportional spacing Facility in printing which takes into account the width of *characters* and the space between them; this makes it possible to *justify* text and make it resemble print in books.

prosopography The study of historical groups, often elites; also called collective biography.

psephology The study of elections and voting behaviour.

pt *Point*.

public domain software Software that is copyrighted but can be used by others without charge.

pull-down menu   A feature of *graphical user interfaces* where the user makes a *menu* appear by pointing and dragging the *mouse*.

punched card   Perforated cardboard cards which were used as a storage device to feed programs and data into a mainframe computer. A common size was 7.4 in. by 3.25 in. Now obsolete.

r   See *correlation coefficient*.

RAM   Random Access *Memory*. The circuits that make up the working memory of the computer, i.e. memory which can be written to and read from by the user (read/write memory). Anything in RAM when the computer is turned off is lost, hence the need for permanent storage devices (*floppy disks*, etc.).

RAM disk   Same as *silicon disk*.

random sample   See *sample*.

range   In statistics, the distance between the highest and lowest values: if the oldest age in a group of people is 72, and the youngest is 3, then the range is 69.

Also, an aggregation of values; '11–20' is a range. See also *recode*.

ratio-scale data   Strictly speaking, *interval-scale data* with an absolute zero point, like age and income.

read   To extract information from a computer's *memory* or from a permanent storage device like a *floppy disk*. The opposite of *write*.

read-only memory   See *ROM*.

rectangular file   Same as a *flat file*.

recode   To change (transform) the data using a computer. For example the text 'male' might be recoded as '1' (or vice versa), or the ages '1', '2', '3', '4', and '5' might all be recoded as the *range* '1–5'.

record   The information about a particular case. In the example of a census database a record might be all the information relating to a particular person. The number of records is one of the basic things to know about a database; database searches are often used to find how many records match particular criteria, e.g. find people with age less than 10 years. All records in a database or *table* have the same structure (i.e. the same *field* structure).

record linkage   Process of linking two *records* in one or more *files* and deciding whether they relate to one and the same person or item. Different versions of the same information have to be taken into account, for example ascertaining whether 'John Smith' in one source is the same as 'John Smyth' in another.

regression   The name of a widely used technique used to describe the relationship between *interval-scale* variables and even to predict the value of one variable from the value of another. Not actually the opposite of 'progression'; the terms comes from the work of Sir Francis Galton (1822–1911) who noted a tendency for 'regression towards the mean' in heredity. See *regression line*.

regression line   A line that expresses the relationship of two *variables* as plotted in a *scattergram*; also called the *line of best fit*. The slope of the line indicates the direction of dependence (positive or negative) between the two variables; up and to the right indicates a positive dependence (older person, more wealth).

relational database   A *database* consisting of several *tables* which may be joined by common *fields* (sometimes called 'pointers'). For example there may be a field in two distinct tables giving people's names; this common field can link the tables together. The relational 'model' is now the standard one in database design. Manipulated by a Relational *DBMS* or RDBMS. See *key table*.

remote host   See *host*.

retrieve   To ask a question of the database, to interrogate it.

RISC   Reduced instruction set computer. Computers, including the modern generation of *workstations*, based on a fast and powerful processor using simplified instructions.

ROM   Read-only Memory. Memory which the user cannot normally alter, e.g. programs built into the computer by the manufacturer. ROM is not lost when the computer is turned off.

row   Horizontal line of data. Often the same as a *record* or *case*.

running head   In *word processing*, text at the head of the page, usually alongside the page number, giving information such as chapter name. Most word processing *software* will print the appropriate running head on each page.

sample   In statistics a sub-group of the total *population*. If the sample is chosen completely at random and the sample is large enough then the characteristics of the sample will be a good indication of the characteristics of the whole population.

sampling error   The extent to which attributes of a *sample* differs from the attributes of the population from which the sample was drawn. A sampling error of ±5% and a sample in which 30% of people were Labour voters could suggest a population in which 25–35% were Labour voters. See also *confidence level*.

save   To send information from the computer's *memory* to a permanent storage device like a *floppy disk*. Like *write*. The opposite of *load*.

scanner   A device for physically scanning an image of any kind (e.g. text or graphics) into the computer's *memory*. If the image consists of printed text, *OCR software* may be used to convert the text into a form which can be used in a *word processor*, etc. Flatbed scanners operate like photocopiers; there are also hand-held scanners.

scattergram   Graph showing relationship between two *interval-scale variables*, with each point representing one *record* (*case*). The base line, or X axis, represents the units of the *independent variable*; the vertical line, or Y axis represents the units of the *dependent variable*. The scattergram gives a good overview of the relationship between the variables, e.g. whether it is positive or negative, *linear* or non-linear. See *regression line*.

secondary analysis Analysis or use of data assembled by another researcher.

serial interface A means of transferring data between *memory* and a *peripheral* (e.g. a *printer*) by which *characters* are communicated in sequence rather than simultaneously. The physical connection on the microcomputer is the *serial port* (RS232). See *parallel interface*.

serial port See *serial interface*.

SGML Standard Generalised Markup Language. A set of agreed conventions regarding the principles of *mark-up* and *formatting*. A file with such mark-up codes would readily be reconstituted when sent from one *environment* to another.

shareware *Software* which is copyrighted but available for evaluation and non-commercial use.

significance See *level of significance, statistical significance*.

silicon disk Part of a computer's *RAM memory* which can be assigned as a storage device. The user can *write* to and *read* from such a disk just like a *floppy disk*, and the process of reading and writing is much faster because there are no moving parts. On the other hand the silicon disk takes up RAM that could be used for other purposes, and anything stored on the silicon disk is lost when the power is turned off. Same as *RAM disk*.

simulation A *program* which simulates a real historical event, allowing users to gain insights into events and look at alternative outcomes. There are simulations of political campaigns and wars.

site licence Licence to use multiple copies of *software* in one location, i.e. at a particular university or school.

skewed Data which is not symmetrical, i.e. differs from a *normal distribution*.

software Computer programs (as opposed to equipment, which is *hardware*).

sort Put records in order, e.g. by individual's last name, by age, etc.

SPARC Scaleable processor architecture. A technology used in Sun Microsystems SPARC *RISC workstations* and their *clones*. Such machines are still substantially more expensive than microcomputers.

spreadsheet A type of *software* designed to hold numerical data in *rows* and *columns* (*cells*). It will calculate row and column totals and, in general, the relationships between cells. In effect a giant pocket calculator. Widely used in business, but with many historical applications. Examples are Microsoft Excel, Lotus 1-2-3, Computer Associates SuperCalc, etc.

SQL Standard Query Language. An international standard command language for *databases*.

standalone A computer that is not part of a *network*.

standard deviation A statistical measure of dispersion which shows the extent to which values are bunched around the *mean*. See *normal distribution*.

statistical package, statistical analysis package Type of *software* used to analyse data statistically. Examples are SPSS, Minitab, and SAS.

statistical significance Measure of probability. This is based on the concept of how likely it is that something (e.g. an observed *value* or association) has occurred by chance. A statistical significance of .05 means a 5 percent chance of an erroneous generalisation.

stratified sampling Weighted sampling where a *sample* is taken of selected sub-groups of a larger *population*; this is used to ensure a sufficiently large size for each sub-group.

string Broadly speaking, a group of *characters* treated as a unit; a word is a string.

string matching Asking the software to select every *string* in a text or database which matches the string defined by the user.

sub-directory See *directory*.

subset Part of a *dataset*; a *sample* is a kind of subset.

superscript Printed text which is slightly above normal text, e.g. in footnote numbers.

support Jargon, for 'to be able to use': 'This *software* supports a *mouse*.' Also to provide technical assistance for specific *hardware* or *software*.

SVGA See *adaptor*, *monitor*.

table Can be a synonym for a *database* or a *data file*, i.e. a group of *records* which have the same *field* structure. For example, a table might be a series of records, each of which is about an individual and gives the individual's name, date of birth and place of birth. The term table is frequently used with *relational databases*, which may contain several tables that can be *joined* together.

tape streamer Device which copies the contents of a *hard disk* on to magnetic tape, usually for *back up*.

TEI Text Encoding Initiative. A standard of textual *mark-up*.

terminal A keyboard and monitor allowing a user to communicate with a large computer, often one located in another room or place.

text analysis, textual analysis Using computers to analyse the content and style of text.

textbase Same as *database*, except that the data consists of free-form text, e.g. one or more historical documents.

textbase manager Software which is to *textbases* what a *database manage-*

ment system (*DBMS*) is to a *database*, i.e. it can be used to isolate and analyse particular parts of the text. See also *concordance*, *keyword*.

text editor   *Software* used to edit raw *ASCII files*. Examples are EDLIN or STEED. Useful for editing or 'cleaning' a *database* or altering short *programs* and *batch files*. A word processor is essentially a fancy and 'friendly' text editor, although there are things a text editor can do that some word processors cannot. See also *editor*.

text retrieval program   See *textbase manager*.

transcribe   To input data into computer (*machine-readable*) form from printed or manuscript sources.

transportable   A portable computer, heavier than a *laptop*.

tweaking   Modifying (fine-tuning) existing *software* to suit particular user needs. Modern *software* often includes a facility for such customisation; see 4GL.

UNICODE   A new standard, much more comprehensive than *ASCII*, to allow the representation of all world alphabets in computing codes.

UNIX   A large and relatively complex operating system, often used to support more specialist applications. Intended to be portable, e.g. usable on different levels of computer, from *mainframe* to *microcomputer*.

user-friendly   *Programs* or *hardware* that are easy to use or easy to learn.

user identification   A number or word by which a particular user is known in a computer network, and which the user types in to get access to the network when he or she logs on. Usually a user also has a *password*, which is secret.

value   A technical way of saying what is contained in a particular field of a record. The value of the name field for a record might be 'John Smith'.

value label   Facility in some *software* to adding a fuller name to a *value*, when producing output, etc. For example, the value '1' might have the value label 'Male'.

variable   See *field*.

variable label   Facility in some *software* for adding a fuller name to a *variable*, when producing output, etc. For example, the variable 'HSIZE' might have the variable label 'Household_Size'.

vdu   Visual Display Unit. The television screen or *monitor* attached to the computer.

vendor   A commercial supplier of *hardware* or *software*.

VGA   See *adaptor*, *monitor*.

videodisk   Large-scale storage device, used especially for storing images.

virus   Malignant and malicious *program* that can spread from one computer to another and which can destroy data or software.

WAN Wide area network. A computer *network* running over several sites, often using telephone lines, data lines, or even satellite links. *JANET* is an example. To be contrasted with a *LAN*; a *LAN* can be part of a WAN.

wild card A special character, often an asterisk (*), used to represent one or more unknown characters.

wimp Acronym describing *graphical user interface* like the *Mac* interface or Microsoft Windows. Stands for: *Windows, Icons, Mouse,* and Pull-down *menu* (or Windows, Icons, Menus, and Pointer).

winchester Same as *hard disk.*

window In effect a 'sub-screen'; several windows can be 'opened' at one time, allowing the user to work with several parts of one *file*, several files or several *programs* at the same time.

Windows The name of a widely used *graphical user interface* produced by Microsoft and similar to that used in the Apple *Mac.* Windows exists in several versions, with 'Windows NT' (New Technology) due to be introduced in 1992–93.

word processor *Program* used for producing and formatting text.

word-wrap In word processing, the way in which the *software* determines where to start a new line.

workstation A common term for a powerful computer, intermediate in size between a *microcomputer* and a *minicomputer.* Often used for *graphics.*

write To send information to a computer's *memory* or to a permanent storage device like a *floppy disk.* Like *save.* The opposite of *read.*

wysiwyg 'What You See Is What You Get', pronounced 'Whizzy-wig'. In *word processing,* the facility to see on the screen precisely how the printed text will appear.

x axis The horizontal line or base line on a graph. Used for the *independent variable.*

y axis The vertical line on a graph. Used for the *dependent variable.*

Select bibliography

A. Books and articles

This bibliography includes some of the more important general works of relevance to the subjects covered in the book. The endnotes to each chapter give additional references on more specific topics, and should be used to supplement this bibliography.

P. Adman, 'Computers and History', in Rahtz ed. (1987), pp. 92–103.

M. Anderson, *Family Structure in 19th Century Lancashire*, London, 1971. Important study based on Preston, combining census data, sampling techniques and a sociological approach to history.

M. Anderson, 'Households, families and individuals: some preliminary results from the national sample from the 1851 census of Great Britain', *Continuity and Change*, III, 1988, pp. 421–38.

D. Andrews and M. Greenhalgh, *Computing for Non-Scientific Applications*, Leicester, 1987. Informative survey.

W. O. Aydelotte *et al.*, eds., *The Dimensions of Quantitative History*, Princeton, 1972.

J. Barzun, *Clio and the Doctors: Psycho-History, Quanto-History and History*, Chicago, 1974. A trenchant critique of the 'new' history.

S. W. Baskerville, ' "Preferred linkage" and the analysis of voter behaviour in 18th-century England', *History & Computing*, I, 1989, pp. 112–20.

L. Benson, *The Concept of Jacksonian Democracy: New York as a Test Case*, Princeton, 1961. A study of early nineteenth-century American politics which pioneered the application of political science quantitative methods to history; as important for political history as Fogel and Engerman were for economic history.

R. E. Beringer, *Historical Analysis: Contemporary Approaches to Clio's Craft*, New York, 1978. Excellent survey of newer trends in history, with strong sections on computing and quantitative approach.

H. M. Blalock, *Social Statistics*, New York, 1960. One of the 'bibles' of statistics for social scientists; relatively advanced.

H. M. Blalock and A. B. Blalock, eds., *Methodology in Social Research*, New York, 1968. Multi-author text, with some chapters on general methodology and sampling which are relevant for historians.

A. G. Bogue, 'The new political history in the 1970s', in *The Past Before Us*, ed. Michael Kammen, Ithaca, 1980. Survey of application of quantitative methods, mainly in American political history.

A. G. Bogue, 'Quantification in the 1980s: numerical and formal analysis in United States history', *Journal of Interdisciplinary History*, XII, 1981–82, pp. 137–75.

E. E. Brent and R. E. Anderson, *Computer Applications in the Social Sciences*, New York, 1990. Useful introductory survey.

L. Burnard, 'Principles of database design' in Rahtz (1987), pp. 54–68.

R. Cobb, 'Historians in white coats', *Times Literary Supplement*, 3 December 1971, pp. 1527f. Witty put-down of quantitative methods and computers by a traditional historian.

P. Denley and D. Hopkin, eds., *History and Computing*, Manchester, 1987. A collection of papers from the first conference of the Association for History and Computing.

P. Denley, S. Fogelvik and C. Harvey, eds., *History and Computing II*, Manchester, 1989. A collection of papers from the second conference of the Association for History and Computing.

Dictionary of Computing, Oxford, 1990.

C. M. Dollar and R. J. Jensen, *Historian's Guide to Statistics: Quantitative Analysis and Historical Research*, New York, 1971. Useful on general approaches to different kinds of quantitative analysis, but technically out of date.

M. Drake, ed., *Applied Historical Studies: An Introductory Reader*, London, 1973. An anthology of eight examples of 1960s 'social science' history, with a useful short introduction.

M. Drake, *The Quantitative Analysis of Historical Data*, Milton Keynes, 1974. An Open University textbook with excellent examples.

M. W. Flinn *et al.*, eds. *Scottish Population History: from the 17th Century to the 1930s*, Cambridge, 1977. Background for the Scottish census studies.

R. Floud, *An Introduction to Quantitative Methods for Historians*, London, 2nd edn., 1979. Widely used textbook originally published in 1973; not adapted to the microcomputer era.

R. Floud, 'Quantitative history and people's history: two methods in conflict', *Social Science History*, VIII, 1984, pp. 151–68. A rather downbeat and defensive piece by a leading British quantifier, comparing a *History Workshop* approach with his own. A good analysis of pitfalls.

R. W. Fogel and G. R. Elton, *Which Road to the Past: Two Views of History*, New Haven, 1983. Two long essays contrasting 'scientific' and 'traditional' history, written by two outstanding practitioners from each school. Not specifically about computer methods, but taken together an excellent balanced general background.

R. W. Fogel and S. L. Engerman, *Time on the Cross*, 2 vols., Boston, 1974. One of the most famous early cliometric studies, based on the economic profitability of American slavery.

D. I. Greenstein, 'A matter of method', *History and Computing*, III, 1991, pp. 210–15. Criticism of mainframe and microcomputer historians' preoccupation with methods, and about their failure to link methods with a conceptual discussion; a plea for the setting of 'historical informatics' in their appropriate intellectual context.

D. I. Greenstein, ed., *Modelling Historical Data*, Göttingen, 1991.

T. Gunton, *The Penguin Dictionary of Information Technology and Computing Science*, Harmondsworth, 1992. Useful reference work.

D. Herlihy, 'Quantification in the 1980s: numerical and formal analysis in European history', *Journal of Interdisciplinary History*, XII, 1981–82, pp. 115–35.

E. Higgs, *Making Sense of the Census: The Manuscript Returns for England and Wales, 1801–1901*, London, 1989.

P. R. Andrew Hinde, 'Household structure in rural England, 1851–81: a multivariate analysis', *History and Computing*, II, 1990, pp. 194–209.

S. Hockey, *A Guide to Computer Applications in the Humanities*, London, 1980. Important text on an area not otherwise well covered.

D. Huff, *How to Lie with Statistics*, New York, 1954.

R. Hunt and J. Shelley, *Computers and Common Sense*, London, 3rd edn., 1983.

K. A. Jarausch and K. A. Hardy, *Quantitative Methods for Historians: A Guide to Research, Data, and Statistics*, Chapel Hill, 1991. The three core chapters (8–10) on multivariate analysis are highly technical but do attempt to give historical examples. The remainder of the book is quite accessible.

J. Johnston, *Econometric Methods*, New York, 3rd edn., 1984. Not computer oriented, but a standard 'technical' university-level textbook on the basic principles involved in econometrics, which are applicable to computer-based economic history.

J. W. Konvitz, 'The study and publication of maps as documents in historical scholarship', *Historical Methods*, XXIV, 1991, pp. 110–15.

J. M. Kousser, 'Quantitative social science history' in *The Past Before Us*, ed. Michael Kammen, Ithaca, 1980. Good survey of 1970s writing by an historian at the 'hard' end of the quantitative spectrum.

G. M. Kren and G. Christakes, *Scholars and Personal Computers: Microcomputing in the Humanities and Social Sciences*, New York, 1988. A clearly written general survey of resources available. Now somewhat dated in parts, but a good introduction for postgraduates and teachers.

I. Lancashire, ed., *Humanities Computing Yearbook*, Oxford, 1989.

I. Lancashire, ed., *Humanities Computing Yearbook, 1989–90: A Comprehensive Guide to Software and Other Resources*, Oxford, 1991. A review of methods and resources, including helpful bibliographies for each subject area.

C. H. Lee, *The Quantitative Approach to Economic History*, London, 1977. A very useful short introduction to the 'new economic history' based on economic theory and statistical analysis.

R. B. McCall, *Fundamental Statistics for Behavioral Sciences*, San Diego, 5th edn., 1990. Useful *ab initio* textbook, explaining simply the maths behind standard statistical operations.

D. M. McCloskey, *Econometric History*, London, 1987.

J. B. Manheim and R. C. Rich, *Empirical Political Analysis: Research Methods in Political Science*, New York, 3rd edn., 1991. Aimed at political scientists, but a clear introduction to techniques usable for historians. The computing section is now out of date.

C. Marsh, *Exploring Data: An Introduction to Data Analysis for Social Scientists*, Cambridge, 1988. Lively, up-to-date and practical first-year textbook, oriented around practical examples and exploratory data analysis. And it's *British*.

F. Mastroddi, ed., *Electronic Publishing: the New Way to Communicate*, Brussels, 1987.

E. Mawdsley, *et al.*, eds., *History and Computing III: Historians, Computers and Data*, Manchester, 1990. A collection of papers from the third conference of the Association for History and Computing.

R. Middleton and P. Wardley, 'Annual review of information technology developments for economic and social historians', *Economic History Review*, 2nd series, XLIV, 1991, pp. 343–72, and XLV, 1992, pp. 378–412.

R. J. Morris, 'Occupational coding: principles and examples', *Historical Social Research*, XV, 1990, pp. 3–29.

M. J. Norusis, *SPSS Introductory Statistics: Student Guide*, Chicago, 1990.

M. Olsen and L.-G. Harvey, 'Computers in intellectual history', *Journal of Interdisciplinary History*, XVIII, 1987–88, pp. 449–64.

J. Palfreman and D. Swade, *The Dream Machine: Exploring the Computer Age*, London, 1991. Not computing in history but the history of computing; an excellent introduction that puts many developments in context.

J. A. Phillips, 'Achieving a critical mass while avoiding an explosion: letter-cluster sampling and nominal record linkage', *Journal of Interdisciplinary History*, IX, 1979, pp. 493–508.

T. K. Rabb, 'The development of quantification in historical research', *Journal of Interdisciplinary History*, XXII, 1992, pp. 711–22.

S. Rahtz, ed., *Information Technology in the Humanities: Tools, Techniques and Applications*, Chichester, 1987.

W. J. Reichman, *Use and Abuse of Statistics*, Harmondsworth, 1964.

S. Reid, *Working with Statistics: An Introduction to Quantitative Methods for Social Scientists*, Cambridge, 1987.

R. S. Schofield, 'Sampling in historical research', in E. A. Wrigley (1972), pp. 146–90. Introduction for historians, explaining the maths involved.

G. Shaw, *British Directories*, London, 1989. Useful bibliography on the raw material for computer-based studies.

E. Shorter, *The Historian and the Computer: A Practical Guide*, Englewood Cliffs, 1971. Technically very out of date, but a number of good points about methods.

H. Southall and E. Oliver, 'Drawing maps with a computer . . . or without?', *History and computing*, II, 1990, pp. 146–54.

D. A. Spaeth, *A Guide to Software for Historians*, CTI Centre for History, Glasgow, 1991. Up-to-date list with comments, organised thematically with helpful introductory comments.

L. Stone, 'Family history in the 1980s', *Journal of Interdisciplinary History*, XII, 1981–82, pp. 51–87. Good overview, but also includes discussion of back projection and other methods.

L. Stone, 'The revival of narrative: reflections on a new old history', *Past and Present*, LXXXV, 1979, pp. 2–34. A well-known British social historian, caught between the 'old' and 'new' history, calls for a certain kind of narrative at the 'cutting edge' of historical writing. Sometimes seen as a harbinger of the 'postmodern' era in historiography.

R. P. Swierenga, ed., *Quantification in American History: Theory and Research*, New York, 1970. An excellent anthology of twenty important articles from the first stages of American computer-based research. Included are both discussions of the usefulness of computers and the quantitative approach and examples of research.

S. Thernstrom and R. Sennett, eds., *Nineteenth Century Cities: Essays in the New Urban History*, New Haven, 1969. Collection of articles which launched the, then, 'new urban history'.

E. R. Tufte, *The Visual Display of Quantitative Information*, Cheshire, Conn., 1983. The classic work on how to present data in graphic form.

E. A. Wrigley, *Identifying People in the Past*, London, 1973.

E. A. Wrigley, *Nineteenth Century Society: Essays in the Use of Quantitative Methods for the Study of Social Data*, Cambridge, 1972. Essential reading, containing a number of very important articles on the census and other sources.

E. A. Wrigley, 'Population history in the 1980s', *Journal of Interdisciplinary History*, XII, 1981–82, pp. 207–26.

E. A. Wrigley and R. S. Schofield, *The Population History of England,*

1541–1871: A Reconstruction, London, 1981. Classic British application of quantitative methods to social history and demography.

H. F. Ziegler, *Nazi Germany's New Aristocracy: The SS Leadership, 1925–1939*, Princeton, 1989. Good example of an 'elite study' combining computer techniques (including modern graphics) with traditional historical approaches.

B. Major relevant journals

Computers and the Humanities (Dordrecht, Netherlands)
Continuity and Change: A Journal of Social Structure, Law and Demography in Past Societies (Cambridge, England)
Craft: The Newsletter of the CTI Centre for History with Archaeology and Art History (Glasgow, Scotland)
Historical Social Research (Cologne, Germany)
History and Computing (London)
Historical Methods (Washington, DC)
Journal of Economic History (New York)
Journal of Interdisciplinary History (Cambridge, MA, USA)
Journal of Social History (Pittsburgh)
Urban History Yearbook (Leicester, England)

C. Data sources

The latest guide to historical data available in computer format is K. Schürer and S. J. Anderson, *A Guide to Historical Datafiles in Machine-readable Form*, London, 1992.

Two especially important central depositories relevant to readers of this book are:

Data Archive of the Inter-university Consortium for Political and Social Research (ICPSR) (PO Box 1248, Ann Arbor, MI 48106, USA) (E-Mail [INTERNET] ICPSR_NETMAIL@UM.CC.UMICH.EDU). Founded in 1962 and located at the University of Michigan. The annual *Guide to Resources and Services* give extensive details of current holdings.
ESRC Data Archive. (University of Essex, Wivenhoe Park, Colchester Essex CO4 3SQ). (E-Mail ARCHIVE@ESSEX.AC.UK) The Archive is funded by the Economic and Social Research Council and Essex University. The *ESRC DATA Archive Data Catalogue* and a monthly *Bulletin* give details of holdings.

Index

This Index contains references to more substantial discussions in the text. For brief definitions of terms, the Glossary is the best place to start.